Study Guide

for use with

jean saindon

Why?
Meaning?
Challenge
Claim
Because
Response

argument
and argumentation

Prepared by JEAN SAINDON
YORK UNIVERSITY

THOMSON

NELSON

Australia   Canada   Mexico   Singapore   Spain   United Kingdom   United States

**Study Guide for use with
Argument and Argumentation**

by Jean Saindon

**Associate Vice President,
Editorial Director:**
Evelyn Veitch

**Editor-in-Chief,
Higher Education:**
Anne Williams

Acquisitions Editor:
Bram Sepers

Marketing Manager:
Shelley Collacutt Miller

Developmental Editor:
James Polley

Copy Editor and Compositor:
Cathy Witlox

Production Coordinator:
Ferial Suleman

Cover Design:
Johanna Liburd

Cover Image:
© M. Thomson/Zefal Corbis

Printer:
Webcom

ARGUMENT AND ARGUMENTATION

STUDENT MANUAL

TABLE OF CONTENTS

MODULE 1: INTRODUCTION

QUICK QUIZ ANSWERS

✍ QUICK QUIZ 1.1
Identifying Arguments

Identify which, if any, of the following are arguments.

1. Mary lied when she said that she had attended the conference.

   This is not an argument. It is simply one claim.

2. Mary did not attend the conference but submitted an expense claim for the conference.

   This is not an argument. Although there are two claims here, one is not offered as a reason or justification for the other.

3. Mary lied because she claimed to have attended the conference although she hadn't.

   This is an argument. There are two claims: "Mary lied" is the conclusion. The other—that Mary claimed to have attended the conference although she hadn't—is offered as a reason for the conclusion.

✍ QUICK QUIZ 1.2
Distinguishing Simple Opinion, Reasoned Opinion, and Evidential Claims

Identify which of the following are simple opinions and which are reasoned opinions. If there is an argument, identify the reason and the conclusion, and determine whether the main conclusion is the kind of claim that can be based on objective evidence.

1. Abortion is wrong.

   As stated, this is simple opinion. No reasons have been offered. If reasons are offered, it could become reasoned opinion.

2. Abortion is wrong because it ends a human life.

   This is reasoned opinion. A reason has been offered for the opinion that abortion is wrong:

   Reason: **Abortion ends a human life.**
   Conclusion: **Abortion is wrong.**

3. I can't stand *American Idol.*

   This is simple opinion.

4. *American Idol* represents the best in contemporary television programming. It appeals to a large audience, has high production values, and gives the audience something they can identify with.

   This is reasoned opinion.

Reason 1:	**It appeals to a large audience.**
Reason 2:	**It has high production values.**
Reason 3:	**It gives the audience something they can identify with.**
Conclusion:	***American Idol* represents the best in contemporary television programming.**

5. Broccoli is good for you; it is high in calcium and some essential vitamins as well as being high in fibre.

   This is an argument—it rests on an evidential claim.

Reason:	**It is high in calcium and some essential vitamins as well as being high in fibre.**
Conclusion:	**Broccoli is good for you.**

✍ QUICK QUIZ 1.3
Applying the Constitutive Rules of Argumentation

Each of the following is a move or response in an argumentation. Explain whether the individuals engaged in the interaction are adhering to the basic principles of argumentation. Identify which constitutive rules are violated, if any.

1. I don't care what your objection is. I know what I believe, and I'm not going to change my mind on the issue.

   By his or her unwillingness to listen to reasons or to accept that his or her position could be wrong, the speaker is violating the argument principle, in effect, refusing to engage in argumentation.

2. So far, your objections haven't undermined my argument. Until they do, I'm not agreeing with you on this.

   This person is adhering to the constitutive rules. Saying that he or she hasn't heard a sufficiently good reason to change positions indicates a willingness to listen to reason (rationality) and admit fallibility.

3. That's just a typical feminist argument. And you know I don't agree with feminists on anything.

This person violates the respect principle by labelling the other person's argument and dismissing it on general grounds. He or she also violates the rationality principle by dismissing the argument without giving relevant reasons.

✍ QUICK QUIZ 1.4
Using the Constitutive Rules

Examine each of the following lines of dialogue from an argument exchange. Identify which constitutive rule the line of dialogue follows or violates and explain why.

1. You have challenged my claim that the government is hiding the remains of a crashed UFO at a secret air base. I admit I don't know where it is. But how do you know they're not hiding one?

This arguer violates the burden of proof rule. The speaker advocates the claim that the government is hiding the remains of a crashed UFO at a secret air base but, having no evidence, defies the challenger to disprove the claim, thereby reassigning the burden of proof.

2. We have been going at this for two hours. I think we have made some progress, and we've both refined our positions and reasons. However, we haven't reached consensus on this. I suggest we go away and think about it.

The above illustrates the suspension of judgment principle. The speaker is recommending that, since the two arguers have not arrived at a successful defence for one position, they suspend judgment on the issue.

3. You know, Fred, we reached agreement on that issue yesterday. I was thinking about it overnight and realized that one of the arguments you used to persuade me just doesn't work. Do you have some time now for me to run my challenge by you?

This is an illustration of the reconsideration principle. Although the arguers reached agreement on the issue, the speaker has found a key flaw in the argument and wants to reopen the issue for reconsideration. He or she is also showing respect for the other by asking if this is a good time to do this.

Identifying Topics, Issues, Positions, and Arguments

A Simple Argumentation Dialogue

Context: The university student council has proposed a referendum on a supplemental health levy to pay for certain items not paid for by provincial health insurance. This includes some prescription drugs, physiotherapy, and chiropractic services. The levy will also provide basic health care for foreign students who are not covered by the provincial health care scheme. Two students are discussing the issue.

A: *I don't think we should support the supplemental health care levy.*

B: *Why not?*

A: *Because most people don't need it.*

B: *So you're saying that since only a few may need supplemental health insurance, we shouldn't support it.*

A: *Yeah.*

B.   *How do you know only a few need supplemental health insurance?*

A: *Because most students are covered by their parents' health insurance.*

B: *How do you know that?*

A: *I just assumed it.*

B: *I have some doubts, but let's suppose for the moment that that is true. So what you are saying is that the only reason to support the additional health levy is if most students don't have supplemental health insurance coverage.*

A: *Yes.*

B: *So you don't think drivers in the province should have to support public transit since the majority of residents don't use it and don't need it?*

A: *I wouldn't agree with that.*

B: *What's the difference?*

For the simple example of argumentation above, identify

1. the topic;
2. the issue;
3. the position taken by A;
4. A's reason(s) for that position; and
5. B's position in this dialogue, if he takes one.

Examine each turn taken by A and B in the dialogue and, using the outline of a basic argumentation dynamic, identify the purpose of each turn in the dialogue—does it identify a position, state a reason, reformulate, challenge, or perform some other function?

1. **The topic: The supplemental health care levy.**
2. **The issue: Should students support the supplemental health care levy? [We formulate the issue as a question.]**
3. **A's position: Students should not support the levy.**
4. **A's reason(s) for that position: Most students don't need it.**
5. **B's position: B does not take a position in this dialogue. Although B elicits reasons and raises challenges, we cannot infer that B defends an alternate position, and we wouldn't know from the dialogue which of several possible alternate positions B might defend. B might even agree with A but be posing challenges and asking for clarification to test A's argument.**

A: *I don't think we should support the supplemental health care levy.*

(A states a position on the issue of whether students should support the supplemental levy.)

B: *Why not?*

(B asks for reasons.)

A: *Because most people don't need it.*

(A gives a reason.)

B: *So you're saying that since only a few may need supplemental health insurance, we shouldn't support it.*

(B paraphrases A's position and checks the paraphrase with A.)

A: *Yeah.*

(A agrees with the paraphrase of his or her argument.)

B.   *How do you know only a few need supplemental health insurance?*

(B probes for information about the reason, in effect, asking for the reason for the reason.)

A: *Because most students are covered by their parents' health insurance.*

(A gives his reason.)

B: *How do you know that?*

(B probes for the reason for this claim.)

A: *I just assumed it.*

(A's response indicates that he or she has no evidence. It is an unsupported claim.)

B: *I have some doubts, but let's suppose for the moment that that is true. So what you are saying is that the only reason to support the additional health levy is if most students don't have supplemental health coverage.*

(B tentatively accepts the claim to see where else it will lead and then restates the argument.)

A: *Yes.*

(A accepts the paraphrase. A might have rejected the paraphrase and said that although only one reason was given, he or she had others.)

B: *So you don't think drivers in the province should have to support public transit since the majority of residents don't use it and don't need it?*

(B issues a challenge to the claim.)

A: *I wouldn't agree with that.*

(A rejects the challenge.)

B: *What's the difference?*

(B asks for reasons for A rejecting the challenge by asking how the challenge differs from B's initial argument.)

EXERCISES

EXERCISE 1.1
Distinguishing Simple Opinion, Reasoned Opinion, and Evidential Claims

Determine whether each of the following is a simple opinion, a reasoned opinion, or an evidential claim. If there is an argument, identify the premise and conclusion.

1. The Matrix was a great movie.

2. The government should not raise tuition fees. It would hinder students from lower-income families from going to university, which would be a bad thing.

3. You shouldn't park on this street overnight. You'll get a ticket. And you don't want to get a ticket.

4. Professor Emmett has a great intro psych class.

5. You should major in psych if you want to practise law. It would give you an insight into people, which would be useful in law.

6. Only half the people who graduate from law school are still practising law five years after they graduate. I don't think law is such a good choice for a career.

7. I don't think we should be doing stem cell research. It requires using human embryos, and that means we are killing potential human beings.

8. We are likely to make some major breakthroughs in stem cell research in the next five years. Not only does this research promise significant insight into our basic understanding of how the human body develops but it promises major medical breakthroughs for a host of diseases for which we currently have no treatments, such as Parkinson's, Alzheimer's, and several disabilities. For all these reasons, we should fund stem cell research.

9. Stem cell research is costly.

10. Not investing in social programs will be more costly down the line. If we don't support education, public housing, health care, and basic welfare programs now, we will have increased social problems in the future. We will have lower productivity, more crime, more people living in poverty, and greater social unrest.

11. iPods can be effective teaching tools. Some universities are using them for audio lectures to free up class time for other, more interactive learning activities.

12. Abortion is justified when it means saving the life of the mother.

13. Abortion is never justified. It kills a living human being.

14. Biker gangs are one of the major sources of the illegal drug trade in the province. I read that in the newspaper.

15. Watching TV doesn't cause violence. In many countries, there is no TV and a great deal of violence.

✍ EXERCISE 1.2
Dialogue 1: Drug Testing

For the dialogue below, do the following:

1. Identify the issue(s) that A and B are disputing. What is the major issue? How did you determine that it is the major issue? Are there subsidiary issues? What are they? How do the subsidiary issues relate to the major issues?
2. Identify the positions taken by A and B in this dialogue.
3. Identify the major arguments given by each side in the dialogue.
4. Determine if there are any moves that mislead or sidetrack the argument. Why do you think they mislead or sidetrack the argument? How could they be effectively handled if someone were to use them on you?
5. Identify the moves the arguers make that effectively advance their positions. Why do you consider them effective?
6. Determine which side, if either, has the best case in the dialogue and why.
7. Brainstorm how each side's argumentation could be improved.
8. Identify the intent or purpose of Person A and of Person B in this encounter.
9. Determine if both A and B are following the constitutive rules of argumentation. Identify key places where they are following them and where they are not.

Context: You are having lunch with two friends, A and B, at work when the following discussion occurs.

A: *I see that the company is going to introduce mandatory drug testing for all employees. I think that's a great idea!*

B: *Are you crazy? That is the dumbest idea I have ever heard! Do you know what that will do to morale around here? Even if they don't catch anyone—but they will—it will simply make everyone nervous and paranoid.*

A1: *What's the matter? Afraid they'll find out you're a doper on the side?*

B1: *I'm not a doper, and you know it. However, I do think it is an infringement on my rights and liberties.*

A2: *Why?*

B2: *The company hires my labour, not my life. This is taking us back to the dark ages of the nineteenth century, when companies dictated the morals and values of their employees, or tried to.*

A3: *You don't know what you're talking about. Companies have never done that.*

B3: *They did, but that is not the point. The issue is whether the company has the right to force me to undergo testing so it can find out what I do on my own time. That's just not right.*

A4: *Sure, it is. If you came to work drunk, the company would have the right to send you home, suspend you, or fire you.*

B4: *Maybe. But only if it got in the way of my doing my job. And that is the point. If I am doing something that interferes with my ability to do my job, then the company has the right to demand that I clean up my act or leave. But drug testing doesn't take into account job performance. It simply looks to see if you have used drugs at some time in the recent past.*

A5: *What's wrong with that? If you've used drugs, it must affect your performance on the job.*

B5: *Not necessarily. You enjoy a few beers while watching the game on Saturday or Sunday, right? If you have a few too many, there still may be traces in your blood on Monday when you come to work. If you can still do the job, should you be penalized for that?*

A6: *That's not the point. Drugs are different from booze.*

B6: *How?*

A7: *Drugs affect you more.*

B7: *How do you know that?*

A8: *If you are a heroin addict, that's all you think about. It dominates your life. Your whole personality changes.*

B8: *How many heroin addicts do you know in this company? That's not what we're talking about. The company wants to test for all kinds of drugs, legal and illegal. From heart medication and insulin to marijuana and cocaine.*

8

A9: *So, what's wrong with that?*

B9: *Everything. The company has a right to know about my medical history only insofar as it affects my ability to perform on the job. What would happen if they found out that someone is diabetic or takes epilepsy drugs or heart medication? Those people could be risks to the company's insurance policy. They could be fired, not because they can't do their jobs, but because sometime in the future they may cost the company money.*

A10: *But what about the real dopers—the pot smokers and coke addicts? They're not doing their jobs, and they're a threat to me if my safety depends on them.*

B10: *All of them? Even people who smoke an occasional joint on the weekends but are straight when they come to work on Monday?*

A11: *Yeah.*

B11: *Look, the tests they are planning on using are extremely sensitive. They can detect substances in the bloodstream or urine that are months old. If someone smokes a joint or two on vacation, and then doesn't have another, the tests can detect the drug a month later. They are also very inaccurate. Do you want to risk losing your job on the basis of a test that may mistake your heart medication for some illegal substance?*

A12: *But the company has a right to protect itself. I don't see why you can't get that through your thick head. You seem so concerned about protecting these dopers and degenerates that I can't help but wonder what you do in your spare time. The company is simply trying to protect itself and us from those people who may pose a threat to our safety.*

B12: *Or to their profit margins!*

A13: *Yeah, so? They have a right to protect their profit margins.*

B13: *But not this way. They are going to get everyone who uses any kind of drugs—legal or illegal. Who knows how they will use that information? What I do on my own time is my own business.*

A14: *Yeah. And what you do on company time is their business.*

B14: *I agree. If someone is coming to work stoned or drunk or wired, then the company has grounds for discipline because, in that case, the person can't do the job he or she is being paid to do. But, if you have a few beers or joints on the weekend, what is it to them? Why should they be concerned? It's not their business.*

A15: *And I say it is their business. People do use drugs on the job, and it affects their performance. I'm not convinced that their using drugs on their own time is not harmful. It's got to affect their overall attitude and work performance. And the company has a right to good performance on the job.*

B15: *(Turning to you) Say, you've been quiet on this whole thing. What do you think about the situation?*

◈ EXERCISE 1.3
Dialogue 2: Huckleberry Finn

For the dialogue below, do the following:

1. Identify the issue(s) that C and D are disputing. What is the main issue? How did you determine that it is the main issue? Are there subsidiary issues? What are they? How are they related to the main issue?
2. Identify the positions taken by C and D in this dialogue.
3. Identify what you consider to be the major arguments given by each side in the dialogue.
4. Determine if there are any moves that mislead or sidetrack the argument. Why do you think they mislead or sidetrack the argument? How could they be effectively handled if someone were to use them on you?
5. Identify the moves the arguers make that effectively advance their positions. Why do you think that they advance the position?
6. Determine which side, if either, has the best case in the dialogue and why.
7. Brainstorm how each side's argumentation could be improved.
8. Identify the intent or purpose of Person C and of Person D in this dialogue.
9. Determine if both C and D are following the constitutive rules of argumentation. Identify key places where they are following them and where they are not.
10. Identify differences between the first dialogue, between A and B, and the second dialogue, between C and D. Consider in terms of both content and process.

Context: A local parents' committee has demanded that Mark Twain's *The Adventures of Huckleberry Finn* be banned from the high school curriculum on the grounds that it is racist. Two students are discussing the parents' demands.

C1: *I think the parents' committee is right. Huckleberry Finn should be banned.*

D1: *Why?*

C2: *Anything that promotes racism and the denigration of people on the basis of their race should not be allowed in the schools.*

D2: *What makes you think that Huckleberry Finn is racist and denigrates black people?*

C3: *The Black Parents' Committee says that the book is racist.*

D3: *Do you always accept everything people say just because they say it is true?*

C4: *No.*

D4: *Well, then, what are their reasons for saying that it is racist?*

C5: *I'm not sure. It didn't say in the press report I read.*

D5: *That's typical of the newspapers. They tell us what people say but usually don't explain the reasoning behind their views. But I heard an interview on the radio in which one of the parents said that the book was racist because it used the word nigger over 200 times.*

C6: *See. They do have good reason.*

D6: *Wait a minute. Have you read the book?*

C7: *No. I don't have to read it to know it's racist. Anything that uses such language about others obviously promotes racism.*

D7: *My dictionary has the term nigger in it. Does it promote racism?*

C8: *That's different.*

D8: *Why?*

C9: *Because the one is promoting racism, whereas the other is simply a reference work.*

D9: *I thought your argument was that any use of the term promoted racism. Obviously, you've changed your position.*

C10: *Not really. It's just that some things do promote racism and some things don't.*

D10: *I agree with you on that. The question is whether the use of the term nigger repeated more than two hundred times in a novel does.*

C11: *How can it not? If you use the term that often, then you are obviously denigrating a whole race.*

D11: *Is that true? Wouldn't it be possible to write a novel in which the term nigger is used a fair number of times but used ironically or in some way to illustrate and at the same time condemn racism? For example, someone could write a novel about South Africa in which the term is frequently used by whites. Yet the novel could be written from the perspective of blacks and demonstrate the inhumanity of a racist system. Would the use of the term in that context be racist?*

C12: *I'm not sure. I'm puzzled now. I started out thinking that the use of the term was automatically racist. Now it seems that there may be some uses that are not racist. In fact, the word could be used in the condemnation of racism. Yet something still seems wrong to me about using the term, even in such a context. Some people could take it as denigrating and react badly to it.*

D12: *It seems as though you are torn between two things. On the one hand, terms such as nigger tend to carry a highly negative connotation, and people react adversely to that connotation. Because of the historical uses of that term, some black people feel that whenever anyone uses the word, it's a personal attack and denigration of them and their race. Yet, on the other hand, there are situations or contexts in which the term can be used to expose and condemn racism.*

C13: *Yeah.*

D13: *So there seem to be several issues here. Does The Adventures of Huckleberry Finn promote or condemn racism? That is, how is the term used in the book? What is the overall intent and effect of its use?*

C14: *That's one. And since neither of us has read the book, we'll have to read it to answer that question.*

D14: Second, even if the novel does not intend to promote racism, even if it condemns it, does the fact that some people, because the term has such emotional meaning, react badly to it, provide sufficient grounds for banning the novel from the classroom?

C15: That seems like the real issue. Whether the novel intends to be racist or not, the real issue is the effect it has on some people.

D15: I would like to see you defend that. Why do you think that is the most important issue, aside from the fact that it lets you off the hook for not having read the book?

C16: Cheap shot. I think it is the most important issue because you can't always determine an author's intent. However, you can determine the effect of a piece of writing. If it makes people feel bad about themselves, or promotes racism and hatred, then that can be measured more easily. And that is a good way of determining that something is racist.

D16: Consider some great works of literature. Even the Bible meets your criteria for racist literature.

C17: How so?

D17: There are passages in the Bible that clearly promote hatred and persecution of others. Is the Bible racist? Oops, there goes the bell. I have to leave for class. Let me just make this one point. You suggest that the real issue is the word's effect, regardless of the intent of the author or the meaning of the text. And if some, many, most, or at least one person finds it offensive, then it should be banned. Consider this for the next time. Any text, even parts of the Bible, can be seen or interpreted by at least one person or even many people as offensive. It seems to me that the real dispute here is which of two principles we should adopt: Do we judge racism in a novel by the intent of the author or the meaning of the text—however that can be established? Or do we judge it by the effects on the readers?

C18: Let's talk about that after school tonight. Get going. You'll be late for class.

☙ EXERCISE 1.4
Two Passages on Mandatory AIDS Testing

Below is a background introduction for two passages. Read the background introduction, then examine both argumentative passages. For each, identify

1. the topic;
2. the main issue and relevant related issues;
3. the positions taken; and
4. the main arguments given for each position.

Which do you think is the better argument? Why?

Background Introduction for Both Passages

The problem of AIDS continues to plague society. The number of people infected with the disease is rising at an exponential rate. As more people become infected, various issues challenge society. One set of issues revolves around the question of what to do about a worker who has the disease. Should coworkers be informed that a fellow employee has AIDS? Should an employer be allowed to require an employee to take a blood test for HIV? Should an employer have the right to dismiss an employee who tests positive for AIDS but does not display the symptoms? Should an employer have the right to dismiss one who does display the symptoms of the disease?

Passage 1: Now Is the Time for Mandatory AIDS Testing

Both employees and employers have a right to know whether anyone in the workplace has AIDS. Someone afflicted with HIV is a threat to others: Even doctors and specialists admit they do not know all of the ways HIV can be transmitted. Since the only means of protecting oneself is to ensure that one does not come into contact with a carrier of the disease, mandatory AIDS testing is an idea whose time has come. Everyone has the right to be protected from indiscriminate exposure to such a lethal disease, especially when the means for detecting and preventing such exposure are obvious— mandatory testing of all employees and the legal ability to terminate anyone who tests positive. No one has the right, deliberately or accidentally, to expose others to a disease that is lethal or for which there is no cure. If there is a way to determine that someone poses a threat to others, this method should be permitted and used. Therefore, an employer should have the right to test all employees for AIDS and to inform other employees if anyone tests positive. After all, we do not allow people with tuberculosis, another contagious disease, to wantonly inflict their illness on others. The employer is responsible not only for the health and safety of workers in the workplace but also for protecting the interests of the company's shareholders, which means ensuring a healthy work force.

Passage 2: AIDS Testing Is a Violation of Basic Human Rights

A basic principle on which our democracy is founded is that no one, least of all the state, has the right to interfere with an individual's rights unless a person poses a clear danger to others. A second basic privilege in a democracy is the right to privacy: As long as a person's actions do not impinge on the rights of others, an individual is entitled to his or her private life. The proposal to introduce mandatory HIV testing in the workplace, to inform all employees of anyone who tests positive, and to fire anyone who tests positive is a violation of those basic rights. What can be more private than our health? Although an individual may test positive for HIV, that does

not mean that he or she will contract AIDS. Mandatory testing and the right to dismiss those who test positive for HIV will only result in ghettoization and discrimination against many individuals who will never get the disease. As such, it is the equivalent of the kind of injustice done the Japanese by this country during the Second World War—the stigmatizing and ghettoizing of many innocent people. Further, even if an individual has AIDS, and not simply carrying the virus, the transmission of the disease requires intimate contact with bodily fluids, especially blood and semen. Such contact is extremely unlikely and infrequent in the workplace setting.

MODULE 2: CLARIFYING MEANING

QUICK QUIZ ANSWERS

✍ QUICK QUIZ 2.1
The Functions of Language

What is the function of each of the following sentences?

1. I'm elated that Canadian women won the gold in hockey.

   Expresses emotion.

2. That is a job well done.

   Evaluates/judges.

3. Wow!

   Expresses emotion.

4. Not one of the women on the team is a professional, but they all played like professionals.

   Not one of the women on the team is a professional [informs], but they all played like professionals [judges, evaluates].

✍ QUICK QUIZ 2.2
The Role of Context

Consider possible alternate meanings for the claims below. Explain how the context might affect the meaning of the key terms or claims. How could they be interpreted in different contexts.

1. Meet me by the bank.

   This could mean meet me near the financial institution or meet me beside the river, depending on what the speaker means by "bank."

2. The president is a man of utmost honour, lives by the highest ethical standards, and tells only the truth.

   Read literally, this could be seen as claiming that the president has these virtues and praising him for them. Read ironically, as though spoken by a critic, this could be saying the exact opposite—that the president is without honour, has no ethical standards, and lies frequently. See Mark Anthony's

speech in *Julius Caesar* in which he praises the assassins of Caesar as "all honourable men."

3. We will ensure that all children have access to child care.

    This appears to be a promise, but it is not clear what exactly is being promised. Spoken by the leader of a political party that supports public daycare, it could be seen as a promise for more daycare spaces. Spoken by the leader of a political party that opposes big government, it could be seen as a promise to supply money or tax breaks to individual families so that one parent can stay home and take care of their children.

4. Liberals are free-spending and irresponsible.

    Read literally, this could be a statement about Liberal spending habits and accountability. Read ironically, it could be a comment that the Liberal party does not have these traits, but the opposition does. As a statement in a political campaign, it could be an unfounded allegation or a charge about past Liberal spending practices.

✍ QUICK QUIZ 2.3
Words, Concepts, Referents, and Connotations

Identify the possible referents and meanings for the key concepts and explain the meaning of the claim in each of the following. Where different referents and meanings are possible, identify these and show how the claims' meanings may be affected.

1. Comment made during the Sponsorgate (Liberal advertising) scandal: The Liberals are corrupt.

    Liberal: There are several possible referents for this, which include the following:

    All or some members of the Liberal Party of Canada.
    All or some politicians in the Liberal Party of Canada.
    All or some members of the Quebec wing of the Liberal Party of Canada.
    All or some members of Paul Martin's Liberal government.
    All or some members of Jean Chretien's Liberal government.

    In fact, the scandal directly involved some members of the Quebec wing of the Liberal party and some members of Jean Chretien's government. However, such claims were commonly used to suggest that Paul Martin's government and all members of the Liberal party were corrupt. This is also an example of a missing quantifier contributing to the confusion.

    In the context of this claim (made about the Sponsorgate scandal), the referents include taking government money for work not done, grossly overbilling for work, and accepting bribes and kickbacks.

16

2. Bikers are members of criminal organizations.

   Bikers could refer to all motorcycle riders or be restricted to members of outlaw motorcycle organizations. The claim is true only of the latter, although some see all bikers as being involved in criminal activity.

   ***Criminal organization* can refer to individuals working together to import drugs, control prostitution, launder money, and so forth.**

3. Intelligence is genetic.

   ***Intelligence* refers to such things as the ability to learn from experience, solve problems, and connect ideas.**

   ***Genetic* refers to genes. Something can be said to be genetic if it is (a) determined by genes or (b) influenced by genes.**

   The claim can mean one of two things: (1) The ability to learn from experience, etc., is directly determined by a person's genes—i.e., the genes of more intelligent people are different from those of less intelligent people; or (2) Genes set the preconditions for intelligence by, for example, establishing the neuronal pathways and the speed with which messages move along such pathways. How individuals use such capacities determines their intelligence.

   In the former sense, a person's genes determine his or her intelligence. In the second, genes only set the framework; environmental factors also have an impact on the development of intelligence.

✍ QUICK QUIZ 2.4
Neutralizing Connotations and Prejudicial Language

In each of the following, identify whether there are terms or claims with strong connotations. If so, neutralize the connotation by dividing the claims into the literal meaning and the emotive force.

1. The anti-choice terrorists have prevented abortion providers from doing their legal work. They have bombed their offices, killed them, and stalked their employees. These enemies of freedom need to be stopped.

   Terms with strong connotations include *anti-choice* and *enemies of freedom*. *Bombed, killed,* and *stalked* also have strong negative connotations. However, we have no terms with neutral connotations to describe these events.

   Neutralized: Anti-abortionists have prevented legal abortion providers from performing abortions by bombing their offices, stalking their employees, and killing them.

If assessing the claim, I would qualify it as referring to "some anti-abortionists."

2. *Spoken by a U.S. commentator:* Those spineless cowards who oppose the valiant U.S. efforts in Iraq are soft on terror and encouraging the murder of our brave fighting men.

   Terms with strong connotations include *spineless cowards, valiant, soft on terror* (a code word)*, encouraging murder,* and *brave fighting men.*

   Neutralized: The critics of the U.S. involvement in Iraq are providing encouragement to those the U.S. is fighting and in so doing are responsible for the deaths of our soldiers.

3. We should be wary of legalizing gay marriage. If we change the definition of marriage to include same-sex marriage, then there appear to be no grounds for limiting marriage to two people or prohibiting it to near relatives. The move to change the nature of marriage could result in legalizing polygamy and incest.

   There are no loaded terms being used to sway the audience in this. Some individuals may react negatively to such terms as gay *marriage, polygamy,* and *incest.* However, these words are not being used in a prejudicial way in this passage. The speaker is presenting an argument about the possible consequences of legalizing gay marriage. Although an arguer may disagree with the argument and its inferences, the argument does not necessarily involve prejudicial use of language.

✍ QUICK QUIZ 2.5
Vagueness

Given the context, which of the following concepts or claims are vague? Explain why and how the vagueness could be corrected. Use the principles for addressing vagueness to make the claims more precise.

1. A police constable, having pulled over a motorist, asks the motorist if he has had anything to drink. The motorist answers, "Just a couple of beers."

   In the context, *drink* is not vague. *Just a couple of beers,* however, is. The constable is trying to determine whether the motorist is intoxicated. "A couple" could mean two, three, or more. Specifying the number, the time frame, and how many in the past hour would be much more precise and would supply the information the constable is seeking.

2. A paper comparing the anatomy of various primates: A gorilla has long arms.

   ***Long arms* is vague in this context. It is a comparison term. How do a gorilla's arms compare to those of other primates? Are the gorilla's arms long in relation to the gorilla's body structure or long compared to the length of the arms of other primates (the gorilla is the largest of the primates)?**

3. *Astrological profile:* You have a strong need to be liked but are fiercely independent. You are strong-willed, with a drive for achievement, yet you take time to stop and smell the flowers.

> **Much of this is vague. *Strong need to be liked, fiercely independent, strong-willed, drive for achievement,* and *take time to stop and smell the flowers* are all open-ended terms. Any individual, given this as a commentary on his or her personality, could identify qualities that fit some or all of these descriptions. It's completely open to interpretation. This is terminally vague: It cannot be made more precise.**

✍ QUICK QUIZ 2.6
Missing Quantifiers and Qualifiers

In the following, identify claims that have missing quantifiers and qualifiers, suggest possible differences and variations among the referents, and provide a more restrictive claim. If there are strong connotations, neutralize them.

1. Universities need to clean up their act. All I read about are students getting out of control, having sex parties, posing for *Playboy,* drinking and uttering racist remarks. The police regularly have to be called to homecoming at Queen's, and McGill was just voted one of the leading "party schools" in North America. What ever happened to going to university to learn?

> ***universities:* All universities or some? Some Canadian universities or all universities in North America?**

> ***students:* A few, some, many, all; some of the time, frequently? Are these beginning-of–term/end-of-term episodes, or do they continue through the term? Are the ones going to sex parties and posing for Playboy the same ones as those uttering racist remarks?**

> **The speaker has observed the behaviour of some of the students at two Canadian universities.**

2. Scientists defending evolution are opposed to religion.

> ***scientists:* With no qualification, this suggests all scientists.**

> ***religion:* All religion, all aspects of religion?**

> **The way this statement is presented, it seems to be claiming that all scientists are opposed to all aspects of all religions. In fact, some scientists, including many who defend evolution, are deeply religious.**

3. *Said by one university faculty member to another:* Students are getting worse. My recently assigned papers were so badly written, I had to hand them back for rewriting. And the incidence of plagiarism is at epidemic proportions.

students: All students or just some of the students in this faculty member's classes?

epidemic proportions: What is "epidemic proportions"? This could be several more than last year or the entire class.

badly written: In what ways were the papers badly written? Poor grammar, poor scholarship, not well argued? Each of these is different and could indicate a different kind of problem.

This could be taken as a voicing of frustration by the faculty member as well as a report of her perception of the changing conditions of her students.

✍ QUICK QUIZ 2.7
Ambiguity

In each of the following, find any terms that are used ambiguously and identify their alternate meanings.

1. The theory of evolution is just a theory. And theories are not factual, just speculative. So the theory of evolution is just a speculation.

   The word *theory* is used in two senses. In science, a theory is a set of interconnected general statements used to unify, explain, and predict phenomena. In everyday language, theory is opposed to fact and means speculation.

2. How can the doctor say that my mother is dead? With the respirator, she is still breathing.

   ***Death* can mean cessation of heartbeat and respiration or cessation of brain activity and function (electrical activity in the brain). The son or daughter is using the heartbeat/respirator definition, while the physician is likely using the brain activity criterion.**

3. Mathematics is a science. After all, it is taught in the faculty of science.

   There are two notions of science here: Science is whatever is taught in a school's faculty of science, and science is a field of knowledge based on observation and empirical knowledge that seeks to explain the physical world. Mathematics is a tool used to explain phenomena in the physical world, but it is not based on observation and is not itself explanatory.

✍ QUICK QUIZ 2.8
Words That Conceal

Translate the following into plain language.

1. *Military:* We made a preemptive reaction strike to neutralize the enemy. However, there was some civilian collateral damage. Several of the coalition forces succumbed to friendly fire.

   We attacked the enemy before he could attack us to prevent him from attacking us. Our attack killed some civilians and some of our own forces.

2. The municipal government is committed to revenue-enhancement measures through cost recovery for nonessential programs.

   The municipal government is going to increase its revenues by getting people to pay for services it considers nonessential.

3. *Corporate email announcement:* George Footloose has left the company effective immediately.

   George was fired. (This is familiar "code" in the context of the corporate world.)

✍ QUICK QUIZ 2.9
Hypostatization

In each of the following, determine if any terms are being hypostatized. If so, identify the term, explain how it is being hypostatized, and state the possible problems that could result because of the hypostatization. If it is possible to treat the terms elliptically, provide an elliptical translation of the claim.

1. Poverty is stalking our nation's children.

   Poverty is likened to a stalker pursuing children. Treating poverty as a single entity could lead to thinking about it as an isolated thing and cause us to ignore the many different factors that contribute to poverty. If this sentence means that many children are either in poverty or risk falling into poverty, this would not be a hypostatization.

2. The male gender believes that women are inferior and seeks to dominate and control them.

   This sentence considers all men as a single entity (the male gender) that has ideas (women are inferior) and a certain intention (to dominate and control women). Treating all men as identical in this way leads us not to see the differences among men and their ideas and attitudes toward women. It also leads us to ignore the various social, economic, and psychological factors that might lead many men to hold such views.

   Saying some (or many) men consider women inferior and seek to dominate and control them is not a hypostatization.

3. The nation demands that every citizen rally behind the war effort.

> **This statement treats the nation as an entity capable of making demands. The nation is composed of many things—leaders, citizens, politicians, opposition groups. What this may be saying is that the leaders of the existing government want people to support the war movement. An unpopular government engaged in an unpopular war might utter such a demand. The sentence may also be saying that leaders of the existing government and some citizens (either a large or small number) want this.**

> **"As a nation, all citizens need to rally behind the war effort" would not be a hypostatization.**

4. The gay community is trying to impose its views about marriage on the rest of society.

> **This sentence treats gays and lesbians as a cohesive single entity (called "the gay community") with one common set of views and intentions.**

> **"Many in the gay community are trying to get the rest of society to support gay marriage" is not a hypostatization.**

✍ QUICK QUIZ 2.10
Metaphors

Identify the metaphors in the following statements and translate them into neutral language. Determine what is under discussion and what it is being compared to. Indicate whether the metaphors in each passage are likely to mislead. Explain.

1. *Politician during an election campaign:* Canadians are staggering under a massive tax burden. If elected, we will relieve the weight borne by the ordinary taxpayer.

> **Taxation is likened to a burden one carries. Burdens may be heavy or light but are generally something people do not voluntarily take on. The metaphor encourages us to think of paying taxes as unpleasant and burdensome rather than, for example, as "dues," "a right," or "an investment in ourselves and our society's future." Each of these alternate metaphors suggests taxes are something positive. As dues, they are payment for what we receive in return. As a right, the focus is on what we gain from paying taxes—the rights we have as a member of society, taxes being the obligation we have in exchange for those rights. The economic metaphor of taxes as an investment turns the focus on improving or increasing our own value and that of our society as a whole. [1]**

---

[1] The metaphor of taxation as a burden comes from George Lakoff:
http://www.berkeley.edu/news/media/releases/2004/08/25_lakoff.shtml.

2. There's a hole in that theory.

   A theory is compared to a container or a ship that doesn't function if there is a hole in it. This could mislead. A hole in a boat or container is a weakness and grounds for rejecting the boat. A hole in a theory, on the other hand, might be an opportunity for further developing the theory.

3. He spends his time wisely.

   Use of time is compared to economic investment. We can use our time prudently or imprudently. Where this has potential to mislead is in what the investment is for and what might count as dividends from the investment. It may also suggest that the use of our time should be measured in terms of profit and loss—of what it achieves. This may not always be a good thing.

✍ QUICK QUIZ 2.11
Identifying Kinds of Definitions

Identify the kind of definition used in each of the following statements.

1. For the purpose of the Income Tax Act, a student is someone who is enrolled in a full-time course of study at an approved educational institution.

   This is an operational definition. It might also be considered a stipulative definition.

2. An environmentalist is someone who wants to preserve the environment at the expense of humans.

   This is a persuasive definition. It slants the definition against environmentalists.

3. In this paper, by *education*, I mean not only formal education but any informal learning individuals undertake to better themselves.

   This is a stipulative definition of education for the purpose of a given paper.

4. A bachelor is an unmarried male.

   This is an essential definition. Being unmarried and a male are necessary and sufficient conditions (together) for being a bachelor.

5. Suicide is the act of intentionally killing oneself.

   This is an essential definition. Intentionally killing oneself is a necessary and sufficient condition for suicide. This is also, probably, a reportive definition.

6. Euthanasia is the unjust killing of another human being.

   This is a persuasive definition. By including unjust in the definition, the writer puts an emotive slant on euthanasia.

7. A student is one who studies.

   This is a reportive definition.

8. For the purpose of this act, a motor vehicle is defined as any vehicle powered by a gasoline engine.

   This is a stipulative definition.

✍ QUICK QUIZ 2.12
Criteria for Good Definitions

For each of the definitions in Quick Quiz 2.11, given the kind of definition each is, explain whether the definition meets the criteria for a good definition.

1. *student:* **As an operational or stipulative definition, this seems reasonable, given the purpose. It defines not students but students eligible for some kind of tax benefit. It is too narrow to be a reportive or essential definition because it excludes individuals who are part-time students or students who are studying at nonapproved institutions.**

2. *environmentalist:* **As it stands, this is not a neutral definition. However, if "at the expense of humans" were deleted, this could be a satisfactory reportive definition.**

3. *education:* **As a stipulative definition, depending on the uses of the term education in the paper, it seems reasonable. Since it includes not just formal education but any learning, if there is a difference between formal education and learning, then the definition would be too broad. The definition also includes the idea that the learning must be to better oneself. Depending on the meaning of "better oneself," this may also make it too broad.**

4. *bachelor:* **This is a good definition and meets all of the criteria.**

5. *suicide:* **This is a good definition and meets all of the criteria. It does, however, exclude some of the extended uses of the term suicide—for example, "suicide by cop" and "assisted suicide."**

6. *euthanasia:* **This is not a neutral definition—the term unjust is prejudicial in this context. It passes judgment on euthanasia. It is also too broad: Not all killing of another human being or unjust killing of a human being is euthanasia. Abortion and murder both fit these conditions without being euthanasia.**

7. *student:* This definition is circular and therefore not helpful to a reader.

8. *motor vehicle:* This is a stipulative definition. However, it is a poor one. It is both too broad and too narrow. It includes riding lawn mowers and excludes diesel-powered vehicles.

EXERCISES

✍ EXERCISE 2.1
Words, Concepts, Referents, and Connotations

In each of the following, identify the possible referents and meanings for the key concepts and explain the meaning of the claim, taking different contexts into consideration. Where various referents and meanings are possible, identify these and show how they affect the meaning of the claims.

1. Cats are playful.

2. *Proposed university policy:* The university prohibits public demonstrations and gatherings in academic buildings.

3. I contend that all speech, not just politically correct speech, is covered by the provisions of freedom of speech. And that includes hate speech.

4. Mary Shelley's work *Frankenstein* is an excellent example of a Romantic-era novel.

5. The widespread use of obscene language on such publicly aired shows as *The Sopranos* violates the Code of Broadcasting Ethics, which prohibits obscenity, nudity, and pornography from being broadcast on the public airwaves.

6. The government does not sanction torture in the interrogation of prisoners of war.

7. *From a student code of conduct:* Students shall show respect for the rights and views of others.

8. Crime in society is increasing.

9. Gender is determined by genes.

10. My cat is lost.

11. The truth shall set you free.

12. The Supreme Court has ruled that capital punishment is unconstitutional.

13. Economics treats human behaviour as based on exchange within a market.

14. Your car needs new tires.

15. Our goal is to restore democracy to the region.

16. The government will fall on Monday.

17. Tom's sex is male, but his gender is feminine.

18. Power resides in wielding legitimate authority. All else is domination.

19. Martin is a good lecturer.

20. All persons of sound religious morals should support our call for teaching religious values in the schools.

🖎 EXERCISE 2.2
Neutralizing Emotive and Prejudicial Language

In the following, identify whether there are terms and claims with emotive or prejudicial language and, if so, neutralize it by identifying the literal meaning and the emotional force of each set of claims.

1. *Spoken by an opponent of the Kyoto Accord:* The pseudo-research by the alarmists claiming that global warming is increasing is just junk science designed to demonize legitimate attempts by those opposed to global warming to tell the unvarnished truth that global warming does not exist.

2. *Spoken by a pro-life advocate:* The murderers who run the abortion industry are solely motivated to murder pre-born babies for profit. The abortion mills are simply the ovens of a modern Holocaust against our most vulnerable citizens.

3. Legalizing gay marriage will lead to demands that all kinds of other unions be made legal, from incest to polygamy to bestiality.

4. Research using live animals is done in the most humane way with an avoidance of as much pain and suffering as possible. Animals that are severely injured in the research are euthanized humanely.

5. *Said in opposition to a proposal to legalize marijuana:* Now the government wants to legalize drugs—drugs that destroy lives—so it can make money off of people's misery through regulation and taxation.

6. *Said in opposition to a proposal to include information on conception and contraception in grade-nine health classes:* The perverts are proposing that we usurp the sacred right of parents and allow uninformed high school jocks to teach our children about sex and abortion.

7. This spend-hungry government knows no restraints when it comes to extorting money from the besieged taxpayer struggling to stay afloat financially.

8. The irrational proposals fail to meet the minimal conditions for sound public policy.

9. The watchdog agencies meant to oversee government decisions are, instead, slavishly jumping to the whims of their political masters.

10. The new city hall is a hideous blot on the landscape.

11. Reasonable people will see through the wrong-headed assumptions being proposed by the dysfunctional city council.

12. We have a sacred obligation to those who have given their lives for the cause that their sacrifice shall not be in vain.

13. *Said by a Holocaust denier:* The language police are trying to suppress the right to freedom of speech of those who, with great intellectual courage, have investigated the tissue of lies about the holocaust.

14. Intellectual integrity and free speech mean that all sides of an issue be aired. I demand that medical schools teach, alongside obstetrics, that storks bring babies.

15. George is a card-carrying member of the American Civil Liberties Union.

16. Reasonable Picard fans and the Kirk fanatics are fighting over which series is the better *Star Trek*.

17. Abortion is a war on the unborn. Abortion doctors commit cold-blooded murder every day. Killing the murderers is not murder. It is self-defence on behalf of the unborn.

18. We need stronger laws to stop those who pirate software and copyright material and destroy the very basis of our capitalist society. We do not sanction theft. And stealing copyright material is simply theft.

19. An elite few at city hall are trying to implement ruinous anti-smoking policies against the wishes of the majority of the population.

20. The supporters of intelligent design, fighting for free speech and intellectual integrity, are valiantly resisting the storm-trooper tactics of evolutionary biologists, who are posting a last-ditch effort to defend their failed and discredited theory.

✎ EXERCISE 2.3
Definitions

Using the criteria for good definitions and an assessment of the appropriateness of certain definitions in certain contexts, assess whether the definitions proposed below are adequate. If no context is given, assume that the definition is used to clarify the meaning of a term used in a conversation.

1. A preacher is someone who preaches.

2. An honest person is someone who rarely lies.

3. Informed consent is when an individual about to undergo a medical procedure is given information about the possible outcomes of the procedure, understands those outcomes, and then gives his or her consent to undergo that procedure.

4. Someone is poor if his or her income is below the median income for a given community.

5. Evolution is the process by which higher forms of life have developed from lower ones.

6. You want to know what a student is? Fred over there is a student. Moshe, standing next to him isn't.

7. Racism is the systematic subordination and subjugation of a minority group that has little social power.

8. *University regulations:* For the purposes of these regulations, a student is someone currently enrolled in a degree program at the university and taking at least one course in the current term.

9. For the purposes of this paper, I define a Romantic novel as any novel written in the Romantic era.

10. A planet is an object that orbits the sun, has sufficient gravity to be pushed into a round ball, and clears other objects out of the way of its orbit.

11. Hockey is a game played on ice.

12. For the purposes of this study, race is defined as a group of people differing from another group by one or more genes.

13. Economics is the study of wealth.

14. Sex is what people do when they are having sex.

15. A CD is a compact disk.

16. A person is hearing impaired if he or she has less than normal hearing.

17. A pen is an implement for writing.

18. Water is a colourless, odourless, binary compound composed of hydrogen and oxygen; at normal room temperature, it is a liquid.

19. A parking infraction, for the purpose of this legislation, is a violation of one of the parking ordinances as detailed in Section 4 below.

20. A hat is something worn on the head to protect the wearer from sun.

🖎 EXERCISE 2.4
Cumulative Meaning Exercise

The following passages may have various problems with meaning, including vague terms, hypostatizations, euphemisms, doublespeak, metaphors that mislead, missing quantifiers, or definitional problems. Where there is a problem of meaning, identify the kind of problem and use the appropriate means for clarifying the meaning. If you cannot make sense of the meaning, explain why. Some of the following may involve metaphorical and other uses of language that do not mislead. If so, indicate that.

1. The paper is full of inaccuracies and substantive errors.

2. Men are male chauvinists.

3. Animals used in learning experiments will be euthanized at the end of the study.

4. The white race has enslaved the black race and now owes it compensation for the injustices it has done.

5. *Television ad:* I will reinvest in myself in my retirement.

6. Cabinet minister responding to challenges that the government did not react quickly enough to a natural disaster: We responded in a timely and appropriate manner to the disaster and are considering further options.

7. The government has its hands in the pocket of every honest citizen and is stealing what is rightfully the individual's.

8. Justice demands that the accused be convicted.

9. *Seen in a job ad:* Applicants must have two years of Canadian work experience or equivalent.

10. Over 60% of the people surveyed report being overworked.

11. *Said by the prime minister of a minority government:* The voters have given us a mandate to bring about substantial changes in the policies that run this country, and we are going to do that.

12. Students are far more computer savvy than they were five years ago.

13. The universe is simply a machine. Scientists are merely identifying the laws that make that machine function the way it does.

14. The province has been hit with a plague of mortgage fraud in the past six months.

15. Runaway climate change threatens to reach a tipping point that will overwhelm our abilities to deal with it.

16. Use of our wonderful anti-aging cream may help combat the effects of aging skin.

17. Technology has become the god of modern society, subsuming all under its sway—values, human relations, and culture.

18. The war between science and religion has taken a new twist with the development of the intelligent design movement and biologists increasing support of an atheism fuelled by evolutionary theory.

19. The study shows that genetic parents are more abusive toward children than stepparents are.

20. The student council has failed in its duties and should be removed from office.

MODULE 3: ANALYZING ARGUMENTS

QUICK QUIZ ANSWERS

✍ QUICK QUIZ 3.1
Identifying Claims

Identify which of the following are claims and which are not. Explain why each is or is not a claim.

1. Is marriage a sacred institution that deserves to be preserved by the state?

    Question (not a claim).

2. You're joking!

    Exclamation (not a claim).

3. You smoke?!

    Combination question/exclamation (not a claim).

4. Canadians tend to be more tolerant than their neighbors to the south.

    Claim.

5. Surely you don't support gay marriage, do you?

    Question (not a claim).

✍ QUICK QUIZ 3.2
Identifying Arguments

Which of the following are arguments? Why?

1. Although objectionable, racist materials should not be banned from schools.

    Two claims in one sentence—racist materials are objectionable; they should not be banned—but not an argument.

2. The fundamental principles of justice demand that gay marriage be legalized.

    One claim—no argument. Had the person elaborated on what the fundamental principles of justice are, this could possibly be turned into an argument.

3. Secondhand smoke causes harm to others. Therefore, it should be banned in any area that the public has access to.

> **Argument.**
> **Premise:** Secondhand smoke causes harm to others.
> **Conclusion:** It should be banned in any area that the public has access to.

4. Marriage is a sacred institution and deserves to be preserved by the state.

> **Ambiguous. If the person is saying that marriage should be preserved because it is a sacred institution, then it is an argument. If the person is saying that marriage should be preserved *and* that it is a sacred institution (that is, not offering its sacred status as a reason for preserving it), then it is not an argument. Seeing the sentence within the context of the whole would help us determine this. Note how paraphrasing the alternatives and addressing each of the alternatives can help in clarifying the meaning of the passage. In this case, the passage is *ambiguous* (has two or more possible meanings), and nothing in the passage helps us resolve which of those alternative meanings is the intended one.**

5. If pornography causes harm, then it should be banned.

> **One claim—no argument. The sentence says that pornography should be banned if it meets a certain condition. We don't know from the passage whether it does or does not meet that condition. Hence, we can't draw any conclusion. This is called a *conditional claim:* It states a conditional relationship between two states of affairs. Conditional claims in themselves are not arguments.**

✍ QUICK QUIZ 3.3
Distinguishing Arguments from Other Prose

Identify whether the passages below contain arguments, explanations, illustrations, descriptions, narratives, or some other kind of discourse.

1. Céline took the job because she needed the money.

> **Not an argument. It offers an explanation (motive) for Céline taking the job.**

2. Céline had been looking for six months. She had numerous initial interviews, but no follow-up interviews, and she was getting desperate.

> **Description of the background conditions.**

3. Some of her friends had had better luck than she. Her friend Johan had gotten a job within three weeks of starting his job search.

> **Description of the background conditions.**

4. Céline told her younger brother not to take philosophy in university, because it wouldn't help him get a job when he graduated.

> **Argument (also offered as advice).**
> **Premise:** Taking philosophy in university won't help him get a job.
> **Conclusion:** He should not take philosophy in university.

✍ QUICK QUIZ 3.4
Identifying Inference Indicators

In the following passages, circle the inference indicator words being used as such. Make note of any inference indicators that are being misused. Identify the premises and conclusions by putting a *P* next to the premises and a *C* next to the conclusions.

1. Marriage is sacred; therefore, it should be preserved.

> **[P] Marriage is sacred; (therefore,) [C] it should be preserved.**

2. We should allow gay marriage because if we don't, we will be discriminating against people unjustly.

> **[P] We should allow gay marriage (because) [C] if we don't, we will be discriminating against people unjustly.**

3. Marijuana should be outlawed. First, it is harmful; second, the claimed medical benefits are bogus; and finally, it undermines productivity and causes safety hazards in the workplace.

> **[C] Marijuana should be outlawed. (First,) [P] it is harmful; (second,) [P] the claimed medical benefits are bogus; and (finally,) [P] it undermines productivity and causes safety hazards in the workplace.**

4. The Tour de France has been happening since 1903; however, it didn't achieve its current international prominence until after 1980.

> **Not an argument.** *However* is not an inference indicator.

5. Abortion is wrong; therefore, the fetus is a person and therefore anything that kills a person is wrong.

> **This is a misuse of the term *therefore*. The author has simply inserted *therefore* in front of his or her claims. But there is a potential argument here. "Abortion is wrong" would be the conclusion. The other two claims (those preceded by *therefore*) are reasons. However, both the sequence of the claims and the connections between them are incorrect. The fetus being a person may be a reason for considering abortion wrong, not the other way around. And anything that kills a person may be a reason for considering abortion wrong. The author has reversed the logical order and made "abortion is wrong" the reason, not the conclusion.**

Identifying Arguments and Providing Cue Words

In the following passages, identify the basic argument, and then provide the appropriate inference indicator words to help the reader follow the passage. You may reorder the sentences or paraphrase where necessary.

1. Abortion should be banned. It is morally wrong to kill an innocent human.

   P: It is morally wrong to kill an innocent human.
   C: Abortion should be banned.

   Abortion should be banned because it is morally wrong to kill an innocent human.

2. Capital punishment does not allow people to be rehabilitated, and it is immoral.

   P: Capital punishment does not allow people to be rehabilitated.
   C: It is immoral.

   Capital punishment does not allow people to be rehabilitated, so it is therefore immoral.

3. Kittens need to be trained. Instinct goes only so far with higher mammals. What is not governed by instinct needs to be taught. Kittens are higher mammals.

   P: Instinct goes only so far with higher mammals.
   P: What is not governed by instinct needs to be taught.
   P: Kittens are higher mammals.
   C: Kittens need to be trained.

   Instinct goes only so far with higher mammals. What is not governed by instinct needs to be taught. Kittens are higher mammals. Therefore, kittens need to be trained.

4. Most people believe that the woolly mammoths became extinct because of the Ice Age. This explanation is not satisfactory. Mammoths have been found entombed whole in glaciers in Siberia. Glaciers form and move too slowly to entomb woolly mammoths suddenly. The glaciers came later than the woolly mammoths. The mammoths were clearly the first alien abductions. Nothing else makes sense.

   P: Glaciers form and move too slowly to entomb woolly mammoths suddenly.
   P: The glaciers came later than the woolly mammoths.
   C: The mammoths were the first alien abductions.

   The woolly mammoths were the first alien abductions. I say this because glaciers form and move too slowly to entomb woolly mammoths suddenly and because the glaciers came later than the woolly mammoths. Their extinction

because of the Ice Age therefore makes no sense. The only alternative is alien abductions.

5. Everyone should wear a seat belt. This should be mandatory. Not wearing one increases the risk of death. When people are injured or killed in car accidents, their families are devastated. We all have an obligation to our family. And we all have an obligation to society. Not wearing a seat belt results in more injuries, which have to be paid for by the rest of society.

> P: Not wearing a seat belt increases the risk of death.
> P: When people are injured or killed in car accidents, their families are devastated.
> P: Not wearing a seat belt results in more injuries, the cost of which the rest of society must bear.
> P: People have an obligation both to their families and to society.
> C: Wearing seat belts should be mandatory.

> Wearing a seat belt should be mandatory for two reasons. First, people have an obligation to their families. Not wearing a seat belt increases the risk of being injured or killed, which would devastate a family. Second, not wearing a seat belt increases the number and seriousness of injuries from accidents, and society has to bear the costs of these.

✍ QUICK QUIZ 3.6
Ordering Claims in an Argument

Below are five claims that make up a single argument. Identify the basic structure of the argument and then, using only these, order the claims so the argument will be easy for the reader to follow. Add cue words to assist the reader. (Hint: Start with the most controversial claim and then look for the reason for that.)

1. Humans and apes have completely different genes.

2. Humans and apes inhabit the earth at the same time.

3. Humans could not be descended from apes.

4. The Bible claims that humans and apes were created distinctly and separately.

5. If two species have completely different genes, one could not have descended from the other.

> I contend that man could not be descended from apes for three basic reasons. First, men and apes live at the same time. Second, men and apes have completely different genes. If two species have completely different genes,

one could not have descended from the other. Finally, the Bible claims that men and apes were created distinctly and separately.

This argument starts with the conclusion and then lists the premises.

✒ QUICK QUIZ 3.7
Portraying Standard Form

Portray the following arguments in standard form.

1. All tortoiseshell cats are female. Felicity is a tortoiseshell cat. Felicity is female.

> **All tortoiseshell cats are female.**
> **Felicity is a tortoiseshell cat.**
> _____
> ∴ **Felicity is female.**

> **This is the best formulation using the principle of charity, which holds that whenever possible, we should assume that the arguer is trying to give a valid and cogent argument. If the first premise is treated as the conclusion and the conclusion as a premise, we have created a form of the fallacy of hasty generalization.**

2. According to reports of the sightings of the Loch Ness monster, it would be an enormous size—at least six metres in length and a ton or more in weight. An aquatic creature of that size would have to eat literally tons of food each month. Yet, the loch has a far smaller food supply than that. The reported sightings must be wrong.

> **Paraphrase: If the Loch Ness monster were real and the sightings' reports factual, the creature would be an enormous size and would require a diet of tons of food per month. The loch does not have such a food supply. So the reported sightings must be wrong.**

> **If the Loch Ness monster were real, the creature would be an enormous size and would require a diet of tons of food per month.**
> **If the sightings' reports were factual, the creature would be an enormous size and would require a diet of tons of food per month.**
> **The loch does not have such a food supply.**
> _____
> ∴ **The reported sightings must be wrong.**

3. Although Lance Armstrong has won seven Tour de France races to Eddy Merckx's five, Merckx is the better cyclist. Armstrong has won only 71 classic races, including the Tour and the five stages he has won within the Tour. Merckx has won 471 classic races, including his stages within the Tour de France. Although they are both amazing and both legends, Merckx is the better all-round cyclist.

**Eddy Merckx has won 471 classic races, including his stages within the
Tour de France, and five Tour de France races.
Lance Armstrong has won 71 classic races, including his stages within
the Tour de France, and seven Tour de France races.**

∴ **Eddy Merckx is the better all-round cyclist.**

4. *Context: A couple had planned to go camping.* "I think we should stay home. It's going to rain all weekend."

It's going to rain all weekend.

∴ **We should stay home (and not go camping) this weekend.**

5. I recommend that we fire Farah. She has been making decisions not within her job description and then contacting other agencies and saying that her decisions are company policy. She has been warned twice that this is unacceptable behaviour and that it contravenes corporate policy, but she hasn't listened or learned. If she continues, she will cause serious problems not only externally to the company's relationships but internally as well. She's got to go.

**Farah has been making decisions not within her job description and
passing them off as company policy.
She has been warned twice that this is unacceptable behaviour and that
it contravenes corporate policy.
She hasn't listened or learned.
If she continues, she will cause serious problems for the company.**

∴ **We should fire Farah.**

✍ QUICK QUIZ 3.8
Using Arrow Diagrams

Portray the arguments in Quick Quiz 3.7 using arrow diagrams.

           1   **2**
1. **[All tortoiseshell cats are female.] [Felicity is a tortoiseshell cat.]**
           3
[Felicity is female.]

$$\frac{1 + 2}{\Downarrow}$$
$$3$$

2. **According to reports of the sightings of the Loch Ness monster, [it would be an**
                                       1
enormous size—at least six metres in length and a ton or more in weight.] [An

2
aquatic creature of that size would have to eat literally tons of food each month.]
3   4
Yet, [the loch has a far smaller food supply than that.] [The reported sightings

must be wrong.]

$$\frac{1 + 2 + 3}{\downarrow}$$
4

3. Paraphrase:

1   2
[Eddie Merckx is the better all-round cyclist] because [he has won 471

classic races to Armstrong's seventy-one.]

2
↓
1

1   2
4. I think [we should stay home.] [It's going to rain all weekend.]

2
↓
1

1   2
5. I recommend that [we (should) fire Farah.] [She has been making decisions not

within her job description and then contacting other agencies and saying that her
3
decisions are company policy.] [She has been warned twice that this is unaccept-

able behaviour and that it contravenes corporate policy] but [she hasn't listened
4   5
or learned.] [If she continues, she will cause serious problems not only externally
6
to the company's relationships but internally as well.] [She's got to go.]

1 = 6   2 + 3 + 4 + 5
↓
6

Interpreting Arrow Diagrams

Explain the meaning of each of the following arrow diagrams by identifying the premises and conclusions:

1.   1   2   3
       ↘   ↓   ↙
              4

   1, 2, and 3 are each independent premises for the conclusion, which is 4.

2.   1 + 2   3   4 + 5
       ↘   ↓   ↙
               6

   There are three independent arguments given here: 1 and 2 are linked premises; 3 is an independent premise; and 4 and 5 are linked premises. 6 is the conclusion of all three arguments.

3.   1 + 2   7
       ↓   ↓
       3   4   5 + 6
         ↘   ↓   ↙
                8

   8 is the main conclusion. Three independent lines of argument lead to 8. In the first, 3 is an intermediate conclusion that acts as a premise for 8 and is the conclusion of two premises, 1 and 2, which are linked. The second line of argument has one premise, 4. The third line of argument has two linked premises that support 8, premises 5 and 6. 5 is further supported by another premise, 7—5 is the conclusion of 7.

✍ **QUICK QUIZ 3.10**
Diagramming Complex Arguments

Portray the structure of following arguments.

1. Marriage is a private matter between the partners in a marriage. The state has no right to interfere in the private affairs of its citizens. Therefore, the state has no right to prohibit gay marriage.

                                  1
   [Marriage is a private matter between the partners in a marriage.] [The state
                                  2
   has no right to interfere in the private affairs of its citizens. ⟨**Therefore**⟩ **[the**
                    3

state has no right to prohibit gay marriage.]

$$\frac{1 + 2}{\downarrow}$$
3

2. The state does have a right to regulate marriage, including gay marriage. The state is entitled to enforce morals and values, and sexual relations between individuals of the same sex are immoral and an abomination to God. Moreover, marriage is fundamentally about conceiving and raising children, and gay couples can't do this. So the state has a right to prohibit gay marriage.

1

[The state does have a right to regulate marriage, including gay marriage.]
2
[The state is entitled to enforce morals and values,] and [sexual relations
3
between individuals of the same sex are immoral and an abomination to
4
God.] Moreover, [marriage is fundamentally about conceiving and raising
5   6
children,] and [gay couples can't do this.] So [the state has a right to

prohibit gay marriage.]

$$\frac{2 + 3}{\searrow} \qquad \frac{4 + 5}{\swarrow}$$
1

Note: Claim 3 could be treated as one claim or two:

3a: Sexual relations between individuals of the same sex are immoral.
3b: Sexual relations between individuals of the same sex are an abomination to God.
If separated, these would form the basis of two distinct arguments.

$$\frac{2 + 3a}{\searrow} \quad \frac{3b}{\downarrow} \quad \frac{4 + 5}{\swarrow}$$
1

Depending on how the passage is interpreted, claims 1 and 6 can be treated as one or as two separate claims. They are not the same, but in the context of this passage, they might be intended to mean the same.

3. The recent dramatic increase in gas prices is a good thing because it will result in less drain on oil reserves. We are running low on oil reserves and need to conserve them.

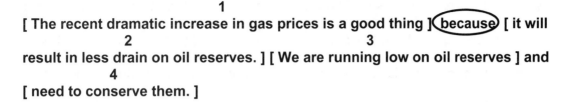

1
[The recent dramatic increase in gas prices is a good thing] (because) [it will
2   3
result in less drain on oil reserves.] [We are running low on oil reserves] and
4
[need to conserve them.]

2 + 3 + 4
↓
1

4. Capital punishment is not effective as a deterrent. It is a form of cruel and unusual
    punishment. And we risk killing innocent people with capital punishment because some
    innocent individuals have been convicted of what would be capital crimes. Therefore, capital
    punishment should not be allowed.

1   2
[Capital punishment is not effective as a deterrent.] [It is a form of cruel
3
and unusual punishment.] And [we risk killing innocent people with capital
4
punishment] (because) [some innocent individuals have been convicted of
5
what would be capital crimes.] (Therefore,) [capital punishment should

not be allowed.]

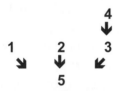

5. The Atlantis portrayed by Plato and on which all later stories of the lost continent are based
    could not have existed. Plato says that Atlantis was in the Atlantic Ocean, that it was
    destroyed by tidal waves and earthquakes and sank to the bottom of the sea virtually
    overnight, and that it was an extremely advanced culture that existed 10,000 years before his
    day. Extensive mapping of the Atlantic Ocean floor reveals neither the kind of rock of which
    continents are made nor a land mass even approximating the presumed size of Atlantis. From
    geology, we know that tidal waves and earthquakes cannot cause a land mass of Atlantis's
    alleged size to sink to the ocean bottom, much less overnight. Nor is there any evidence for
    any kind of advanced civilization existing 10,000 years before Plato. Plato's story is a myth.

    Paraphrase:
    1
    [Plato's Atlantis could not have existed.] [Plato claims that Atlantis was an
    2
    advanced civilization that existed 10,000 years before his day and that it was

destroyed by earthquakes and tidal waves and sank to the bottom of the sea

3

virtually overnight.] [Neither of these claims is true.] [Earthquakes and tidal

4

waves cannot cause a land mass of Atlantis's alleged size to sink to the

5

bottom of the ocean overnight.] And [there is no evidence of an advanced

civilization anywhere 10,000 years prior to Plato.]

$$\frac{4 + 5}{\downarrow}$$
$$\frac{2 + 3}{\downarrow}$$
$$1$$

✍ QUICK QUIZ 3.11
Identifying Arguments in Passages with Extraneous Material

In the following passages, identify whether or not there is an argument. If there is no argument, explain why. If there is an argument, identify the basic argument. Be especially attentive to extraneous material and do not include it in your analysis. If there is extraneous material, explain why the material is irrelevant to the argument.

1. 1 Transgender people are individuals who believe that their proper gender is different from the sex of the bodies they inhabit. 2 Some transgender people seek to change their bodies to conform to what they feel is their proper gender identity. 3 Some psychiatrists have argued that these individuals have a serious personality disorder and that such attempts at transformation are signs of this. 4 I disagree. 5 They don't have a personality disorder at all, and 6 psychiatrists have provided no evidence that this is the case. 7 Moreover, if it were, transgender people would have the various characteristics of a personality disorder. 8 And they don't. 9 This is just another example of psychiatrists trying to impose their narrow values on anyone they see as different.

   1. [Defines transgender people.]
   2. [Explains transgender sex change.]
   3. [States a position taken by some psychiatrists and identifies a possible issue.]
   4. [States the author's position.]
   5. [Denies that transgender people have a personality disorder.]
   6. [Denies that there is evidence for the position of some psychiatrists.]
   7. [States the conditional that if transgender people have a personality disorder, they would display the characteristics associated with it.]
   8. [Denies the consequent in 7.]
   9. [Comments on psychiatrists.]

   Paraphrase: 1 Some psychiatrists have argued that attempts by transgender people to change their body to that of another sex are a sign of a serious personality disorder. **2 This is not the case. [=Transgender people do not have a serious personality disorder.] 3 Psychiatrists have not supplied any evidence for their position. Furthermore, 4 if transgender people have such a personality disorder, they would display the characteristics associated with it. And 5 they don't.**

```
   3        4 + 5
    ↘        ↙
        2
```

2. 1 Marijuana, like heroin and cocaine, is an addictive drug. 2 It has become widely available in Canada. 3 Much of the marijuana available in Canada is grown domestically. 4 Once grown only in fields, it is increasingly being grown in grow-houses, houses taken over by drug dealers and used to grow marijuana. 5 Because it is addictive, 6 marijuana should not be legalized for either medical or recreational uses. 7 There are far more effective drugs that could be used medically. 8 And because it is addictive, 9 it should not be used recreationally.

Claims 1 through 4 provide background information. The argument is contained in 5 and 7, which are reasons; 6 is the conclusion. Claim 8 repeats 5, and 9 simply says it should not be used for recreational uses, which repeats the conclusion.

> **Marijuana is addictive**
> **There are far more effective drugs that could be used medically.**
> _____
> **∴ It should not be legalized for either medical or recreational uses.**

3. 1 Hate speech should not be prohibited. 2 It is simply speech. 3 Some people find what is called "hate speech" upsetting. 4 However, many people find many things upsetting. 5 For example, some people find particular ads upsetting. 6 Others find violence in movies upsetting. 7 Some people find couples being the same sex upsetting. 8 Some find even the mention of such things upsetting. 9 That is not sufficient grounds for the prohibition of anything. 10 If we did that, we would prohibit all kinds of unpopular ideas and beliefs. 11 Hate speech is simply speech. 12 And all speech, even unpopular and unpleasant speech, should be tolerated. 13 It is far better to counter such verbal communication with good arguments than to suppress it. 14 No, hate speech should not be suppressed.

1 = 14.

Finding something upsetting is not sufficient grounds for suppressing it (= 9). This is supported by 5, 6, 7, and 8.

```
  5  6  7  8
   ↘ ↘↓ ↙
      9 + 10   11 + 12 + 13
        ↘          ↙
             14
```

Diagramming Challenges and Responses

Diagram the following arguments using the notation for challenges and responses.

1. A: (1) *The Adventures of Huckleberry Finn* is racist because (2) it uses the n-word over 200 times and (3) that is offensive to many people.

    B: (4) The dictionary uses the n-word, and it is not racist.

    A: (5) The dictionary is defining the term; (6) *The Adventures of Huckleberry Finn* uses the term to refer to a group of people.

2. A: (1) Euthanasia is immoral because (2) it denies an individual autonomy.

    B. (3) It does not deny an individual autonomy; rather, (4) it allows the individual to choose how and when he or she will die, and (5) that is upholding an individual's autonomy.

3. A. (1) Pornography is degrading to women because (2) it shows women in sexual positions.

    B: (3) It shows men in sexual positions. (4) Is it not degrading to men as well?

    A: No. (5) Men have positions of power in society and cannot be degraded, whereas women are degraded by being shown in sexual positions.

EXERCISES

🖎 EXERCISE 3.1
Identifying Claims

In the following, identify the claims and distinguish them from nonclaims.

1. You don't want to fail your driver's test simply by not knowing the road signs, do you?

2. You can't do that!

3. By the powers vested in me, I hereby declare you a citizen of Canada.

4. The distance between San Diego and Atlantic City is 3052 miles. And the winning four-man bicycle team in the Race Across America rode it in five days, eighteen hours and fifteen minutes.

5. Evolutionary theory has been well established.

6. I tell you that you are not going to the party. That's final.

7. You're not going to the party, are you?

8. Evolutionary theory is an abomination in the sight of God.

9. Mice! We have mice!

10. I confer upon you the authority of a law enforcement officer with all of the powers and responsibilities that the law accords.

🖎 EXERCISE 3.2
Identifying Arguments and Cue Words, and Portraying Structure

For each of the following,
a. identify if the passage contains an argument;
b. identify any cue words by circling them;
c. portray the structure of the argument; and
d. explain why the passage does not contain an argument if you believe it doesn't.

1. You should study economics rather than philosophy or English because economics is more likely to lead to a job.

2. If free speech is a key value in our society, then we need to protect it regardless of the issue, even those we disagree with, like pornography.

3. Capital punishment is final and irreversible. Over the years, a substantial number of individuals have been wrongly convicted and executed. In addition, the burden of capital punishment has tended to fall on blacks and Aboriginals. Nonetheless, capital punishment should not be abolished.

4. Once reason has failed, we need to resort to violence to defend ourselves. And reason has failed. The only conclusion is that we must resort to violence.

5. Although certainty is a valuable quality, it is not to be found in science, for all scientific knowledge is based on human observation and judgment, and human observation and judgment can be wrong.

6. The tuition fees of the province's universities will go up significantly next year, while course selection and student access to faculty will decrease.

7. If the doctors strike, they will only harm their patients, themselves, and the people of Ontario, while making the government look good.

8. Harry should not be ashamed of what he did, for he simply broke a promise when it was inconvenient to keep it. And it is always permissible to break promises when keeping them is not convenient.

9. Thirty-five thousand people die each day from hunger. By the end of the year, thirteen to eighteen million people will die. Seventy-five percent of these will be children. At the present time, we have enough food to feed seven billion people. There are only five billion people on the earth.

10. Censorship exists simply to prevent anyone from challenging current concepts and existing institutions. However, progress is initiated by challenging current concepts and brought about by replacing existing institutions. Therefore, censorship stands in the way of progress. (based on a theory of G. B. Shaw)

11. You should not take alcohol and tranquillizers together; it may cause a fatal overdose.

12. If autonomy (the right of individuals to make and act on their own decisions) is a key value in our society, then we need to protect it regardless of individuals' decisions, even those that we disagree with. We need to respect an individual's right to make bad choices.

13. Abortion is final and irreversible. Most women who choose abortion are young and incapable of making a reasoned decision. In addition, the women contemplating abortion often do not get adequate counselling about options other than abortion. Nonetheless, abortion should not be banned or restricted.

14. Once evidence about the existence of God has been shown *not* to prove the existence of God, then we need to resort to faith. And evidence has failed. The only conclusion is that we must resort to faith.

15. Although freedom of speech is a valuable quality, it is not to be found in the Canadian political system, for all parties require party loyalty, and being loyal to a political party means that the party members are not free to speak their minds on issues.

16. The only way of paying down the deficit is to raise taxes. And raising taxes will harm our party's chances in the next election. But if we don't address the deficit, the country will suffer.

17. Although biotechnology has serious risks, it also offers significant benefits, and the benefits outweigh the risks. So we should go ahead with trying to genetically engineer an ice-resistant citrus crop.

18. One hundred people participated in the survey. Twenty-five claimed they did not feel stressed in their jobs; seventy-five claimed they were under increased stress at work in the past year. Of those who claimed they were under increased stress, thirty percent said they had control of their working conditions, whereas seventy percent said they did not.

19. The province is changing the math requirements for graduation and will be requiring a calculus credit as of next year. We should, therefore, raise our entrance requirements to reflect the higher standards.

20. You should vote to reelect Rockford as mayor. Although his opponent has made some nice promises, she has not shown an ability to put together a coalition to implement her platform, whereas Rockford has. Although Rockford is not as flashy, he can get things done. That is why I am voting for him.

✎ EXERCISE 3.3
Interpreting Argument Diagrams (Labelling Arrow Diagrams)

For each of the following argument diagrams,
- identify each separate argument;
- identify the reasons, main conclusions, and intermediate conclusions within each argument; and
- identify challenges and responses to challenges.

1.
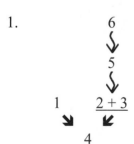

2.

```
              8
              ↓
  3 + 4    5 + 6    7
    ↘        ↓      ↙
              2
```

3.

```
   8
   ↓
   7
   ↓
   1      3     4+5
   ↓      ↓     ↙
   2
   ↘
          6
```

4.

```
         13       16
         ↓        ↓
         12      14   15
         ↓        ↓    ↓
  1 + 2   5     6 + 7   8
    ↘    ↙       ↘     ↙
    3 + 4          9 + 10
      ↓              ↙
          11
```

5.

```
              15        17
              ↓         ↓
              14        16
              ↓         ↓
  4 + 5   6   7     8 + 9    10
    ↘    ↙    ↓       ↓      ↙
    2 + 3    11    12 + 13
      ↓      ↓        ↙
              1
```

✎ EXERCISE 3.4
Argument Analysis

For each of the passages below, do the following:

    a. If the passage contains an argument, portray the structure of the argument using either standard form or arrow diagrams. If you use arrow diagrams, identify each claim by drawing square brackets around the claim and numbering it. Circle cue words.

b. If the passage does not contain an argument, explain why it is not an argument.

Note: You may paraphrase.

1. In all wars there is the chance innocent people will be killed, and we should never kill innocent people, even for a good cause. So, we should not participate in this war.

2. Some people justify deception as simply a part of good business practice. However, good business practice is built upon trust. And trust is undermined by deception. So, good business practice should not be built upon deception.

3. Whenever we find evidence of this kind of erosion, we know that it has taken many millions of years for the rock formation to develop. Therefore, we know this rock formation developed over many millions of years.

4. An ethics committee should be impartial. If it is appointed by and answers solely to those it is monitoring, it cannot be impartial. So an ethics committee must be appointed by and answer to an independent source.

5. Deregulation of electrical power in California brought tremendous increases in the cost of electricity; in some cases, increases of three thousand percent were common. The proposal to deregulate electrical power in Ontario is likely to produce even worse consequences, for Canada is surrounded by American states that have higher energy costs, and those states will rapidly drive up the cost of electricity within Ontario.

6. Never buy a car more than five years old. The repair costs are too high.

7. Canadians consider health care a basic right, and rightly so. Health is fundamental to people's ability to contribute to and benefit from this society. It is important for us as a society to ensure that every member can contribute to society in the best way he or she can. Public health care helps ensure this. Furthermore, guaranteeing that every member of society has access to universal health care ensures that every person is treated as an individual and as part of the society. It does not set artificial barriers based on money, need, or age. If the health of the citizens is important to the members of the electorate, then this needs to be communicated—and soon—to the various regional bodies.

8. We should all work to control global warming. If we don't, the world will be uninhabitable by humans within fifty years. My opponents contend that this would be costly. Yet recent studies by the European Union estimate that it would take less than one percent of Gross National Product to implement such reforms. Such an investment would not be costly considering the alternative.

9. We shouldn't ban books in the schools. It undermines free thought and it limits what we can teach. To those who object, arguing that this would allow racist and other unacceptable books in the schools, I reply that such works, if taught to expose racism and sexism, can have a positive role in the curriculum.

10. We should legalize marijuana. It would have many benefits. It would give chemotherapy patients access to a drug that would help alleviate their symptoms. It would allow police time to chase more "deserving" criminals. It would give people a recreational drug that is far safer than tobacco or alcohol. To those who assert that it would justify impaired driving, I reply that this is not the case. Alcohol being legal does not mean that a person can legally drive under the influence. If a person is going to smoke up and drive, then that person is under the influence and should be charged. Legalizing marijuana does not inherently mean that we justify its abuse.

11. She's been married since last June.

12. She married Tom since she thought he would be a good father to her children.

13. Everybody has needs. You don't fulfill mine. So I'm splitting.

14. Definitions cannot, by their very nature, be either "true" or "false," only more or less useful. For this reason, it makes relatively little sense to argue over definitions.

15. She won't get the promotion. She has antagonized virtually everyone on the committee.

16. I'll be glad to tell you my opinion of sex education in the public schools. It stirs up interest where it didn't exist before; it encourages immorality by making sex seem natural and nothing to be uptight about; and it gives the schools a job that is the responsibility of the parents. It is a filthy communist plot.

17. If people are keenly interested in their work, then they are not likely to be distracted from it.

18. If he brags about himself all evening, Joan will be miserable. Poor Joan!

19. Nobody can corrupt government. It does that by itself.

20. Humans are limited as far as wisdom is concerned. That is why they need the support of a social group to offset their limited individual capacities.

21. If the fetus has no legal rights, then a pregnant woman cannot be forced into a substance-abuse program against her own will, even if her behaviour will result in harm to the child when it is born. And, according to the laws in Canada, a fetus has no rights. So there is nothing we can do to protect a fetus from the substance abuse of its mother.

22. Society is best served by educated people, so cutting spending on education is a shortsighted solution to economic problems.

23. Cheating on exams can sometimes be justified because not all courses are part of a student's major program or related to the student's career plans. Besides, it is just as important to have a high grade point average as it is to be competent in one's area of specialization. My opponents will object that we are teaching students to be unethical by allowing such cheating. However, I reply that we are only fitting them for the work force they are preparing to enter.

24. In view of the fact that George is taking the introductory class in abnormal psychology this semester, it is not surprising that George believes that he has a neurosis, because everyone taking the introductory course in abnormal psychology ends up believing that he or she has a neurosis. (Those who take the advanced course believe they are psychotic.)

25. Statistical studies establish that the incidence of forced rape is lower in places where prostitution is tolerated than in places where it is not. Therefore, prostitution should be completely decriminalized. Reduction in the incidence of rape is a desirable social end. So laws that make prostitution a criminal offence should be repealed. To the objection that decriminalizing prostitution will spread disease, I reply that we can control disease by mandatory licensing. Moreover, studies show that the spread of disease from prostitutes is lower than from other people engaging in casual sex.

26. There is no life on Venus because there is no water on Venus.

27. Women make up over fifty-one percent of the population. Women, however, make up only twenty-three percent of all university faculties. Of those on faculty, over two-thirds occupy the lower academic ranks of instructor and assistant professor. This is a clear indication that women have been discriminated against in the university system.

28. Homosexual acts involving only consenting adults have no victims. Without a victim, there is no crime. So how can you call homosexual acts crimes?

29. Jones will never be a success in business, for he is just as concerned about the social impact of his operations as he is about the earnings of his stockholders. No one who is concerned about the social impact of his business can be a success in business.

30. No children under the age of eighteen should engage in sex education because it tends to encourage them to think about and do things they would not otherwise think about or do.

31. Whenever we find evidence of this kind of erosion, we know that there was glacier activity within the past twenty thousand years. There are many signs of this kind of erosion in this area, so there must have been glacier activity here within the past twenty thousand years.

32. Emile Durkheim, in his classic work *Suicide,* argued that suicide was linked to social forces, particularly social cohesion. The tighter an individual is bound to a group, the lesser his risk of suicide, and the less tight the bonds to the group, the greater his risk of suicide. Durkheim established this through detailed statistics showing that suicide rates among single men, Protestants, and the chronically unemployed were higher than those among married men, women, Catholics and Jews, and the employed. The former all have looser social ties than the latter.

33. The candidate for mayor is proposing taking all of the homeless off the streets either by warehousing them or shipping them elsewhere. Both of these "solutions" violate the basic rights of the homeless. Therefore, other measures must be sought.

MODULE 4: ASSESSING ARGUMENTS: DEDUCTIVE ARGUMENTS

QUICK QUIZ ANSWERS

✍ QUICK QUIZ 4.1
Identifying Deductive and Inductive Arguments

For each of the following,

- portray the structure of the argument;
- identify whether the argument is inductive or deductive; and
- assess whether the premises are relevant and sufficient to establish the conclusion.

If the argument is inductive, assess whether the premises strongly or weakly support the conclusion.

1. Daphne is a cat. All cats are playful. Therefore, Daphne is playful.

> **Daphne is a cat.**
> **All cats are playful.**
> _____
> ∴ **Daphne is playful.**

Deductive argument.
Relevance: *Daphne* and *playful* are mentioned in both the premise and the conclusion.
Sufficiency: Daphne being a cat and the fact all cats are playful are sufficient to establish that Daphne is playful.
The premises are relevant and sufficient to support the conclusion.

2. Nigel is a dog. Some dogs are playful. So Nigel is playful.

> **Nigel is a dog.**
> **Some dogs are playful.**
> _____
> ∴ **Nigel is playful.**

Deductive argument.
Relevance: The premises are relevant to the conclusion that Nigel is playful. It is mentioned that Nigel is a dog and that some dogs are playful.
Sufficiency: The premises are not sufficient. We know only that *some* dogs are playful. The premises do not establish that Nigel is one of the dogs that are playful.

3. The defendant knew the victim. She had the motive to want him dead. She was in possession of a weapon that could have been the murder weapon. She was in the vicinity where the victim was killed. She was seen by three eyewitnesses talking to the victim just before he was killed. Therefore, she must have killed him.

> **The defendant knew the victim.**
> **She had the motive to want him dead.**
> **She was in possession of a weapon that could have been the murder weapon.**
> **She was in the vicinity where the victim was killed.**
> **She was seen by three eyewitnesses talking to the victim just before he was killed.**
> _____
> ∴   **She must have killed him.**

> **Inductive argument.**
> **Relevance:**   **The premises are all the kinds of things that are relevant to helping establish that the defendant could have been the murderer.**
> **Sufficiency:** **The premises are not sufficient to establish that she is the murderer. All of the information quoted in the premises could be true and the conclusion could be false without a contradiction. However, the argument is reasonably strong. These facts together increase the probability of the conclusion being true.**

4. If something is immoral, it should be illegal. Adultery is immoral. So it should be illegal.

> **If something is immoral, it should be illegal.**
> **Adultery is immoral.**
> _____
> ∴   **It should be illegal.**

> **Deductive argument.**
> **Relevance:**   **The premises need to establish the conclusion that adultery should be illegal. The claim that anything that is immoral should be illegal is clearly relevant. The second claim is also relevant: It establishes that adultery is immoral.**
> **Sufficiency:** **The two claims together are sufficient to establish the conclusion. We cannot accept the premises and deny the conclusion. It is a valid argument.**

5. I didn't receive any mail last week, yet there were no holidays. My mailman must be falling down on the job.

> **I didn't receive any mail last week.**
> **There were no holidays.**
> _____
> ∴   **My mailman must be falling down on the job.**

Inductive argument.

Relevance: That I didn't receive mail and that there were no holidays would both be relevant reasons why my mailman is falling down on the job.

Sufficiency: It is possible, however, given the premises, that no one sent me any mail. The premises are relevant but not sufficient to establish the conclusion.

✍ QUICK QUIZ 4.2
Validity Comprehension

Which of the following claims are true and which are false? If the claim is false, explain why.

1. A valid argument can have true premises and a false conclusion.

   False by definition. A valid argument cannot have true premises and a false conclusion.

2. A cogent argument must be valid.

   True

3. A cogent argument can have false premises.

   False. A cogent argument must be valid, and a valid argument cannot have true premises and a false conclusion.

4. A valid argument must have a true conclusion.

   False. A valid argument can have a false conclusion if the premises are false. If the premises are true, it must have a true conclusion.

5. Validity is an indication of the truth of the claims in the argument.

   False. Validity is an indication of the relation between the premises and conclusion. By itself, it tells us nothing about the truth or falsity of the conclusion.

6. Cogency is an indication of the truth of the claims in an argument.

   True

7. Validity is concerned with the relationship of the claims to one another.

   True

Identifying Logical Terms and Content

Identify the logical terms and content terms in each of the following, and then turn the content terms into variables.

1. Either I study for the exam or go partying with my friends.

   Logical Term: **Either *a* or *b* (one term)**
   Content Terms: **a: I study for the exam**
                         b: I go partying with my friends

2. Some stars are relatively cool compared to our sun.

   Logical Term: **Some *a*'s are *b*'s**
   Content Terms: **a: stars**
                         b: things that are relatively cool compared to our sun

3. No stars are as cool as a planet.

   Logical Term: **No *a*'s are *b*'s**
   Content Terms: **a: stars**
                         b: things that are as cool as a planet

4. If I am late for the interview, I won't get the job.

   Logical Term: **If *a*, then *b***
   Content Terms: **a: I am late for the interview**
                         b: I won't get the job

5. All cats chase mice.

   Logical Term: **All *a*'s are *b*'s**
   Content Terms: **a: cats**
                         b: things that chase mice

✍ **QUICK QUIZ 4.4**
Identifying Antecedents and Consequents

In the following, identify the antecedents and the consequents.

1. If the sun is powered by nuclear fusion, then its life span is far longer than anyone expected.

   If (the sun is powered by nuclear fusion) [antecedent], then (its life span is far longer than anyone expected) [consequent].

2. We will go to the party if I can borrow the car.

   (We will go to the party) [consequent] if (I can borrow the car) [antecedent].

3. If the province raises tuition fees, fewer students will be able to go to university.

   If (the province raises tuition fees) [antecedent], (fewer students will be able to go to university) [consequent].

✍ QUICK QUIZ 4.5
Translating Claims into Conditionals

Translate the following claims into conditional claims.

1. No students like tuition increases.

   If someone is a student, then he or she does not like tuition increases.

2. Only the ignorant take action without considering the consequences.

   If someone takes action without considering the consequences, then he or she is ignorant.

3. He will graduate unless he fails critical thinking.

   If he fails critical thinking, then he will not graduate.

4. He will graduate only if he passes critical thinking.

   If he passes critical thinking, then he will graduate.

✍ QUICK QUIZ 4.6
Determining Validity: Conditionals

In each of the following, portray the structure of the argument and then determine whether or not the argument is valid or invalid. Show validity or invalidity by labelling the claims with variables and identifying the argument pattern.

1. If Watson's fingerprints are found on the money, then he committed the robbery.

   His fingerprints are not on the money.

   ―――――――――――――――――――――――

   ∴ **He didn't commit the robbery.**

a	*b*
If (Watson's fingerprints are found on the money), then (he committed the robbery).	If *a*, then *b*
(His fingerprints are not on the money.)	not *a*

∴   He didn't commit the robbery.   not *b*

Invalid; denying the antecedent.

2. If the moon has an atmosphere, then there would be few signs of impacts with meteors.

    There are signs of a large number of meteor impacts on the moon.

    ∴   **The moon does not have an atmosphere.**

a	*b*
If (the moon has an atmosphere), then (there would be few signs of impacts with meteors.)	If *a*, then *b*
(There are signs of a large number of meteor impacts on the moon.)	not *b*

∴   **The moon does not have an atmosphere.**   not *a*

Valid; denying the consequent.

3. If Mars is inhabitable, we would find water on Mars.

    We found water on Mars.

    ∴   **Mars is inhabitable.**

a	*b*
If (Mars is inhabitable), (we would find water on Mars.)	If *a*, then *b*
(We found water on Mars.)	*b*

∴   **Mars is inhabitable.**   *a*

Invalid; affirming the consequent.

4. If I park here overnight, I will get a ticket.

    I have to park here overnight.

    ∴   **I will get a ticket.**

a	*b*
If (I park here overnight), (I will get a ticket.)	If *a*, then *b*
(I have to park here overnight.)	*a*

∴   **I will get a ticket.**   *b*

Valid; affirming the antecedent.

✍ QUICK QUIZ 4.7
Identifying Necessary and Sufficient Conditions

In the following, identify the necessary and sufficient conditions.

1.   If something is a whale, it is a mammal.

> **Being a whale is a sufficient condition for being a mammal.**
> **Being a mammal is a necessary condition for being a whale.**

2.   All critical-thinking instructors have Ph.D.s.

> **Being a critical-thinking instructor is a sufficient condition for saying someone has a Ph.D.**
> **It is not clear whether having a Ph.D. is a necessary condition for being a critical-thinking instructor or simply an accidental feature of this group of critical-thinking instructors. If it is a requirement of the position, then it is a necessary condition. If it is merely an accidental feature of this collection of critical-thinking instructors, then it would not be a necessary condition.**

3.   No reptiles live in arctic climates.

> **Its living in an arctic climate is a sufficient condition for saying that a species is not a reptile.**
> **Being a reptile is a sufficient condition for saying that members of that species do not live in arctic climates.**

4.   Some logicians are mad.

> **There are no necessary or sufficient conditions in this claim.**

We are not assessing the truth of these claims. Rather, we are determining, from the claims themselves, whether one condition is being identified as a condition for another.

✍ QUICK QUIZ 4.8
Assessing Disjunctive Arguments

In the following, portray the structure of the argument and identify whether the argument is valid or invalid.

1.   Either Harris did it or his wife is lying. His wife is not lying. So he must have done it.

<u>a</u> **<u>b</u>** **Either Harris did it or his wife is lying.** **His wife is not lying.**	**Either _a_ or _b_** **not _b_**

∴ **He must have done it.**	**_a_**

Valid form; denying a disjunct.

2. Either the fuse is faulty or the TV's picture tube has gone. The fuse is faulty. So the picture tube is OK.

<u>a</u> **<u>b</u>** **Either the fuse is faulty or the TV's picture tube has gone.** **The fuse is faulty.**	**Either _a_ or _b_** **_a_**

∴ **The picture tube is OK.**	**not _b_**

Invalid; affirming a disjunct.

3. Either we improve our response time in getting to fires or more people are going to die needlessly. I guess more people are going to die needlessly because we can't improve our response time.

<u>a</u> **<u>b</u>** **Either we improve our response time in getting to fires or more people are** **going to die needlessly.** **We can't improve our response time.**	 **Either _a_ or _b_** **not _a_**

∴ **More people are going to die needlessly because we can't improve our** **response time.**	 **_b_**

Valid; denying a disjunct.

✍ QUICK QUIZ 4.9
Complex Argument Patterns

Consider the following patterns. Are they valid or invalid? Explain.

1.   If *a* then *b* or *c*.
        not *b*

    ∴ not *a*

    Although this initially looks like a valid pattern—denying the consequent—it is not. The consequent is "_b_ or _c_." To show that this _a_ is false, we would have to show that both _b_ and _c_ are false. All we know from the argument is that _b_ is false.

2.   Either *a* or *b*
            not *b*

        —————————————

∴ *a*
            If *a,* then *c* or *d*

        —————————————

∴ *c*

                Either *a* or *b*
                not *b*

                —————————————

                ∴ ***a***   **Valid; denying a disjunct.**
                If *a*, then *c* or *d*

                —————————————

                ∴ ***c***   **Valid; affirming the antecedent.**

3.   If *a* or *b* or *c,* then *d* or *e*
            a
            not *d*

        —————————————

∴ *e*

                If *a* or *b* or *c,* then *d* or *e*
                a   **Valid; affirming the antecedent.**
                not *d*

                —————————————

                ∴ ***e***   **Valid; denying the disjunct.**

4.   If *a* and *b,* then *c* or *d*
            a
            b
            not *c*

        —————————————

∴ *d*

                If *a* and *b,* then *c* or *d*
                a
                b   **Valid; affirming the antecedent**
                not *c*

                —————————————

                ∴ ***d***   **Valid; denying the disjunct.**

5.   If *a,* then *c* and *d*
            a
            not *d*

        —————————————

∴ *c*

If *a*, then *c* and *d*	
a	Valid; affirming the antecedent.
───────────────	
∴ *c*	Valid; if we have a conjunction, *c* and *d*, then both conjuncts must be true for the conjunction to be true. From a conjunction, we can infer either of the conjuncts.

✒ QUICK QUIZ 4.10
Identifying Topics

Identify the topics in the following claims and arguments.

1. Adultery is immoral.

   Adultery is **immoral**.

2. Anything that is immoral should be illegal. Adultery is immoral. So it should be illegal.

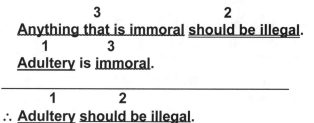

```
              3                    2
   Anything that is immoral should be illegal.
         1              3
   Adultery is immoral.
   ─────────────────────────────────────
              1            2
   ∴ Adultery should be illegal.
```

3. Whatever is gained easily is not valued. University degrees are becoming too easy to achieve. As a result, they will not be valued.

```
              3                     2
   Whatever is gained easily is not valued.
            1                   3
   University degrees are becoming too easy to achieve.
   ──────────────────────────────────────────
              1                 2
   ∴ University degrees will not be valued.
```

4. You ought to study economics. Of all the options, it is the only one with real-world application.

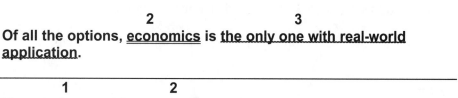

```
                    2                      3
   Of all the options, economics is the only one with real-world
   application.
   ────────────────────────────────────────────
             1            2
   ∴ You ought to study economics.
```

5. Personal testimony based on experience, though vivid, is often not reliable. Our perceptions and memory are often flawed and limited in perspective.

3   **4**

<u>**Our perceptions and memory**</u> **are often** <u>**flawed and limited in perspective.**</u>

---

1   **2**

∴ <u>**Personal testimony based on experience**</u>**, though vivid, is** <u>**often not reliable**</u>**.**

✍ QUICK QUIZ 4.11
Determining Validity Using the Topics Model

For the exercises that consist simply of a claim in Quick Quiz 4.10, identify the two questions that would have to be addressed if that claim were the conclusion of an argument. For the exercises that contain arguments, identify the two questions that need to be asked of the conclusion.

1. Q1: Under what conditions should something be illegal?
   Q2: Does adultery meet those conditions?

2. Q1: Under what conditions should something be illegal?
   Q2: Does adultery meet those conditions?

3. Q1: Under what conditions will something not be valued?
   Q2: Do university degrees meet those conditions?

4. Q1: Under what conditions should one study something?
   Q2: Does economics meet those conditions?

5. Q1: Under what conditions is something not reliable?
   Q2: Does personal testimony based on experience meet those conditions?

✍ QUICK QUIZ 4.12
Using Argument Counterexamples to Show Invalidity

For each of the following arguments, provide a counterexample.

1. All logicians are mad. Saindon is not a logician. Saindon is not mad.

   logicians = *a*
   mad = *b*
   Saindon = *c*

Pattern: All *a*'s are *b*
c is not an *a*

_____

∴ *c* is not *b*

Substitute: *a* = cat
b = mammal
c = dogs

This yields true premises and a false conclusion. The argument is invalid.

2. Some logicians are mad. Saindon is a logician. So Saindon must be mad.

logicians = *a*
mad = *b*
Saindon = *c*

Pattern: Some *a*'s are *b*
c is an *a*

_____

∴ *c* is *b*

Substitute: *a* = women
b = CEOs (chief executive officers)
c = any woman who is not a CEO; e.g., a student in this class

This yields true premises and a false conclusion. The argument is invalid.

3. Anyone who works hard will pass the course. I haven't worked very hard. It looks as though I won't pass.

anyone who works hard = *a*
someone who will pass the course = *b*
I (me) = *c*

Pattern: All *a*'s are *b*
c is not an *a*

_____

∴ *c* is not a *b*

Substitute: *a* = cats
b = mammals
c = Fido (a dog)

This yields true premises and a false conclusion. The argument is invalid.

4. If you don't have perfect attendance, then you won't be entitled to a bonus at the end of the year. I had perfect attendance. So I will get the bonus.

you don't have perfect attendance = *a*
you won't be entitled to a bonus at the end of the year = *b*

Pattern: **If *a*, then *b***
                      not *a*
_____
                      ∴ not *b*

Remember the difference between affirming and denying a claim.

Substitute: ***a* = someone who is not a student at York University**
                         ***b* = someone who cannot graduate from York University**

Being a student at York does not guarantee that a person will graduate from York. It is a necessary, not a sufficient, condition. This yields true premises and a false conclusion. The argument is invalid.

5. Treating animals kindly is a sign that individuals will treat other people kindly. Michael doesn't treat his dog very well. He must not treat his wife very well.

Someone who treats animals kindly = *a*
Someone who will treat other people kindly = *b*

Pattern: **If *a*, then *b***
                      not *a*
_____
                      ∴ not *b*

This has the same pattern as the preceding and the same substitution will show that it is invalid.

✍ QUICK QUIZ 4.13
Using Valid Patterns to Supply Missing Premises

1. We want to reduce speeding, so we should use red-light cameras.

If we want to reduce speeding, we should use red-light cameras.	**If *a* then *b***
We want to reduce speeding.	***a***

                      ∴   We should use red-light cameras.   ***b***

Valid; affirming the antecedent.

2. If he is a good lawyer, he reads the fine print in contracts. So he is not a good lawyer.

If he is a good lawyer, he reads the fine print in contracts.	If *a,* then *b*
[He does not read the fine print in contracts.]	not *b*

∴　**He is not a good lawyer.** 　　　　　　　　　　　　　　　　not *a*

　　Valid; denying the consequent.

3.　If something is intellectually challenging, it is not designed for a mass audience. So university is not designed for a mass audience.

If something is intellectually challenging, it is not designed for a mass audience.	If *a,* then *b*
[University is intellectually challenging.]	*a*

∴　**University is not designed for a mass audience.** 　　　　　*b*

　　Valid; affirming the antecedent.

4.　If he is a good lawyer, he reads the fine print in contracts. So he doesn't read the fine print in contracts.

If he is a good lawyer, he reads the fine print in contracts.	If *a,* then *b*

∴　**He doesn't read the fine print in contracts.** 　　　　　　not *b*

There is no way to make this into a valid argument from the material given. The most obvious missing premise would be "not *a*," but that would result in denying the antecedent, creating an invalid argument.

✍ QUICK QUIZ 4.14
Using the Topics Model to Supply Missing Premises

Portray the structure of the following arguments and use the topics model to supply the missing premises for each argument. Identify the two questions for each conclusion and show how the stated premise and missing premise answer those questions.

1.　Fred shouldn't be allowed to drive. He drives dangerously.

　　　　1　　　　　3
　　　　Fred drives dangerously.

　　　　1　　　　　2
∴　**Fred should not be allowed to drive.**

Q1:　Under what conditions should someone not be allowed to drive?
Q2:　Do those conditions apply to Fred?

The stated premise says that certain conditions apply to Fred, namely that he drives dangerously. This answers Q2.

The missing premise should connect 2 and 3: Someone who drives dangerously should not be allowed to drive. This answers Q1, making the argument valid.

2. Creationism should not be taught in biology classrooms because it is not science.

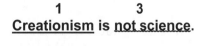

           1   3
Creationism is <u>not science</u>.

_____

           1   2
∴   Creationism <u>should not be taught in biology classrooms</u>.

Q1:   Under what conditions should something not be taught in biology classrooms?
Q2:   Does that apply to creationism?

The stated premise answers Q2: It specifies that certain conditions apply to creationism.

What needs to be connected are 2 and 3, which will answer Q1. The missing premise is "Things that are not science should not be taught in the biology classroom." With this, the argument becomes valid.

3. Stem cell research can help in the search for a cure for Alzheimer's. Therefore, we should support stem cell research.

           2   3
<u>Stem cell research</u> <u>can help in the search for a cure for Alzheimer's</u>.

_____

           1   2
∴   <u>We should support</u> <u>stem cell research</u>.

Q1:   Under what conditions should we support (scientific) research?
Q2:   Do those conditions apply to stem cell research?

The stated premise answers Q2. What needs to be connected are 1 and 3, This will give us the answer to Q1. The missing premise is "We should support scientific research that leads to cures for serious diseases" (or for Alzheimer's). The former is a more general premise. The argument is valid with this premise.

✍ QUICK QUIZ 4.15
Assessing Cogency

Assess the following arguments for cogency using the skills developed thus far. Give reasons for both your assessment of validity and of cogency.

1. Teachers should not be allowed to strike because their going on strike disrupts students' learning.

                   1   **3**
Teachers' going on strike <u>disrupts students' learning</u>.

_____

                 1   **2**
∴ **Teachers' going on strike** <u>should not be allowed</u>.

Q1:   Under what conditions should someone not be allowed to strike?
Q2:   Do these conditions apply to teachers?

Missing premise: **a.** **Something should not be allowed if it disrupts students' learning.**
         or **b.** **Someone should not be allowed to strike if it disrupts neutral third parties. (This would need an additional premise that students are neutral third parties.)**

    1. **{ If (anything disrupts students' learning) [a], (it should not be allowed) [b] }**
    2. **Teachers' going on strike disrupts students' learning. [a]**

_____

∴ **3.** **Teachers should not be allowed to go on strike. [b]**

Valid; affirming the antecedent—see the pattern above.

Not cogent. The missing premise (1) is false. Many things can disrupt students' learning that we would want to allow: for example, teachers' professional development days, holiday celebrations. and fire drills (counterexamples).

One presupposition of the missing premises is that students' learning should take precedence over everything else. This can be challenged. Teachers are employees, not serfs.

A simple denial of a claim (teachers' going on strike does not disrupt students' learning) is not sufficient. We need to provide at least one reason for the denial, which would require a counterargument—that is, an argument supporting the denial. Alternatively, we can give a counterexample as we did in this case.

Confirmation bias. **One problem encountered in assessing arguments is** *confirmation bias*—**looking for reasons to confirm or support a belief or claim. Finding examples of how strikes disrupt students' learning does not prove the claim to be true in all cases. Many strikes do disrupt students' learning. However, in some cases, strikes can lead to improved overall learning in the long run by, for example, improving the teaching conditions or reducing class size. We can usually find confirmations, even for false beliefs. If the evidence is anecdotal rather than systematic, what we end up with is a trading of** different hypothetical situations—I can think of an example that confirms my belief; you can think of one that disconfirms it. If we take as a rule of evidence that any confirming instance proves a claim, then, since we can find evidence both for and against many beliefs we hold, those claims are both true and false. There is an asymmetry in evidence. While we can find confirming instances for false claims, we cannot find disconfirming instances for true claims.

Consider the following claim:

> All swans are white.

I can find many examples of white swans. If confirming instances make a claim true, then this claim is true. However, I can also find black swans (in Australia). The claim is therefore false.

Argument strategy. This tells us something important about critical reasoning and our basic *argument strategy:* Simply finding confirming instances for our claims is not sufficient to guarantee that they are true. We need to test claims critically by looking for possible negative instances and, when we find them, modify our claims accordingly. We can modify our swan claim as follows:

a. Most swans are white.
b. All swans outside of Australia are white.
c. Swans are usually (normally) white.

Each of these makes the claim more likely true, although each does it in a slightly different way. a qualifies the scope of the claim by limiting its range of application ("most," not "all"). b qualifies the claim by noting important exceptions. c qualifies the claim in a different way, but we haven't worked through the difference yet.

In terms of argument strategy, if we want to make sure that our claims are true, not only do we need evidence that they are true but we need to test them to find out if there are negative or disconfirming instances that would require us to modify or possibly abandon our claims.

Argument critical strategy. In critically examining an argument, we need to choose which premise to challenge. We are most likely to find the fundamental flaws in an argument by examining (a) the missing premise and (b) the general premise. These are often the same. In this case, premise 2 is talking about the specific: teachers' strikes. Premise 1 is more general: It is talking about anything that disrupts student learning. We have a greater chance of finding disconfirming instances for the general claim than for the specific claim. If the specific claim is false, then, obviously, we should challenge it. However, it is usually the general claim where we find the problems with the argument. This is why I emphasize missing premises and supplying a complete argument for critical analysis. Even the person presenting the argument frequently will ignore the general claim that underlies it (the missing premise) and neither make it explicit nor defend it. And more often than not, it is defective in some way.

2. We should censor anything that is crude and offensive. And much of rock music is certainly crude and offensive. So we should censor it.

> 1. **We should censor anything that is crude and offensive. (= If something is crude and offensive, then we should censor it.)**   If *a*, then *b*
> 2. **Much of rock music is crude and offensive.**   *a*
>
> ---
>
> ∴ 3. **We should censor (much of) rock music.**   *b*

> **The best critical strategy in this is to challenge the general premise (1). There are many things that are crude and offensive that we don't particularly want to censor—for example, much advertising.**
>
> **One tendency in criticizing the argument is to challenge the argument by challenging the second premise. However, simply identifying *some* rock music that is not crude and offensive doesn't really counter the argument. If the argument is that we should censor those things that are crude and offensive, then pointing to something that is not crude and offensive doesn't counter the claim. (This might be a particular form of a red herring fallacy.) To show that a qualified claim (e.g., Much of rock music is crude and offensive) is false, we have to show not just that one or a few instances are not crude and offensive but that *much* of it is not. And that is harder to do.**

3. The novel *The Adventures of Huckleberry Finn* uses language that many consider racist. Therefore, the novel is racist and promotes racism.

> 1. **(If a piece of literature uses language that many consider racist, then it is racist and promotes racism.)**   If *a*, then *b*
> 2. **The novel *The Adventures of Huckleberry Finn* uses language that many consider racist.**   *a*
>
> ---
>
> ∴ 3. **The novel is racist and promotes racism.**   *b*

> **With the missing premise, the argument is valid: It affirms the antecedent.**
>
> **But the argument is not cogent. The fact that something uses racist language does not mean it is racist and promotes racism. A novel set in a racist society may use racist language to portray the racism while condemning that society and the racism in it.**
>
> **A second way of attacking this would be to develop a counterexample that shows that what many people consider racist is not necessarily racist.**

EXERCISES

☒ EXERCISE 4.1
Identifying Topics

Assume the following are conclusions of arguments. Identify the topics and the questions that would need to be answered for the claims to be established by argument.

> *Example:*   *Logicians are not quite sane.*
>
>   *Q1:*   *Under what conditions is someone not quite sane?*
>   *Q2:*   *Do logicians fit those criteria or conditions?*

1. Teachers should not be allowed to strike.

2. Prostitution is immoral.

3. Children with AIDS should not be allowed to attend public schools.

4. Doctors have an obligation to maintain the confidentiality of their conversations with their patients.

5. Affirmative action is a form of discrimination.

6. Nuclear energy is a safe form of energy.

7. John-Paul Rocquefort's work on race and IQ is neither academically respectable nor morally acceptable.

8. Education is merely a subtle form of indoctrination.

9. Statistics Canada's ethnicity categories are not to be trusted.

10. The university's classrooms are overcrowded.

11. None of the mayoralty candidates will benefit the city.

12. Student tuition should be frozen for three years.

13. We should use more technology, such as podcasting, in the classroom.

14. Affirmative action is necessary to establish equality.

15. We should buy this wheat cat litter rather than clay litter.

🐦 EXERCISE 4.2
Assessing Structure Using Conditional and Disjunctive Patterns

In the following, using conditional or disjunctive patterns, identify the logical structure of the arguments and determine whether the arguments are valid. To determine the validity of those arguments for which we have clear patterns, identify the pattern. Supply missing premises where necessary.

> *Example: It is not surprising that Saindon is quite mad. After all, he is a logician.*

(If someone is a logician, [a] then he is mad. [b])	If a, then b
Saindon is a logician.	a
∴ He is quite mad.	∴ b

This argument is valid, after supplying the missing premise—it affirms the antecedent. Note that in supplying the If a, then b, I have generalized the premise to anyone, rather than just Saindon. If I use "Saindon," then I am just repeating myself. The arguer is appealing to a broader claim—all logicians are quite mad.

1. If I study well, I do well on the exam. I didn't do well on the exam, so I must not have studied well.

2. Either the government is corrupt or inept. We know it is not inept. Therefore, it must be corrupt.

3. If we reject radiocarbon dating, then we must reject the rest of physics. Scientific creationists reject radiocarbon dating. Therefore, they must reject the rest of physics.

4. Whenever we find evidence of low morale, we know that there is mismanagement at upper levels. There must be mismanagement at upper levels in this organization. *[A underlined "we find evidence of low morale"; B above "there is mismanagement at upper"] If A, then B / A / B* [Con]

5. I can go either to dinner or to a movie. I need to eat and must go to dinner, so I cannot go to the movie. *Either A or B , A , ∴ Not B Affirming Disjunct (invalid)* [Dis]

6. If abortion is universally accepted, then it should be legal. But it is not universally accepted, so it should not be legal. *If A, then B*

7. Euthanasia kills a human being. Therefore, it is murder. *A: kills a human being ∴ B (valid)* [Con]

8. Business is not like the rest of society, so it should not be subject to the same moral principles that govern the rest of society.

9. Business has a responsibility only to its shareholders. If a company has a responsibility only to its shareholders, then it has no social responsibility. Therefore, business has no social responsibility.

A *B*

Dis 10. Either we pay our workers a decent wage or we pay our stockholders a decent dividend. If we
A pay our workers a decent wage, then the stockholders will replace the board. If we pay our
B stockholders a decent dividend, then the workers will go on strike. Ladies and gentlemen, we
are faced with either replacing the board or dealing with a strike.

Con 11. I don't see how you can censor the Internet. There is no way to enforce your prohibitions on
Internet sites that originate in other countries. And if you can't enforce your prohibitions,
then you can't censor. *IF A, then B* *A ∴ B*

12. If I don't pay the bill on time, my credit rating will suffer. I don't want my credit rating to
suffer, so I guess I'll have to find some way to pay the bill on time.

13. In order to get into law school, I need to get a high mark on the LSAT exam. I guess I am not
going to law school.

14. We should respect a person's choices. Therefore, if a person chooses to die by euthanasia to
end his or her suffering, then we should respect that choice.

15. If we put the course on the Internet, then we will lose some of our traditional student
population. It will cost less to put the course on the Internet. So we should resign ourselves to
losing some of our student population.

16. All attempts to keep specific materials from people are doomed to failure. People just set up
black markets. Therefore, we should not ban hate literature.

17. If something causes harm, then it should be banned. Hate literature has not been clearly
shown to cause harm. Therefore, it should not be banned.

18. If Hoyle's theory of the universe is correct, then the universe had no beginning in time. But
Hoyle's theory is not correct. Therefore, the universe has a beginning in time.

19. If she was involved in the murder, she won't testify at the trial of her lover. She won't testify
at the trial. Therefore, she was involved in the murder.

20. Capital punishment does not deter murder. If capital punishment deters murder, then the
murder rate should increase when capital punishment is abolished. And the murder rate does
not increase when capital punishment is abolished.

Test Questions largely on this q

☒ EXERCISE 4.3
Assessing Structure Using the Topics Model

Identify the structure of the following arguments and supply any missing premises. Assess the
arguments for relevance and sufficiency using the topics model.

Example: A businessperson is justified in lying in business because everyone else does it.

Everyone else in business lies.	*a*
(If everyone else in business lies, then a person is justified in lying in business.)	*If a, then b*
∴ *A person is justified in lying in business.*	*b*

Q1:   Under what conditions is someone justified in lying in business?
If everyone else in business lies.
Q2:   Does this apply to businesspersons?
Yes, because everyone else in business lies.

Without the missing premise, the premises are relevant to the conclusion but not sufficient. With the addition of the missing premise, the arguments' premises are relevant and sufficient to establish the conclusion.

1. There have been more reported cases of fraud in scientific research over the past ten years. This shows that the ethics of scientists are declining.

2. The Aptek 4000 is a better computer than the Wintex 2000 because it is cheaper.

3. Playing sports builds character in children. Children who play sports have to work as a part of a team, practise patience, and learn that winning is not everything.

4. I don't see how you can believe in astrology. It is based on a form of astronomy that puts the earth at the centre of the universe and was discredited by Copernicus 450 years ago.

5. We should not outlaw prostitution because to do so is to legislate morality.

6. In a way, even Hitler was a moral person, because he did what he thought was morally right.

7. Atheists cannot be moral because morality requires a belief in God, which is what gives individuals reasons for obeying the laws of morality.

8. Because standard IQ tests ignore differences in cultures, they are discriminatory. And if they are discriminatory, they should not be used in school or work settings.

9. Marijuana should be legalized. Although it has some harmful effects, these are outweighed by its beneficial effects and by the fact that prohibiting it is an unjust imposition on people's freedom of choice.

10. Sex should not be discussed publicly. It is a private and intimate act. That is why it should not be taught in schools. Aside from making public what is private, it usurps the role of parents in teaching values.

11. Not all opinions deserve the right to be heard in the court of public opinion. Opinions that cause harm to others, involve disrespect to others, or incite hate violate the basic principles of

a decent society. And anything that violates such principles does not have a right to a public hearing.

12. Marxism is a false philosophy. The Soviet Union was based on Marxism, and it failed after fifty years. That clearly shows there is no truth in Marxism.

13. Why outlaw pornography? We know now that it does no psychological harm. And surely naked bodies are not evil per se.

14. It is clear that sexism is on the decline and women are no longer being discriminated against. There are more women in university than men and the numbers of women in professional programs such as law and business is increasing yearly. A woman even ran to be leader of the Liberal party. How can you say that sexism is alive and well?

15. It is obvious that children need two parents. That is why gay marriage should not be made legal.

EXERCISE 4.4
Assessing Cogency

Assess the following arguments for cogency (validity and acceptability of the premises). Identify the structure of the arguments by putting them into standard form, add any missing premises, and explain your analysis.

1. My friend Mary had her horoscope cast by an astrologer, and it was incredibly accurate. So there must be some truth to the claims of astrology.

2. If the aim of higher education is to produce an enlightened citizenry, then a broad-based, liberal arts education is best for achieving this. However, if the aim of higher education is to produce jobs for people, then a sophisticated form of technical training would be best. The two forms of education, however, have a fundamental incompatibility.

3. To be moral, one must be religious. Morals are founded on values. And there are only two possible bases for grounding values—nature or God. Nature contains no values in itself. So values must be based on God. So one must believe in God to be moral.

4. Playing sports is valuable because it teaches people teamwork.

5. Workers should share in management decisions. They are affected by those decisions, and often they know as much or more about the running of the plant than do the senior managers who usually make the decisions.

6. Although many college faculty members are reaching retirement age, universities are tending to hire older rather than younger scholars to replace them. Therefore, the universities will not revitalize themselves.

7. The number of unmarried adults in Canada is continuing to rise. If there is an increase in people unsupported by the bonds inherent in the nuclear family, there are increases in alcoholism, drug abuse, and suicide. So there will be an increase in alcoholism, drug abuse and suicide.

8. Football should be discouraged because it makes people aggressive.

9. Cigarette smoking in public places should be discouraged because it forces nonsmokers to risk their health against their will.

10. John withheld information; therefore, he lied.

11. We shouldn't allow doctors to reveal the gender of a fetus when parents request it. If we allow such disclosure, then some parents will abort a fetus simply because of its gender. And that is not a good reason for abortion.

12. Tourists have a good time at Disney World; therefore, they are not being exploited.

13. I don't see how you can call Miles Davis a great jazz musician. He uses one basic technique and fluffs half of his notes. Those aren't characteristics of a great jazz musician.

14. The novel *The Adventures of Huckleberry Finn* uses language that many consider racist. Therefore, the novel is racist and promotes racism.

15. The primary purpose of a university education is to train people so they can get well-paying jobs. Liberal arts courses such as critical thinking, sociology, and philosophy do not help people get well-paying jobs. So these courses should not be part of a university education.

16. Those who argue for equal rights for everyone are ignoring the fundamental facts of human nature. Not everyone is equal. So why should we be forced to treat everyone as equal?

17. Christmas celebrations and symbols should not be allowed in the public schools because they pertain to only one religion and culture, and ours is a multicultural society.

18. We are justified in torturing and even killing terrorists without trial or due process. Terrorists have no concern for the rights of the innocent citizens they slaughter. Therefore, we should not grant them any rights once we have caught them.

19. Subsidizing the pill helps prevent unwanted pregnancies and reduces the population explosion. So, industrialized countries should help subsidize the pill for developing countries.

20. Students should not be held accountable for plagiarism and cheating, for most don't know what these are.

21. More people are living together and fewer are getting married. This shows that fewer people in society are interested in getting involved in committed, long-term relationships.

22. If media portrayals of violence incite real violence, then we should see evidence of more violence in societies that have widespread media portrayals of violence than in societies that do not. But that is not what we find: Many societies with no media portrayals are much more violent than some societies that do have such portrayals. So, media portrayals of violence do not incite real violence.

23. In the Bermuda Triangle, there have been many mysterious disappearances over the past one hundred years. Most of these disappearances cannot be explained by any known natural cause. There must be some kind of unknown force or power operating within this area to cause the disappearance of so many ships, planes, and people.

24. You know, it is uncanny how the stock market predicted the election results. The day before the election, the market rose significantly. Analysts claimed that this was a sign that the market expected a Liberal majority government. And that is exactly what we got.

25. In a democracy like ours, the government should do whatever the majority want. The majority want prayer in public schools. So, the government should institute prayer in public schools.

26. Burying garbage is wasteful and harms the environment. Burning garbage, although initially more expensive, is both more ecologically sound and, in the long run, cheaper. We should burn our garbage.

27. No opinion should be suppressed. If an opinion is false, then its being aired allows us to judge it and discover why it is false. If it is part true and part false, then allowing it to be aired gives us the opportunity to challenge it and discover what is beneficial and what is harmful. If the opinion is true, and it is not challenged, then it risks becoming a dead dogma, whose truth we do not understand. (Mill, John Stuart. *On Liberty*. Markham: Penguin Books. 1987.)

28. Advertising systematically misleads and misrepresents. So, it is not trustworthy and should therefore be ignored.

29. Professional athletes who use steroids to enhance performance should be banned from competition for at least two years. Not only do such athletes undermine the basic idea of fair competition, but they set a bad example for young people who admire them.

30. Since the university is going to accommodate Christian, Jewish, and Islamic holidays by not having exams on those days, then it should accommodate every religious holiday, including those in Wicca (modern witchcraft), Scientology, and other less mainstream religions. That is only fair.

31. Since advertising does not pretend to be argumentation, it should not be held to the logical and truth conditions of argumentation. After all, it is simply a form of persuasion, not argumentation.

✍ EXERCISE 4.5
Additional Exercises for Assessing Cogency

Go back to Exercises 3.4, 4.2, and 4.3 and, where the arguments are deductive, assess the arguments for cogency.

MODULE 5: ASSESSING INDUCTIVE ARGUMENTS

QUICK QUIZ ANSWERS

✍ QUICK QUIZ 5.1
Assessing Inference-to-the-Best-Explanation Arguments

Formulate the following arguments. Assess each argument in terms of strength—very strong, strong, weak—and explain why you assess it that way. Use the criteria for assessing inference-to-the-best-explanation arguments.

1. Raj and Janet are friends. They have studied together all year. They sat next to each other in the exam. Not only did they both get the same letter grade on the exam, but both got the same questions right and most of the same questions wrong. They must have cheated on the exam.

   1. **Raj and Janet are friends.**
   2. **They have studied together all year.**
   3. **They sat next to each other in the exam.**
   4. **Not only did they both get the same letter grade on the exam, but both got the same questions right and most of the same questions wrong.**

   ∴ 5. **They must have cheated on the exam.**

   That Raj and Janet have similar right and wrong answers may simply establish that they have studied together and therefore have a similar understanding of the material, both correct and incorrect. If their other work is also similar, there would be support for the alternative hypothesis—that they didn't cheat. If their other work is quite dissimilar, one being an A student and the other a D student, there would be more to support for the existing hypothesis.

   The premises provide weak support for the conclusion. The alternative conclusion is at least equally as probable.

2. The Loch Ness monster must exist. Hundreds of people have seen the creature over the centuries. Furthermore, there are photographs and even videotapes of the monster.

   1. **Hundreds of people have seen the creature over the centuries.**
   2. **There are photographs and even videotapes of the monster.**

   ∴ 3. **The Loch Ness monster must exist.**

   Many people have claimed to have seen things that we know don't exist— dragons, fairies, elves, witches flying through the air, Sasquatch. Such claims don't prove that these things exist. They show that if people believe something, they may tend to interpret strange experiences in terms of what

they believe. The photographs and videotapes are unclear and ambiguous, and a few have been shown to be hoaxes. These sightings are based on interpretations.

The original argument is weak. More information about the photos and videotape and about the eyewitness testimony might strengthen it. As it stands, without this information, the premises provide inadequate support.

3. Gasoline prices go up at the beginning of a long weekend and down just after. And this happens all over the country. This shows that the major oil companies are controlling gas prices.

> 1. **Gasoline prices go up at the beginning of a long weekend and down just after.**
> 2. **And this happens all over the country.**
>
> ---
>
> ∴ 3. **The major oil companies are (unfairly) controlling gas prices.**

> **An alternative explanation might be that this is coincidence. However, if the pattern persists over many months or several years, the coincidence argument wears thin. It might be that on holiday weekends there is increased demand, which puts increased pressure on the supply. That would provide a reasonably plausible alternative explanation. If the oil companies could show that their costs increase and/or that their corporate profits do not go up when there are price jumps, then the argument would be less plausible. As it stands, I would rate this argument possible but needing substantially more evidence to draw this conclusion.**

4. The developer withdrew $25,000 from his business account. He then immediately called a local city alderman and met him fifteen minutes later in an underground parking garage. Over the next week, $23,000 was deposited to the alderman's account in five deposits. All deposits were in $100 dollar bills. The alderman claims that the money was a gift from his father-in-law. However, there is no evidence of withdrawals from the father-in-law's account and no independent evidence for the source of the money. The alderman spoke strongly for a proposal favouring the developer over the next few months and convinced many of his colleagues to support the developer's proposal. I contend that the alderman took a bribe from the developer.

1. The developer withdrew $25,000 from his business account.
2. He then immediately called a local city alderman and met him fifteen minutes later in an underground parking garage.
3. Over the next week, $23,000 was deposited to the alderman's account in five deposits.
4. All deposits were in $100 dollar bills.
5. The alderman claims that the money was a gift from his father-in-law.
6. There is no evidence of withdrawals from the father-in-law's account and no independent evidence for the source of the money.
7. The alderman spoke strongly for a proposal favouring the developer over the next few months and convinced many of his colleagues to support the developer's proposal.

∴ 8. The alderman took a bribe from the developer.

The reasons provide strong evidence for the conclusion. The alderman has offered an alternative—that his father-in-law gave him the money—that has not been supported. Of the two alternatives, the bribe explanation is the stronger.

✒ QUICK QUIZ 5.2
Assessing Generalizations

In the following, identify the population and the sample, and assess whether the sample is likely representative of the population. Using the criteria specified in the text, how reliable would you judge the conclusions reported? Justify your reasoning.

1. Most people think that the government should lower the taxes on gas.

   No numbers in terms of population or sample are given. This is an unsupported generalization. We have no way of assessing its reliability.

2. A radio journalist interviews five people at a parking lot in the city about their views on what the government should do about rising gasoline prices. Four of the five think that the government should intervene to lower the gas tax. The journalist reports that eighty percent of the population think the government should lower the gas tax.

   Sample: Five people at a parking lot in the city; no demographics given.
   Population: Uncertain. They could be all city residents, all drivers, all residents of the province.

   Since only five people in a parking lot were questioned, the sample is too small and likely unrepresentative even of all drivers in the city. At best, this might represent drivers or, more narrowly, commuters, who have a vested interest in the question. So, these are people who would probably favour lower gas prices and lower taxes on gas. The sample ignores transit riders, cyclists, noncommuters, and ecologists. This is an unreliable generalization.

3. A student surveys a class of sixty students on whether they approve of a proposal to introduce a student health levy. Forty-five of the sixty students interviewed agree with the proposal. The student concludes that seventy-five percent of the ten thousand students at the university support the proposal.

> **Sample:** Sixty students in one class; no demographics given.
> **Population:** 10,000 students at the university.
>
> **The sample is likely not representative of the student population. Without knowing the year of study of the class, whether or not the class is composed of students who already have health insurance, or other relevant factors, it is difficult to determine how representative this sample is. A sample of sixty is small, but, with some effort, could be somewhat representative. This has low reliability.**

4. A student surveys a cross-section of two hundred students, balanced for year of study, gender, ethnicity, and major, on whether they approve of a proposal to introduce a student health levy. One hundred and fifty students agree with the proposal. The student concludes that the majority of the 10,000 students at the university are likely to support the proposal.

> **Sample:** Two hundred students, cross-section, balanced for gender, ethnicity, major, and year of study.
> **Population:** 10,000 students at the university.
>
> **This is fairly reliable. The surveyor has attempted to address within the sample relevant variables, including year of study, gender, ethnicity, and major. Two key variables missed might be income (family and student) and access to existing health insurance. With these limitations, it is a fairly reliable generalization.**
>
> **One objection commonly raised is that a sample of two hundred is "too small." Without specifying why, this is a weak criticism. The size of a representative sample depends on a number of factors, including the degree of variation and frequency of variation of the units in the sample. National surveys of political opinion for Canada, for example, are often based on samples of fifteen hundred people. These samples are balanced for relevant variables—age, socioeconomic status, gender, region—and they tend to be correct nineteen times out of twenty. Doubling the sample size does not increase reliability.**

✍ QUICK QUIZ 5.3
Defending General Claims and Generalizations

Qualify each of the bolded claims below by limiting the scope to make it a more defendable claim in the context of the passage. (You are not being asked to supply reasons or justifications.)

1. The Sponsorship Scandal shows that **politicians are corrupt.** [The Sponsorship Scandal involved a number of politicians and civil servants allied with the Liberal party providing government advertising contracts for little or no work and, in return, receiving kickbacks to the Liberal party in Quebec.]

    In order of increasing defensibility:

    - **All politicians are corrupt.**
    - **Some politicians are corrupt.**
    - **All Liberals are corrupt.**
    - **A few Liberal politicians in the Chrétien government were corrupt.**
    - **About a dozen Quebec-based liberal politicians and civic servants in the Chrétien government involved in the Sponsorship programme were corrupt.**

    The first is clearly an overgeneralization. As we move down the list, the claims become more defensible based on the information given. The last claim is the most specific and most defensible based on the information provided in the passage.

2. I was in Montreal for a month and saw really bad driving. Drivers ignore the rules of the road. They speed, run red lights, and go through crosswalks as children are crossing. **Society is becoming more lawless.**

    At best, the passage applies to drivers in Montreal, not to all of society. We might offer the following:

    Some drivers are ignoring the law more frequently.

    The passage extends significantly beyond the evidence in two ways: (1) It involves a comparison statement—society is becoming *more* lawless—which suggests a comparison between two states, the current observations in Montreal and a previous set of observations; however, no comparison state is given. (2) It applies to all drivers, although the observations are based on Montreal.

    A better formulation might be:

    Drivers in Montreal ignore the rules of the road.

    This claim suggests that all or most drivers ignore all rules of the road. That seems unlikely. It's doubtful that drivers run red lights or drive through crosswalks as a common practice. We could further qualify the claim, as follows:

    Many of the drivers I observed when I was in Montreal tended to ignore some of the basic rules of the road.

Based on the original passage, this claim is more defensible. It does not, however, establish that society is becoming more lawless. Minimally, to establish such a claim, we would have to come up with a baseline with which to compare the current state. The poor driving I observed in Montreal may simply indicate that the drivers in Montreal engage in such behaviour. It is possible they have always behaved in such a way, not that they have gotten worse. Also, we can't deduce from a person's driving behaviour that the person would engage in other kinds of law-breaking behaviour.

3. I read in the *New York Times* (online version Nov 16, 2005) that **many young urban professionals are self-medicating.** In interviews with a number of people under thirty-five, the *Times* found that these people are trading prescription medications both with friends and via the Internet. Some of them fake symptoms to get the prescription medications they want.

> **Nothing in the description justifies the claim that it is "urban professionals" who are self-medicating. Also, it is not made clear whether this activity is a New York phenomenon or if it is more broadly based. The article provides no statistical information or information about samples, which makes it impossible to determine how representative this claim is.**

> > **In interviews with the *New York Times* in 2005, some individuals under the age of thirty-five reported that they self-medicate using prescription drugs.**

> **This is more defensible.**

✍ QUICK QUIZ 5.4
Assessing Causal Connections

In the following, identify whether or not a causal connection is being claimed. If one is being claimed, identify the claimed cause and effect and then assess whether a satisfactory causal connection has been established.

1. Taking large doses of Vitamin C prevents colds. My whole family took twice the recommended daily doses of Vitamin C every day, and none of us had a single cold all winter.

> **A causal connection is being claimed.**

> **Cause: taking large doses of Vitamin C**
> **Effect: prevents colds**

> **A satisfactory causal connection has not been established. At best, this statement establishes a limited correlation, not a cause. The claim meets the conditions of temporal and spatial proximity; it does not establish covariance. In order to do that, an arguer would have to show that those who did not take large doses of Vitamin C got colds more frequently than those who did. This is a common error. We often draw conclusions about correlation and cause**

when we haven't even established covariance. To establish covariance, we need to establish not only that when one event occurs, the other occurs, but also that when one event does not occur, the other does not occur. This argument does not suggest a reasonable mechanism.

2. Surveys show that teens are reporting using drugs and having sex at a younger age than was reported five years ago. Sociologists suggest that this is due to increased pressure on them to succeed and the fewer opportunities they have.

   The term *due to* suggests a causal connection is being claimed.

   Cause: increased pressure to succeed and fewer opportunities
   Effect: using drugs at a younger age
   having sex at a younger age

   A satisfactory causal connection has not been established. A possible cause has been proposed, but no covariance has been shown and no mechanism suggested.

3. In November 2005, some of the poorer immigrant areas of France erupted in violent riots. Most of the rioters were young males between sixteen and twenty-five, unemployed and subjected to discriminatory behaviours from authorities. Experts suggested that the riots were a natural outcome of the conditions and pointed to the social law that when young males are marginalized, deprived of opportunities, and feeling little hope, given an opportunity, they often resort to antisocial, antiestablishment, and illegal behaviour—drug use, crime, and, sometimes, revolutionary activity. As one expert pointed out, we do not see these reactions in middle-class areas where individuals are not marginalized and do have hope.

   A causal connection is being proposed:

   Cause: marginalization, deprivation of opportunities, and little hope and an opportunity to act out against authority
   Effect: the riots in France in November 2005

   This argument presents a reasonable causal connection. There is spatial and temporal priority, covariance, and a reasonable mechanism.

✍ QUICK QUIZ 5.5
Assessing Appeals to Experts

Treat each of the following claims as an appeal to authority. Identify what body of knowledge is being appealed to and who is being appealed to as an expert. For each of the following claims, determine, using the criteria for a proper appeal to authority, whether the person being appealed to would qualify as an appropriate authority for the claims being made.

1. News broadcaster gives his opinion on a current political event.

   Expert: news broadcaster
   Body of knowledge: a current political event

It is not clear that this is an issue about which there is a body of knowledge. There may be. For example, if we were talking about the current legal ramifications of stem cell research, there is a substantial body of knowledge on the legal impact of that. It would be unlikely that most journalists would have that body of knowledge, but a specialist on stem cell research might. On the other hand, a political commentator might well know whether the NDP would support the minority Conservative government on a crucial vote and be able to give an informed opinion on that. But ultimately, he or she would have to back any arguments with reasons.

2. The author of a popular book on negotiating strategies makes claims about the most effective way to negotiate. He bases his claims on twenty-four years' of negotiating in various contexts.

Expert: author of a book on negotiating strategies who has twenty-four years of personal experience
Body of knowledge: the author's personal experience

The author has personal experience, but there is no indication that he has systematically studied the field (i.e., the available research in the field) nor that there is a body of knowledge. This is informed opinion, not expertise.

3. Pollution Probe (an environmental organization opposed to nuclear energy) testifies at a public hearing on the reopening of Ontario's nuclear generating facilities that such a move would be costly and environmentally unsound.

Expert: Pollution Probe
Claim: reopening Ontario's nuclear generating facilities would be costly and environmentally unsound

The issue is a policy decision: Should Ontario reopen its nuclear generating facilities? The choice ultimately rests on ethical and political considerations. While there is a body of knowledge about the costs, risks, and environmental consequences of reopening such facilities, the final decision is a political/ethical one. If Pollution Probe is testifying about the body of knowledge, and granting its members are experts in this area (I will grant that they are or that the group will have experts who will testify on its behalf), the issues it is testifying about are controversial. Since estimates differ about the risks, costs, and environmental impact, they cannot testify as experts; rather, they can offer informed opinion and arguments.

4. Wayne Gretzky, a hockey superstar, claims in an advertisement that Motrin is a good medication for arthritis.

Expert: Wayne Gretzky
Claim: Motrin is effective for treating arthritis

If Gretzky were talking about hockey, I would grant him expert status. But since there is nothing to indicate he is an expert in the treatment of arthritis, he fails to meet the criterion of being an expert in the field. The advertisement is using what psychologists call "the halo effect": An individual who is seen as having something good about them (e.g., beauty, expertise in one area) is assumed to be an authority in other areas.

5. A management consultant who teaches negotiation is called as an expert witness to testify at a trial about whether a contract was negotiated in good faith.

> **Expert:** management consultant who teaches negotiation
> **Issue:** whether a particular contract was negotiated in good faith

> The fact that the person teaches negotiation establishes nothing about his or her knowledge of the field. Many people set themselves up as self-styled consultants. We would need to know on what the person's claim to expertise in the field is based. Assuming there is a body of knowledge on negotiation (there is), nothing about the information given in the context establishes that the person is an expert in the field.

✍ QUICK QUIZ 5.6
Assessing Experts

What expertise would be required to establish someone as an expert on the following topics? Be as specific as you can be. To the best of your knowledge, are these fields of knowledge about which expert testimony is possible?

1. The claims of astrology

> An astrologer or an academic who has studied astrology would likely know the claims of astrology, and, although there are many, I doubt that they comprise a coherent field that would constitute a body of knowledge. Different astrologers have widely varied approaches and interpretations of astrological charts.

2. The truth of astrology

> There is no clear field, no consensus, and no clear expertise. Various groups would have things to say about this, but we have to examine their arguments, not rely on their expertise.

3. The origins of humankind

> The relevant academic fields are anthropology, archaeology, and paleontology. A scholar of human origins in these fields would be helpful as an expert. Others that might be useful would be comparative anatomists and geologists. There is controversy about various aspects of human origins. In those areas, experts could be cited about the state of the controversy but not its resolution.

4. International banking policy

   This is a field of knowledge insofar as what the policies are. The experts are economists. If the issue is what policies should be adopted, that is normative and there is controversy.

5. The effects of the Roe v. Wade decision (a United States Supreme Court decision on the legal acceptability of abortion)

   The primary effects are legal, social, and political, so I would consider the experts to be legal scholars, sociologists, political scientists, and historians. There is a field here of the effects of this decision, but it crosses academic disciplinary boundaries. Experts would likely disagree about the legal implications, in which case what we would need are arguments, not an appeal to authority.

✍ QUICK QUIZ 5.7
Experts, Informed Opinion, and Opinion

In each of the following, identify whether the appeal is made to expert opinion, informed opinion, or just opinion. Explain.

1. My brother, who has worked as a motorcycle mechanic for thirty years, says that Harley-Davidson motorcycles are more reliable than Suzukis.

   This is at least informed opinion. Someone who has been a motorcycle mechanic for thirty years (assuming he has worked on both kinds of bikes) surely can be considered reliable in this field. The only question is whether there is a body of knowledge and a consensus in the field on that body of knowledge. If these two conditions were met, I would grant that this is expert knowledge.

2. Based on an extensive survey of motorcycles, Consumers Union reports that Harley-Davidson motorcycles are more reliable than Suzukis.

   This is difficult. Although Consumers Union has surveyed motorcycles, it is not clear whether it has surveyed consumers, mechanics, recalls by manufacturers, or anything else. There is probably a body of knowledge on the reliability of various kinds of motorcycles. A well-conducted survey would likely reveal which is more reliable. If this were a well-conducted survey, I would consider it expert knowledge.

3. Dr. Hamm in the physics department says that Harley-Davidson motorcycles are more reliable than Suzukis.

   Personal opinion: Even if there is a body of knowledge, nothing in the passage indicates that Dr. Hamm is an expert on that body of knowledge.

EXERCISES

🖎 EXERCISE 5.1
Assessing Inferences to the Best Explanation Arguments

Formulate the following arguments. Assess each argument in terms of strength—very strong, strong, or weak—and explain why you assess it that way. Use the criteria for assessing inference-to-the-best-explanation arguments.

1. Mark has been doing poorly in school this term. His behaviour has become more erratic lately, and he alternates between being hyper and being moody. He has also started hanging out with his former roommate, Fred, who was suspended from school for using drugs. I can only conclude that Mark has started using drugs.

2. Roy's sailboat disappeared off the coast of Puerto Rico in the area called the Bermuda Triangle. His last radio transmission was November 9. A severe hurricane went through the area on November 10. It is now December 10, and no one has heard from him for four weeks. His projected landfall was November 15. His sailboat was probably lost during the hurricane.

3. The weather was clear with none of the conditions that would cause wind shear or other atmospheric problems. There were no mechanical defects found in the reconstruction of the plane. No drugs or other factors that would indicate pilot impairment were found in the autopsy. The investigatory board concludes that the crash was most probably due to pilot error.

4. Eva must have taken the money from petty cash. It was there when I looked at 11:00. I left my office for only ten minutes. When I got back, Eva was there, standing near where the petty cash is kept. She acted suspicious. When I asked her if she had seen anyone else in the office, she said no. Although earlier she had said she had to go to the bank at noon to get money for lunch, she didn't go, yet she had money to buy her lunch.

5. The full-moon effect states that there is a relationship between the full moon and such things as increased violence, police arrests, accidents, and psychiatric episodes. In a study of the alleged full-moon effect, a researcher examined all of the police arrest, hospital emergency, and psychiatric records in a major metropolitan area for a three-year period. He correlated these with the moon's cycle, allowing a margin of several days on either side of the full moon. He discovered that although most of the incidents recorded did occur during a full moon, at least forty percent of the dates with the highest number of incidents happened nowhere near this lunar phase. He found, however, that these tended to coincide with weekends. When he rechecked his original data, he found that ninety percent of the high number of incidents he had classified as full-moon reports also occurred on weekends. He concluded that the full-moon effect is actually a weekend effect: Weekends, rather than the

moon's cycle, were a far better predictor of violent actions, police arrests, emergency room admissions, and psychiatric admissions.

6. Fatima's car was found unlocked and parked by the side of the road. The keys were in the ignition. Her purse and cell phone were untouched inside the car. Last week, two other people disappeared in the same area. Then two days later, they turned up and reported that they had been abducted by aliens. There have been two other such cases in the area in the past six months. Fatima was obviously abducted by aliens.

7. There were three food-product recalls yesterday. I checked and found there has been an average of one a day for the past year. Ten years ago, there was an average of one every ten days. The average number of recalls has been increasing steadily over the past ten years, but they have particularly escalated in the past three years. It seems that our food system is far less safe than it was ten years ago, despite increased regulation and monitoring.

8. The theory of evolution was not widely taught in American schools until 1963, with the introduction of new biology textbooks. Throughout the 1950s, there was little social upheaval and disorder in American society. Everyone knew the rules for a well-ordered society and followed them. Immediately after the widespread teaching of evolutionary theory, society disintegrated into chaos—crime rates rose; blacks, women, adolescents began challenging all authority and engaging in violent protests; pornography became rampant; abortion became legal; illegitimacy rates rose dramatically. It is clear that teaching evolutionary theory destroys any sense of morality.

9. The allegedly fictional Atlantis probably existed but not in the form described by Plato, the source of the legend. Plato told the story as an allegory about an advanced civilization that runs afoul of the gods. According to Plato, the Atlanteans were an advanced, seagoing civilization that controlled the Mediterranean. Atlantis was a large island, destroyed overnight by violent eruptions and the rising of the sea about ten thousand years prior to Plato. We know that humans at that time did not have the advanced capabilities described by Plato. However, the Minoans, who lived about one thousand years before Plato, did. And they were an advanced, seagoing civilization that controlled the Mediterranean and were destroyed by the volcanic eruption of Santorini, not overnight, but over an approximately fifty-year period. It is clear that Plato used the history of the Minoans to relate his story about the mythical Atlantis that runs afoul of the gods.

10. The power must be off in the whole neighbourhood. When the lights went out, I checked the main fuse box, but all of the fuses and circuit breakers were OK.

🖎 EXERCISE 5.2
Assessing Generalizations

In the following, identify the population, the sample, and whether the sample is likely representative of the population. Using the criteria specified in the text, how reliable would you judge the conclusions reported to be? Justify your reasoning. If a general claim is too broad, limit the scope so that the claim is more defensible.

Population: Restaurant
Sample: Your experience eating there.
Representation: Reviews

1. On Thursday I went to that new gourmet restaurant that opened last week, and the food was quite poor. The reviews that it is an excellent restaurant are obviously wrong.

Representation: Not very reliable Generalization.

2. Only thirty percent of registered voters voted in the recent city elections. This shows that citizen concern with politics is very low. Most people don't care what politicians do or who represents them.

Population: Citizens (Registered voters)
Sample: Recent election (people don't care)

3. I don't think I should major in economics. Economics requires a strong background in math, which I don't have. I barely made it through high school math and had serious trouble with my first-year math course. I am just not good in math.

4. Montreal is a really ugly city. I took the train from Quebec City to Montreal then to Ottawa. While the countryside was spectacular, Montreal was full of abandoned warehouses, with litter all over the place. I didn't leave the train station. Montreal sure was a disappointment.

5. Four of the major leaders of modern evolutionary theory—Richard Dawkins, author of *The Selfish Gene;* Francis Crick and James Watson, who together won the Nobel Prize for discovering the structure of DNA; and E. O. Wilson, founder of sociobiology—are not only atheists but argue that evolutionary theory shows that religion is not only unnecessary but harmful. It is clear both that evolutionary theory is atheistic and that biologists are atheists.

6. My three best friends all took economics and got great jobs upon graduation. Even though I am not great at math, I had better take economics. It will lead to a great job.

Representation: Biased opinion or survey.

7. Most Canadian postsecondary students are spending five to ten hours a day outside of class working on their schoolwork, contrary to what many teachers claim. A survey of one hundred and seventy-five students at the University of British Columbia found that one hundred and thirty of the students reported spending five to ten hours a day on schoolwork; thirty admitted to spending less time; and fifteen, more time. The survey was done of students emerging from the undergraduate library on three consecutive weekday evenings in November.

Population: Most secondary student
Sample: Student are always studying. (Post)

8. My sister has a white cat with blue eyes, and it is deaf. My cousin has a white cat with blue eyes, and it is deaf. And my nephew has a white cat with blue eyes that is deaf. I guess all blue-eyed, white cats must be deaf.

9. For the past month, I have often parked on the street overnight. Every Tuesday, I've gotten a ticket for parking illegally, but I haven't received a ticket on any of the other nights I have parked on the street overnight. The parking authority must be targeting this street on Tuesdays right now.

10. Three times last semester, the university administration allowed both the Palestinian and Israeli student organizations to set up information tables in the Student Centre. Each time, there were outbreaks of violence. I don't think we should allow them to have information tables in the Student Centre this term.

Each time there is an outbreak of violence.

Population: Palestinian and Israeli students
Sample: Three times the information tables were set up.

Representation: Is three times adequate to conclude they always get into fights? inadequate Repre

EXERCISE 5.3
Assessing Causal Inferences

In the following, identify whether or not a causal connection is being claimed. If one is being claimed, identify the claimed cause and effect and then assess whether a satisfactory causal connection has been established.

1. Since the reintroduction of the death penalty in 1982, Texas has executed three hundred and seventy-eight prisoners. At the same time, the violent crime rate has continued to increase at an alarming speed. The murder rate nearly doubled between 1982 and 1996 and has since remained at that level. The rape rate has also risen dramatically. This proves that capital punishment does not serve as a deterrent to those crimes for which the death penalty is invoked. *(Not a Causal Connection)*

2. Jim is fifty and smokes heavily. We know that smoking causes cancer. The causal mechanisms have been clearly established, and fifty percent of all smokers will die of cancer. Therefore, it is probable that Jim will die of lung cancer. *(Causal Connection, Smoking and Cancer) Weak argument.*

3. Overall grade profiles at the university started to decline when we started admitting more nontraditional students (mature students, foreign students, students whose family members had never attended university). The nontraditional students are responsible for the decline in grade profiles.

4. Fourteen people came down with food poisoning after eating the potato salad at the family picnic. No one who did not eat the potato salad suffered from food poisoning, and there was nothing else that those fourteen people all ate. The potato salad probably caused the food poisoning. It is being tested now.

5. Whenever there is a full moon, the number of violent crimes and admissions to emergency wards and psychiatric units skyrocket. It is obvious that the full moon has an adverse effect on people's behaviour. *(causal argument) Not a Strong Argument Is this systemically observed?*

6. Green tea may help prevent cancer. A recent study of five thousand people, half of whom have been drinking at least three cups of green tea daily for twenty years or more compared to the other half, who drink coffee or black tea, has shown there is twenty percent less incidence of stomach and esophageal cancer in the green tea drinkers. Researchers have recently isolated a chemical in green tea that acts to inhibit the growth of cancer tumours in mice.

7. Whenever I visit my sisters in Ontario and Quebec in the summer, my allergies go crazy. I never have any trouble in B.C. or Alberta. I've got to stay away from Ontario and Quebec in the summer. *(Causal Argument) Not a strong Argument, what is causing Allergies?*

8. There have been three serious school-based shootings in Montreal in recent memory. Marc Lépine killed fourteen women at L'École Polytechnique in 1989; Professor Valerie Fabrikant killed four colleagues at Concordia University in 1992; and Kimveer Gill killed one at

Dawson College in 2006. It is clear that the government's attempts to restrict access to guns are not working.

9. After two years of disappointing performances and rained-out sessions, the last four Montreal Jazz Festivals have been huge successes. Since the weather is supposed to be good this year, I expect that this year's will also be a huge success.

10. Incidents of violence among people twelve through twenty-one have been increasing over the past twenty years. During that same period, *The Simpsons* has become one of the most popular TV shows among people in that age group. By teaching a disrespect for authority, *The Simpsons* is clearly contributing to the rise in violence.

✎ EXERCISE 5.4
Assessing Experts and Informed Opinion

For each of the following claims, use the criteria for an appeal to authority or to informed opinion to determine whether a proper one has been made. Explain your answer.

1. From a student paper defending the use of genetically modified foods: James Watson is one of the discoverers of the molecular structure of DNA, was head of the Human Genome Project, and was chancellor of Cold Spring Harbor Laboratory. If anyone knows the values of genetics, it is James Watson. He asserts that genetically modified crops are safe and that they hold the only hope for the future of the human population.

2. According to Professor Jay Stanton of the university's astronomy department, Pluto is much smaller than the other eight planets and co-orbits around its moon, Charon. Professor Stanton explains that these characteristics are what fuelled the move to "delist" Pluto as a planet.

3. Mike, my mechanic, has been working on cars for twenty-five years and has never steered me wrong. If he says I need a front-end alignment, I need a front-end alignment.

4. According to Richard Twassen, an evolutionary psychologist, males seek to mate and marry young, fertile women, and females seek men of high social status. Twassen says this is genetic. Other evolutionary psychologists agree.

5. When I was filling my new eyewear prescription, my optician recommended getting a separate set of glasses for computer use. She said it would ease eye strain. Although they are somewhat expensive, because of the complexity and specialized nature of my prescription, maybe I should get them.

6. Dr. Lynn Margulis recently wrote a literature review article on the status of research on single-celled organisms that appeared in *Science,* the journal of the American Association for the Advancement of Science. The article clearly shows that the current received opinion among microbiologists is that eukaryotic cells evolved from prokaryotic cells through a symbiotic process.

7. Dr. M. L. Link of the psychology department of the University of Northern Ireland has been investigating the relationship between race and IQ for over thirty years. According to Dr. Link, there is a definite relationship between IQ and race, and this connection is genetic, as it appears to persist from generation to generation.

8. According to Richard Compton, a leading expert on crop circles, the circles have been around for at least fifty years, and, to date, no credible natural explanation has been offered for them.

9. Dr. Craig Allen, an ethicist at San Diego State University, testified at the trial that, despite various studies showing a correlation between breast implants and the development of cancer, the generally received opinion in the field is that no causal connection exists. His own research, funded by Dow Corning, makers of one of the most widely used implants, has shown no correlation. He testified that it was his expert opinion that no such correlation exists.

10. Hillaire St. Croix, a journalist who has been covering Quebec affairs for the past twenty years and has written two books on Quebec politics, says that it is unlikely that Quebec will support the Tories in the next election.

✍ EXERCISE 5.5
Analyzing and Assessing Inductive Arguments

Formulate the argument and assess for support (strength). Justify your assessment using the relevant criteria. Identify any additional information that would make the argument stronger or weaker.

1. My neighbour must have lost his job. He was home three days last week.

2. The incidence of syphilis has gone up in the past five years. At the same time, the teaching of sex education has moved from the upper grades to grades eight and nine. To stop the spread of syphilis, we have to stop teaching sex education.

3. The number of people killed or severely injured by guns and gun-related crimes has increased by ten percent in each of the past three years. We can look forward to another increase of ten percent this year.

4. Most people downloading movie files from the Internet do so illegally. Mia has been downloading music files from the Internet. So she is doing something illegal.

5. More than half of all Canadians are overweight. Antony is a Canadian. So he is overweight.

6. Only one in one thousand people undergoing this kind of surgery experience serious complications. So you are not likely to suffer serious complications.

7. Canadians are generally friendlier than their American counterparts. I visited Halifax, Winnipeg, and Vancouver this summer, as well as Chicago, New York, and Miami. The people in Canada were far friendlier than those in the States.

8. The number of cyclists and pedestrians killed or seriously injured on the roads has gone up by thirty percent in each of the past three years. It will only increase significantly this year unless we do something to control dangerous drivers.

9. Twenty percent of my students are ESL students. Twenty percent of the students in my course did poorly on the first exam. I can only conclude that the exam was poorly designed for ESL students.

10. Days before he was executed, serial killer and rapist Ted Bundy admitted to an interviewer that pornography had started him off on his life of rape and murder. Paul Bernardo, the Scarborough rapist and murderer of two Toronto schoolgirls, also used pornography. This shows that pornography causes men to commit rape.

11. In the past four years, the education minister has scheduled a press conference on March 1. At that conference, he has announced a tuition hike for university and college students. I see that he has scheduled another press conference for March 1. Students had better start digging deeper in their pockets; tuition is going up.

12. The average mental power of men is greater than that of women. If we were to make a list of all the eminent people in virtually any field—science, the arts, business, politics, philosophy—it would be clear that males dominate the list. If men are more renowned than women in so many areas, then the average mental power of men must be greater than the average mental power of women. (Charles Darwin, *Origin of Species,* paraphrased)

13. Airline food service has gotten really bad. I flew to Winnipeg and then to Calgary on different airlines. On both flights, the food was of poor quality and the airlines charged for it.

14. Professor Samardjich gave a really dynamite third-year course on Near Eastern archaeology last year. I hear he is giving a course this year on New World archaeology. I've got to sign up for it. It will be awesome.

15. Women now outnumber men in colleges and universities by a ratio of fifty-seven to forty-three. This shows that women are making great strides in moving into professional fields such as law, medicine, and engineering.

16. Most incumbents in city council races are reelected unless they have a strong opponent. Mayor Marge Simpson is the incumbent, and her main competitor, Bart, is not a strong opponent. So Mayor Simpson is likely to be reelected.

17. A survey of two hundred and fifty of the twenty-five hundred first-year students at the university showed that seventy percent preferred that their instructors make podcasts of their lectures and make them available to students. This shows that nearly three-quarters of all students at the university prefer that lectures be podcasted as well as delivered live.

18. Crop circles are elaborate patterns that appear overnight in cereal crops. The stalks of the crops are bent over to form patterns when seen from the air. Thousands have been discovered since they began appearing in Britain in 1978. Many people interested in the paranormal have claimed that the circles are too elaborate to have been made by humans, especially in such a short period of time, and that the making of the circles would require advanced technology. Some of the patterns are extremely intricate, ruling out natural explanations as well. The only alternative is the presence of some unknown advanced civilization, not of this world.

19. Professor Murwal has shown that between 1960 and 1990, there was a rise in the number of illegitimate births—from five percent to thirty percent of births. Since 1990, the number of illegitimate births has stabilized at thirty percent. Concurrently, the average score on IQ tests dropped by six points. Dr. Murwal contends that this can be explained by linking IQ and illegitimacy rates. He suggests that if IQ is genetic, then the only way of reducing the illegitimacy rates would be to increase the average IQ of the population.

20. One hundred and seventy-five societies, ranging from small, simple agrarian societies to large, complex industrialized ones, were surveyed worldwide. Only eight did not show evidence of same-sex sexual behaviour. All of those societies are extremely sexually repressive. I think it is safe to conclude that same-sex sexual behaviour is nearly universal, if not universal, in humans.

21. Dr. Harold Benjamin of the Dalhousie Law School and a leading expert on the Constitution has said that the Conservative motion in the House of Commons to recognize the Quebecois as a nation within a nation would have no constitutional standing and would not give more power to Quebec. He also claims that this would serve only as a symbolic gesture.

22. I haven't received a single e-mail all weekend, and normally I get about thirty. I also couldn't get into the online library when I tried to do some research. The university server must be down for maintenance.

23. According to Statistics Canada, the employment rate for the past quarter has increased by 2.4%. The unemployment rate has declined to 6.2%, after adjusting for seasonal averages. This shows that the economy is improving.

24. Radiation causes mutation in genes. Hans Mueller established this by exposing fruit flies to X-rays. Mueller divided his flies into two groups. One group he exposed to X-rays; the other group he did not. The more radiation the flies were exposed to, the more mutations there were per generation, whereas the control group showed no mutations. Mueller hypothesized that radiation altered something at the gene level, although at the time, the exact biochemical nature of the gene was not known.

25. The fire was caused by arson. There was extensive use of accelerant throughout the first floor. Although it was midwinter, several windows had been left open to allow oxygen to enter. The owner had been refused permission by the city to tear down the building and put

up a new one because the building was designated a historic site. And the owner had just days before tripled the insurance on the building. It all points to arson by the owner or someone acting on his behalf.

MODULE 6: ASSESSING CLAIMS

QUICK QUIZ ANSWERS

✍ QUICK QUIZ 6.1
Preliminary Quiz: Kinds of Claims

Before continuing, examine this list. For each claim, consider how you would establish that it is true (acceptable) or that it is false (unacceptable). Identify the specific evidence that would be required to prove or disprove each of the following claims. Be as specific and detailed as you can be. You do not need to gather evidence. Rather, you are being asked *what would count as evidence* for or against the claim. If you are unsure about what kind of evidence would be relevant, explain your uncertainty. If there are several possible interpretations of the claim's meaning that would affect how you would assess the acceptability of the claim, explain. Having identified the specific evidence that would count for or against each of the claims, examine your list and analyze it to see what different *kinds* of evidence are used.

1. The chalkboard in my critical thinking classroom is green.

   Observation: I simply examine the chalkboard in the classroom.

2. Every chalkboard on this campus is green.

   Observation: I can look at every chalkboard on campus. I could search for a single non-green chalkboard. It is easier to find a negative instance (a counterexample) for a generalization than to look at all of the chalkboards on campus. I could ask the person in charge of maintenance (an expert) whether there are non-green chalkboards on campus. That person's answer would be based on his or her experience.

3. Every chalkboard ever made has been green.

   Generalization: This is based on my (and possibly others') observations.

4. It is in the nature of chalkboards to be green.

   Not an observation: This is giving information about the nature of the thing itself. It claims that there is something in the nature of chalkboards that makes it impossible for them to be any colour other than green. This could be definitional if something is not a chalkboard unless it is green.

5. Caesar crossed the Rubicon in 49 B.C.E.

   Inference based on observations: Someone observed and reported Caesar crossing the Rubicon, and that has been included in various accounts passed down through history. We can check the original documents and reports to

get information that is as close as possible to the original observation. A significant number of historical events are misreported, partially reported, or simply inaccurate. Stories often get changed in the telling of them.

6. The earth is 4.5 billion years old.

   Inference based on observation of effects and inference from scientific laws: Although I would probably check this by asking an authority—a geologist or astronomer—ultimately, that person's assessment is based on observations and subsequent inferences. Although no human was present, we can make inferences based on our accumulated knowledge of the laws of nature. However, it is worth noting that scientists have disagreed about the age of the earth. They point to various observations they have made and the inferences from these in an effort to resolve such disputes.

7. Water boils at 32 degrees Fahrenheit (0 degrees Celsius).

   Observation: Originally, this was determined by people boiling water and measuring its temperature at boiling. This has since become a scientific law. As a scientific law, it defines the boiling point of (pure) water at sea level. In fact, water boils at different temperatures at different atmospheric pressures. Scientific laws are abstractions from the complexity of conditions encountered in the real world. They specify what happens under specified or ideal conditions. Water with impurities boils at a different temperature than pure water.

8. The atomic number of gold is 79.

   Scientific law based on observation: This was originally discovered by observation. Now that we understand the underlying processes and mechanisms of elements, it has become a scientific law. Ultimately, however, it is still based on observation.

9. Scientists believe that AIDS is not one single virus but several kinds of viruses.

   Observation: This is a claim about what scientists believe, not necessarily a claim about AIDS. Its truth or falsity is established by observation of what scientists believe. What they believe and what is true may be different.

10. AIDS is caused by HIV.

    Observation and inference: This is a claim about the cause of AIDS. Not being a biologist or medical researcher, we would probably ask an expert. However, the expert's opinion should be based on observation, inference, and the scientific community's best understanding of the cause of AIDS.

11. Getting unauthorized information about an exam prior to that exam is cheating.

    Definition: This definition of *cheating* relates to an academic context and identifies one kind of cheating. To check the meaning, we would examine the appropriate academic documents to see if this is how cheating is defined in this context.

12. This classroom is overcrowded.

> **Judgment: Not quite an observation, this involves a judgment, an evaluation of whether the room is or is not overcrowded. To make that judgment, we have to invoke some criterion for "overcrowded." The criterion for overcrowding may vary based on whether it is being set by instructors for pedagogical reasons or the fire marshal for safety reasons. It is an evaluative claim.**

13. *Pornography* is any depiction of sex or nudity that degrades women or children.

> **Definition: The italicization of *pornography* indicates that it is being used as a term, not a thing, and helps us infer that the writer is providing a definition— explaining how he or she is going to use the term. To challenge this, we may point out uses of the term that do not conform to this. We may also demonstrate that it is not useful as a definition.**

14. Pornography degrades women and children.

> **Observation and judgment: This is a claim about the effects of pornography. In order to assess it, we need to know the meanings of both *pornography* and *degrades*. Once we know those, we can examine the world to see if the claim is true. This requires a mixture of understanding the meaning and then judging the truth of the claim through observation.**

15. Prostitution is immoral.

> **Judgment: Establishing the truth or falsity of this involves making a judgment or evaluation about prostitution. In order to assess the claim, we need to know what criterion of value the author is using to evaluate prostitution. However, we cannot simply observe morality or immorality; our evaluation of whether prostitution is immoral will depend on the criteria we have for morality.**

16. Humans are, by nature, selfish.

> **This is an odd claim. Although it looks like one we could prove true by observation, that is not the case. We can find examples where the claim is true, but we can also find examples where the claim is apparently false. The claim that humans are, by nature, one way or another suggests that the counterexamples can be explained away and/or don't really count. This is not a generalization from experience. If it were, a single counterexample would show it to be false. If a person holds on to such a claim, despite observational evidence, and uses it in making life choices, then it is functioning as some other kind of claim. We call this kind of claim "metaphysical": It functions more as an organizing principle in a person's life and is beyond empirical refutation.**

Kinds of Evidence Used

1. evidence based on observation, which I will call empirical

2. evidence based on the meaning of concepts, which I will call conceptual

3. evidence based on criteria used to evaluate, which I will call normative

✍ QUICK QUIZ 6.2
Assessing Empirical Claims

In each of the following, identify the empirical claim, the evidence offered for it, and how reliable each claim is based on the evidence.

1. Last year when I was in Scotland, I visited Loch Ness and saw a number of photographs of the Loch Ness monster. It is a forty-foot-long dinosaur-like creature that lives in the loch.

   I saw a number of photographs. **The inference is that they were of the Loch Ness monster (or so was reported to me). Since I did not directly observe the creature, the second sentence is merely an inference that the monster is forty feet long, dinosaur-like, and lives in the loch. Whether I would judge the inferences as reliable or unreliable would depend on how clear the photographs were, the provenance of the photographs, who took them, under what conditions, etc.**

2. Although there are no photos of the Loch Ness monster before 1900, we have over a dozen drawings. All of these show a seagoing dinosaur-like creature.

   The claim that there are no photographs from before 1900 is based on the testimony of those who have studied the monster. It is probably reliable, both since no photographs have shown up and since photographing the monster using cameras made before 1900 would be extremely difficult because of slow shutter speeds and the large size of the cameras. The drawings may show a seagoing creature; however, there is no way of telling how accurate the drawings are or what the artist actually saw.

3. Ancient dinosaur-like creatures must exist because they have been seen. The Loch Ness monster is a good example of one.

   Ancient dinosaur-like creatures must exist **is an inference based on the claim that "they have been seen." Whether they have actually been seen or whether people have projected their assumptions on such sightings needs to be determined. Unfortunately, we have no independent evidence of the existence of such creatures, and the claim that they must exist is not reliable based on the evidence cited.**

✍ QUICK QUIZ 6.3
Assessing Conceptual Claims

Identify which of the following are conceptual claims and explain why.

1. Objectifying women is wrong.

   The basic claim is normative. There may be subsidiary questions about the meaning of the term *objectifying women*.

2. Objectifying women means to treat them as less than human.

   This is a conceptual claim: It offers a definition of *objectifying women*.

3. Objectifying women results in their being treated as less than human.

   This is an empirical claim: It identifies the results of treating women in a certain way.

✍ QUICK QUIZ 6.4
Distinguishing Normative Claims

Determine whether each of the following is a factual claim, preference normative claim, or criterial normative claim, and explain why. If you are undecided, explain your indecision.

1. Ken Dryden was a better goalie than Patrick Roy.

   Normative claim: A judgment is being made about who is the better goalie. No criteria are provided, so we cannot determine whether it is preferential or criterial.

2. Despite their respective records, the Toronto Maple Leafs is a better team than the Montreal Canadiens.

   Normative claim: A judgment is being made about which is the better team. No criteria are provided, so we cannot determine whether it is preferential or criterial.

3. I like the Leafs better than the Canadiens.

   Preference normative claim: This is just a statement about which team the person likes better.

4. The Canadiens have scored more goals this year than the Leafs.

   Empirical claim: The claim appeals to a matter of fact—who has scored the most goals.

Assessing Normative Claims

For each of the normative claims below, identify (1) the kind of normative claim; (2) the purpose of the evaluation, if it can be determined; (3) the criteria used; and (4) other possible criteria that might challenge these criteria.

1. This book is poorly written. It is very difficult to understand, and the author's language is highly technical.

Normative claim:	**This book is poorly written (argument's conclusion)**
Purpose of the evaluation:	**Not stated, not made clear**
Criteria:	**How easy it is to understand; how technical the language is**
Alternative criteria:	**1. Quality of the book's contents**
	2. Importance of the book's ideas and argument

If the text is technical, the criteria being used may not be the most suitable. Using these criteria would, at best, offer a stylistic criticism, not a substantive one. What would be more important is the quality of the book's contents. If, on the other hand, the book is intended for a general audience, then its writing quality might be a significant criticism, although other criteria might outweigh the difficulty of the language.

2. *Said in a discussion between a couple deciding where to vacation this year:* "I think we should go camping and cycling in Quebec this summer rather than visit my sister in Calgary. We both like camping and cycling, and it would be cheaper. Besides, we saw her last year, so it's her turn to visit us—and cycling and camping would be more relaxing than staying with family."

Normative claim:	**1. We should go camping and cycling in Quebec this summer. (conclusion)**
	2. We both like camping and cycling. (reason, preference claim)
	3. Cycling and camping would be more relaxing than staying with family. (reason, preference claim)
Purpose of the evaluation:	**To decide where to vacation this summer**
Criteria:	**1. Preference for cycling and camping**
	2. Cost
	3. Turn-taking (sister's turn to visit)
	4. What is more relaxing
Alternative criteria:	**1. Possible family obligations and commitments**
	2. Visiting family

3. *Said in an election campaign:* "You should elect the Conservatives because they will form a better government. They will interfere less in the lives of citizens."

Normative claim:	1. We should elect the Conservatives. (conclusion)
	2. The Conservatives will form a better government. (intermediate conclusion)
Purpose of the evaluation:	To influence voting.
Criteria:	1. Who would form a better government (normative claim)
	2. Who would interfere less with the lives of citizens
Alternative criteria:	1. Fiscal responsibility
	2. Social policies
	3. Visions for the country

✍ QUICK QUIZ 6.6
Identifying Ethical Claims

For each of the ethical claims below identify (1) the ethical claim being argued for; (2) the criteria being invoked; and (3) other possible criteria that might challenge these criteria.

1. The U.S. should be condemned for systematically using torture in its conducting of the war on terror and the war in Iraq. Torture violates the basic human rights of its victims.

Claim:	The U.S. should be condemned for systematically using torture in its conducting of the war on terror and the war in Iraq.
Criterion:	Torture violates the basic human rights of its victims. Which human rights are violated is not specified but could be inferred.
Other criteria:	One might justify torture on the grounds of safety or protection of others from harm at the hands of terrorists.

2. Paying women less than men for doing the same job is immoral. Therefore, we shouldn't do it.

Claim:	We shouldn't pay women less than men are paid for doing the same job.
Criterion:	No criteria are offered. The claim is simply made that it is immoral (possibly meaning unethical) and is treated as self-evident. Simply saying that something is immoral without providing a criterion for immorality is not giving a sufficient reason. It is a variant of a formulaic reason. However, we could relatively easily generate a criterion for this claim.
Other criteria:	We might justify differential treatment based on differential productivity, differential costs in training and development of staff, and differential costs in benefits.

3. A student charged with a breach of the rules of the university should have the right to a fair hearing before a disinterested party and the right counsel at such a hearing. This is only a matter of natural justice.

Claim:	A student charged with a breach of the rules of the university should have the right to a fair hearing before a disinterested party and the right counsel at such a hearing.
Criterion:	Having a fair hearing before a disinterested party and the right to counsel are a matter of natural justice.
Other criteria:	We might claim that some breaches of the rules pose a threat to the health and safety of other members of the community and justify overriding the principle of natural justice. In this case, we would be invoking protection of the health and safety of other members of the community.

We might challenge this by arguing that the university is not the same kind of setting as the broader society, that the university stands in a different relationship to its members and that principles of natural justice do not apply.

✍ QUICK QUIZ 6.7
Identifying Mixed Claims

Identify any mixed claims below. Determine which are conceptual–empirical and which are conceptual–normative. Explain what would be required to determine the claim's acceptability.

1. The Conservatives have the best policy on child care.

    This is a mixed claim. We need to know what the arguer means by "best policy," a conceptual claim, before we could assess the overall claim, which is normative—it is using criteria to evaluate the best policy on child care.

2. Feminism is making a comeback among female university students.

    This is a mixed conceptual–empirical claim. The basic claim is empirical. However, in order to measure it, we need to know what the claimant means by "feminism," which calls for a conceptual clarification.

3. Low-income earners have greater health problems and lower life expectancies than middle- and high-income earners.

    The basic claim is empirical. However, we need to clarify how "low-income earners," "greater health problems," and "middle- and high-income earners" are defined by the claimant.

✍ QUICK QUIZ 6.8
Counterexamples

For each of the following claims, identify at least one possible counterexample.

1. All SUV drivers are a menace on the roads.

Some police forces use SUVs. Are the officers who drive them menaces?

[I have framed this as a question, which I would do in a face-to-face situation to pose a challenge to my argument partner. In a written context or non-face-to-face situation, I would formulate the counterexample as I do in question 2.]

2. If a person is a financial success, then he or she is a good person.

   Some members of the Hell's Angels motorcycle gang are financial successes. They have achieved this through murder, extortion, and other forms of criminal activity. They would not normally be considered "good persons."

3. In making all of their decisions, chief executive officers have in mind the best interests of the stockholders.

   If this is a claim about the actual behaviour of chief executive officers, then there are numerous examples of CEOs who have been found guilty of corrupt practices to the detriment of their stockholders and employees. The heads of Enron come to mind.

   If this is a claim about the normative rules of what a CEO should do, then there are various counterexamples: Should CEOs not be concerned about what is legal, what obligations they have to their employees, the safety of their products, etc.? The claim as stated seems to suggest that serving the best interests of the stockholders overrides other considerations. These counterexamples serve as reminders of those other considerations.

4. Everyone who uses a public roadway should have a motor vehicle licence or be banned from using it.

   Should fourteen-year-olds on bicycles, twelve-year-olds on skateboards or Rollerblades, and sixty-seven-year-olds in motorized wheelchairs all have motor vehicle licences?

✍ QUICK QUIZ 6.9
Presuppositions

Identify the presuppositions in the following claims. Using the list of kinds of presuppositions might be helpful here. Identify at least one claim related to the claims in the passage that is not a presupposition of the claim given.

1. You need to replace your engine. It has over 350,000 km on it.

   Presuppositions:
   1. **You have a vehicle that has an engine.**
   2. **This person knows the mileage on the engine.**
   3. **Having 350,000 km on an engine is a sufficient (relevant) reason for replacing it.**

   Not a presupposition:
   Your vehicle is a car. [It could be a motorcycle or a truck.]

2. Kidnapping, torture, and extortion are legitimate strategies in waging war.

Presuppositions:
1. **There are legitimate and illegitimate strategies in waging war.**
2. **Kidnapping, torture, and extortion are strategies used in warfare.**

Not a presupposition: The speaker is talking about the war in Iraq.

3. Marijuana should be legalized for medical reasons.

Presuppositions:
1. **Marijuana is currently illegal.**
2. **Marijuana has medical uses.**

Not a presupposition: Marijuana's medical uses outweigh its medical harms.

✍ QUICK QUIZ 6.10
Corollaries

Identify the implications and consequences for the following claims/situations.

1. Situation: Marijuana is going to be legalized for medical reasons.

Consequences:
1. **Some patients will be able to relieve their pain more easily now.**
2. **Some people without medical grounds will likely use this to gain access to marijuana.**
3. **Canada will set up a means for growing and distributing medical marijuana.**
4. **Health plans will need to consider whether they will pay for medical marijuana.**

Implication: **The United States will see this as another weakening of the Canadian moral fabric.**

2. Situation: A student is trying to get an exemption from the rule that he can't take a particular course without first taking its prerequisite. In talking with an advisor, he is caught lying about his grade in a previous course and why he got the low grade.

Consequences:
1. **The student's advisor will likely not trust the student.**
2. **The student will likely not get the exemption he wants.**
3. **The student may not be able to graduate on time.**
4. **The student will likely have to do the prerequisite first.**

Implication: **Social relations are increasingly based more on what one wants and can get away with than on personal integrity.**

3. Claim: Tuition for general undergraduate education will increase next year by ten percent.

Consequences:	1.	**Students will have to work more to pay for their university education.**
	2.	**Students will take longer to complete their degrees.**
	3.	**Students who borrow to finance their education will face even more debt.**
	4.	**Students will likely increasingly demand more quality in their education.**
	5.	**Students will likely move to programs and majors that promise job-related skills.**
Implication:		**The government values other things more highly than education.**

EXERCISES

EXERCISE 6.1
Identifying Kinds of Claims

Identify the kinds of claims in the following. Briefly identify the kind of evidence that would be used to prove or disprove the claim. Be as specific and detailed as you can.

1. All bachelors are unmarried males.

2. Prostitution is immoral.

3. Prostitution is legal in Canada.

4. Prostitution should not be legal.

5. A falling body descends at the rate of 32 feet per second per second.

6. Echinacea (a natural healing agent) is ineffective in building the human immune system.

7. According to the Pope, genetic engineering is immoral.

8. Most people in Canada are opposed to genetic engineering.

9. Genetic engineering is immoral.

10. Genetic engineering will lead to widespread ecological disasters by creating monocultures.

11. Margaret Atwood's *The Handmaid's Tale* is a well-written political novel.

12. Anything that degrades human beings should be banned.

13. It's raining.

14. The weatherperson says it's going to rain.

15. Abortions are legal in Canada.

16. Abortion kills a person.

17. Abortion is wrong.

18. Abortion stops a beating heart.

19. A fetus is a person.

20. A fetus is a human being.

21. A fetus is genetically human.

22. Athletes shouldn't take banned substances such as steroids.

23. Capitalism produces the greatest good for the greatest number.

24. Women are equal to men.

25. Good negotiators are good listeners.

26. Anything unnatural is bad for your health.

EXERCISE 6.2
Presuppositions and Corollaries

Identify the presuppositions and corollaries for each of the following passages. What kinds of claims are each of the presuppositions and corollaries?

1. How often have you cheated on your taxes before this?

2. AIDS is changing the sexual behaviour of single Canadians.

3. Employees who know of illegal or unscrupulous tactics on the part of their companies are duty bound to speak up—to blow the whistle.

4. It is hard to get ahead around here without cheating a little bit.

5. How many times have you deliberately lied during this past week? On how many of these occasions did you sincerely believe that lying was justified?

6. Why outlaw pornography? We know now that it does not cause psychological harm. And surely naked bodies per se are not evil.

7. The increase in speeding and recklessness on the highways is responsible for fifty percent of the increase in traffic injuries and deaths last year.

8. Although the 2010 Winter Olympics in Vancouver are supposed to pay for themselves, there are already cost overruns that will guarantee that the budgets run a deficit.

9. The government's uncompromising hard-line policy on human rights is endangering trade and closer ties with China at a critical point in the relationship between the two countries.

10. I prefer cycling in the few hours before sunset. The heat of the day has passed, and the wind tends to drop, which makes cycling easier.

☜ EXERCISE 6.3
Counterexamples

Provide one or more counterexamples for each of the following claims. The counterexamples can be real instances or hypothetical cases.

1. Dogs are unfriendly.

2. People convicted of spousal abuse tend to be naturally violent people.

3. Mature university students generally work harder at their studies than students just out of high school.

4. Unions are generally hostile to management.

5. If I take the exam, I will pass the course.

6. The staff members of this university don't care about students.

7. Anyone who commits suicide is insane.

8. Being a good citizen means always obeying the law.

9. Over seventy-five percent of the heroin addicts in Canada started out by smoking marijuana. Therefore, over seventy-five percent of the time, smoking marijuana leads to taking heroin.

10. If I drop this chalk and it doesn't break, then there must be something wrong with the chalk.

11. *Euthanasia* means killing the innocent.

12. The elderly shouldn't be allowed to drive.

13. If censorship did what it was supposed to, then it would eliminate all of the material it was trying to censor.

14. *Euthanasia* means the taking of a person's life without their consent.

15. Deception is never morally justified.

✍ EXERCISE 6.4
Claim Analysis

In the following passages, identify the main claim, the kind of claim it is, and whether or not the support being offered for it is adequate. Explain.

1. Using animals in research is immoral because it causes the animals needless pain and suffering.

2. A planet is defined as something that orbits the sun, is spheroidal, and clears all other objects from its path. Pluto fits only the first condition. So it is not a planet.

3. Instructors should not deduct marks for late papers. If the point of marking a paper is to evaluate how well the student has done on an assignment, then when the student turns the paper in is irrelevant.

4. I know that what I saw last night was a UFO. It moved quickly across the sky, faster than any plane could; it made no noise; and it seemed to be performing intelligent manoeuvres as it flew. No natural phenomenon or plane could do that.

5. Many reliable witnesses have seen UFOs. They must exist.

6. This year, the province has started patrolling the rivers and lakes, and charging boat operators who are impaired. The number of people who have drowned in boating accidents this year has decreased by fifteen percent. Therefore, enforcing the law against impaired boating has been effective.

7. Women are increasingly making up a greater percentage of secondary-education students. Across Canada, since 1998, women have outnumbered men in postsecondary enrolments, increasing by 1.7% per year.

8. Wayne Gretzky claims that the teams most likely to be in the finals this year are Ottawa and Vancouver.

9. After the shootings at Dawson College in Montreal, in which Kimveer Gill killed one student and wounded nineteen, the news reported that a psychiatrist claimed that Gill's playing of violent video games could not be seen as a cause of the rampage.

10. Although the murder rate for the city is relatively unchanged over the past ten years, the nature of those killed and of those doing the killing has changed substantially. Ten years ago, over sixty percent of the killings were domestic incidents and fewer than twenty-five percent were gang or crime related; only fifteen percent involved guns. These figures have changed steadily. Now over seventy-five percent of the killings are gang or crime related and eighty percent involve guns. Gangs have become more violent and more pervasive in our society.

11. A researcher has found that where written alphabetic languages have become dominant, women have tended to be treated as unequal. And the more dominant the use of such an alphabet, the greater is the subordination of women. On the other hand, the more widespread the use of nonalphabetic languages, such as the pictographs of Chinese or the hieroglyphs of ancient Egypt, the more egalitarian is the relationship between the sexes. The researcher hypothesizes that with the greater use of media and decreased use of written alphabetic languages, the relations between the sexes will become more egalitarian. [2]

12. A sociologist argues that cohabitation is not consistent with women's liberation. The sociologist, a women's studies professor, claims that cohabitation and women's best interests do not coincide. Basing her findings on fifteen hundred autobiographies written by students in her women's studies classes over the past thirty years, the instructor claims that the trade-off is unequal. While the men get access to sex, they are reluctant to make a commitment. The women report feeling used. The sociologist concludes that cohabitation is simply one more thing that tends to keep women in subordinate positions.

13. *Gerrymandering* is the process of redrawing electoral boundaries to favour the party in power in the next election.

14. We don't know if genetically engineered crops will be harmful. Therefore, we should not allow them.

15. Based on geological principles and the extent of erosion observed, it took the Colorado River over twenty million years to make the Grand Canyon.

✎ EXERCISE 6.5
Assessing Normative and Ethical Claims and Arguments

For each of the ethical claims below, identify (1) the normative or ethical claim being argued for, (2) the criteria being invoked, and (3) other possible criteria that might challenge the stated criteria.

1. Driving while impaired, whether on drugs or alcohol, is dangerous and, therefore, should not be allowed.

2. This is a better novel. The writing is more elegant than in the one we read first.

3. I don't think you should buy the SUV. It is less safe and costs substantially more than the van you are considering.

4. We should take our winter break in Aruba. I can get a great deal on the flight.

---

[2] Shlain, Leonard. *The Alphabet and the Goddess.* New York: Penguin Books. 1998.

5. I don't think you should tell the boss that Raj is cheating on his expense account. You don't want to get him in trouble.

6. Student to instructor: "I object to submitting my essays to TurnItIn.com [a plagiarism-checking site]. It's an American company subject to the Patriot Act. The U.S. government could force the website to give access to the database. That would compromise my privacy."

7. It's OK to lie by omission. It doesn't really hurt anyone.

8. You shouldn't eat meat because killing animals is murder, and murder is never justified.

9. We shouldn't patronize the big-box stores. They are not unionized, and they exploit their workers.

10. Psychology 101 is a good course. The instructor is interesting and the exams are fairly easy.

11. The major video chain store is better than the specialized local video store. It carries more copies of the most popular movies.

12. Capital punishment is justified because it costs a lot to keep those convicted of capital crimes in prison for the rest of their lives.

13. You should go to the conference. It has a good lineup of main speakers and the workshops sound good.

14. The university is a good employer. It has decent leadership and the morale among the staff and faculty is high.

15. Same-sex marriage should be legalized. It is the only way of treating gays and lesbians as equals in our society.

For additional exercises on conceptual claims, see Modules 2 and 9.

MODULE 7: FALLACIES

QUICK QUIZ ANSWERS

✎ QUICK QUIZ 7.1
Understanding Fallacies

For each of the following, state whether the claim is true or false.

1. A fallacy as used in this text is a false claim.

   False

2. All bad arguments are fallacies.

   False

3. In challenging a fallacy, one should attack the person for making a mistake in reasoning.

   False

4. A fallacy is a violation of one of the constitutive rules of argumentation.

   True

5. In challenging a fallacy, it is sufficient to be able to name the fallacy committed.

   False

6. Any error in reasoning is a fallacy.

   False

7. All fallacies are bad arguments.

   True

✎ QUICK QUIZ 7.2
Context

For each of the following, identify a possible context in which the claim or argument would be an *ad hominem* fallacy and a possible context in which it would not be. Explain the difference.

1. You have lied in the past. How can I trust what you are saying now?

   Not an *ad hominem* fallacy: If said between two persons, one of whom is challenging the truth of a current claim, this would not be an *ad hominem*

fallacy. For example, a creditor is challenging a debtor who in the past has lied about having an income and promised to pay the debt. Said as a comment between a courting couple, it could be an expression of distrust for past behaviour. The challenge is relevant to trusting what the person is saying is true. Said in a public hearing where a person's testimony relies on truthfulness, it would not be an *ad hominem.* Challenging the person's integrity is relevant.

Ad hominem fallacy: If said between two persons in a meeting where the person being attacked has presented data and an argument, and if this is being used to dismiss the data and argument, it would be a poisoning the well fallacy.

2. Of course she would say that. She is a feminist.

   Not an *ad hominem* fallacy: After a person expresses puzzlement about what a third party has said, his friend makes this comment to explain the speaker's remarks. In such a situation, there is no intent to dismiss the third party's remarks but merely to explain them by putting them in context.

   Ad hominem fallacy: Made as a response to her arguments, this would be an *ad hominem* fallacy.

3. A stockbroker has been charged with insider trading. After hearing the stockbroker's lawyer's explanation, the investigator says, "Of course you'd have an explanation. You're a lawyer."

   Not an *ad hominem* fallacy: Said as a joke between two people who know each other, this would be an innocuous comment.

   Ad hominem fallacy: Said as a dismissal of the stockbroker's defence without addressing the defence, it would be an *ad hominem* fallacy.

✍ QUICK QUIZ 7.3
Appeal to Force or Threat

Which of the following arguments is an appeal to force or threat? For those that are, explain how the criteria for this fallacy apply in the example. For those that are not, formulate the argument and explain why you do not consider it to be a fallacy of appeal to force or threat.

1. *A professor to a student who has challenged her argument:* "I suggest that you remember who is marking your paper before you continue this line of reasoning."

   This is an appeal to force or threat.

If you continue challenging my argument, I may mark your paper down.

∴ **You should not continue this line of reasoning.**

An appeal to force is committed when someone uses force or the threat of force to coerce someone to do something instead of offering rational reasons for the person to take such actions. In this case, rather than responding to a challenge, the instructor tries to silence the student's criticisms by subtly threatening her with a lower mark if she continues to challenge the instructor's position.

Consider possible conditions under which a similar utterance might not be an appeal to force.

2. *Spoken by a Canadian cabinet minister:* "If the United States continues to engage in unjust and unfair restrictions on Canadian softwood lumber imports, Canada will have no choice but to take the issue to arbitration and to impose countervailing restrictions on U.S. imports to Canada."

This could be formulated as follows:

> **If the United States continues to engage in unjust and unfair restrictions on Canadian softwood lumber imports, Canada will have no choice but to take the issue to arbitration and impose countervailing restrictions on U.S. imports to Canada.**
> **[We hope that the U.S. does not want to go to arbitration and face countervailing duties.**

∴ **We hope that the U.S. will not continue to engage in these actions.**

This is not a fallacy of appeal to threat, but a warning about what the Canadian government will do if the U.S. persists in a given course of action. The U.S. still has the option of continuing its actions. Canada is merely defending its rights and indicating how it will react if the U.S. maintains its restrictions on softwood lumber imports. That is different from uttering a threat.

3. *Manager to employee:* "I don't care if you think the 1-2-3 accounting program will do a better job and cost less. Remember that you are working for me, and if you don't support it, I will give you a bad performance appraisal."

This is a clear appeal to force.

The arguer is threatening to give the employee a poor performance appraisal if he or she doesn't support using the 1-2-3 accounting program.

The appeal is based entirely on the threat of a poor performance evaluation. This violates the principle that we must provide relevant reasons for our claims.

Appeal to Emotion

Which of the following passages are appeals to emotion? For those that are, explain how the criteria for this fallacy apply in the example. For those that are not, portray the argument and explain why you do not consider it to be a fallacy of appeal to emotion.

1. *Tenant to landlord:* "I know that I am six months behind on my rent, but I lost my job and then my wife left me. You've got to let me stay until I can get back on my feet."

   This is a clear appeal to emotion. The person is trying to elicit the landlord's sympathy by using his circumstances—not having a job and his wife having left him—as grounds for remaining in his apartment and not paying his rent.

2. I know that my client has admitted killing his parents, but consider the effects of sending him to prison for this. This poor, homeless orphan, without anyone to turn to, will wither and become a shell of himself. Do you want that on your conscience?

   This is a clear appeal to pity. The defence lawyer is appealing to the jury's sympathy for an orphaned child to encourage them to excuse the defendant's criminal actions.

3. Children are dying in Africa every day. Just pennies a day can help save a child from malnutrition. Send your money today.

   In this argument, we are being urged to send money to alleviate starvation of children in Africa. While there is an appeal to emotion—no one wants to see children starve—this is not a fallacy. The appeal is to an underlying value: We should do what we can to prevent starvation in children. While there is emotion involved in the appeal, reasons relevant to the conclusion are given. Although this argument could be better developed, there is enough here to warrant not calling it a fallacy of appeal to emotion.

   Children are starving and dying in Africa.
   [Money can help prevent children from starving and dying.]

   ∴ **You should send money to prevent a child from starving and dying.**

   Although the argument, as formulated, is not yet cogent, it is clearly an argument, and it appeals not simply to emotion but to an underlying implicit value—of preventing pain and suffering.

Ad Hominem

In the following, identify whether an *ad hominem* fallacy has been committed. For those that are *ad hominem* fallacies, explain how the criteria for this fallacy apply in the example. For those that are not, portray the argument and explain why you do not consider it to be an *ad hominem* fallacy.

1. *George Bush speaking about John Kerry in the 2004 U.S. presidential election campaign (paraphrased):* "My opponent is simply repeating the liberal tax-and-spend ideas that have proved bankrupt in the past." (Implication: You should not vote for him.)

   This is an abusive *ad hominem* in the context of U.S. politics, where being a liberal is seen by a substantial part of the public as a bad thing. Rather than addressing what is wrong with Kerry's ideas, Bush simply calls the ideas "liberal" and dismisses them on those grounds.

2. *John Kerry speaking of George Bush (paraphrased):* "I would urge you to look at George Bush's policies over the past four years. He has taken the nation from a substantial surplus to a massive deficit. He is the first president since the Depression to preside over a net loss of jobs. He has led the nation into an unjustified and costly war that is taxing the American economy. He has enriched the wealthiest ten percent at the expense of the middle class and poor. This is the policy of a compassionate conservative? Are these the policies you want continued for another four years?"

   This is not an abusive *ad hominem*. Kerry is arguing that George Bush should not be reelected because his policies have been disastrous. The comment about Bush being a "compassionate conservative," while perhaps a jibe at Bush's self-identification, is not part of the argument.

3. Dr. Khan was a member of the committee who authored the report. I doubt that we can accept anything he has to say in favour of it.

   This is a circumstantial *ad hominem*. The arguer is dismissing what Dr. Khan has to say on the grounds that he helped write the report and, presumably, is in favour of it. That someone has been involved in writing a report does not establish that his or her arguments are bad (or good). The only thing that can establish that is an examination of the arguments.

✍ QUICK QUIZ 7.6
Poisoning the Well

In the following, identify in which of the passages a poisoning the well fallacy is committed and explain how it is committed. If a poisoning the well is not committed in the passage, explain how it might be confused as one.

1. My opponent is a vulgar opportunist who will say and do anything to get elected and in so doing corrupts the entire electoral process.

   This is a poisoning the well fallacy. It attempts to discredit anything the opponent says by characterizing him or her as a vulgar opportunist who will say anything to get elected. The implication is that the opponent is not to be believed because he or she will not follow through on promises made.

2. Lawyer in summation to a jury: "We need to consider carefully anything that the witness has to say. She has already been shown to have lied under oath on numerous occasions to serve her own interests."

   This is not a poisoning the well. It is a legitimate questioning of the witness's credibility based on past experience. As part of a charge to a jury, it is a caution, not a poisoning of the well.

3. Anyone who doubts the president's approach to the war on terror is only helping the terrorists.

   This is also a poisoning the well. It seeks to discredit any critics of the president's approach as, in effect, helpers of the terrorists. It silences the opposition, not allowing its views to be heard.

✍ QUICK QUIZ 7.7
Shifting the Burden of Proof

In the following, identify whether one of the persons involved has shifted the burden of proof and explain how it is done. If the burden of proof has not been shifted, explain why the argument might be confused with a shifting the burden of proof fallacy.

1. The advocates of gay marriage keep claiming that the legalization of gay marriage is necessary to ensure civil rights. Yet they have not shown what these rights are nor how legalizing gay marriage ensures them. Before we can continue, they must support those claims.

   This does not shift the burden of proof. Advocates of gay marriage are campaigning for a change in the status quo. The burden of proof is on them to establish their case. The arguer in this passage is simply demanding that they live up to their obligations under the burden of proof—the advocates must establish their case. There is a difference between legitimately pointing out that someone has not made his or her case and claiming that an argument partner must disprove one's claims.

2. You will have to show me why I shouldn't believe in astrology before I will consider giving it up.

118

This is a form of shifting the burden of proof. The speaker has assumed that astrology is correct and suggested that the critic must provide reasons not to believe in it. However, the principles of astrology are contentious and need to be defended. The burden of proof should be on the person advocating astrology.

3. I don't believe that man ever went to the moon. What evidence have you got to show that he did?

This is a form of shifting the burden of proof. The evidence for the landing on the moon is fairly widespread and substantial. The belief that man did not go to the moon is more contentious. The skeptic needs to make his case.

✍ QUICK QUIZ 7.8
Self-Evident Truth

In the following, identify whether one of the persons involved has committed a fallacy of self-evident truth and explain how it is done. If there is no fallacy, explain why the argument might be confused with a fallacy of self-evident truth.

1. Evolution is clearly true. No one doubts that.

   This is a fallacy of self-evident truth. No reasons are presented why evolution is clearly true. It is simply taken as obvious.

2. The evolutionists either ignore or can't answer the basic questions of origin. It is obvious that their theory is incomplete and therefore false.

   This is not a fallacy of self-evident truth. A reason has been given for the conclusion, so it is an argument. "It is obvious" is being used as an inference indicator.

   > **The evolutionists either ignore or can't answer the basic questions of origin.**
   > **[If evolutionists ignore the question or can't answer it, their theory is incomplete.]**
   > **[If a theory is incomplete, it is false.]**
   > _____
   > **∴ Evolution is false.**

3. I am absolutely convinced that God made the world in six days. I don't understand why others don't accept this.

   Fallacy of self-evident truth. No reasons are given for the claim. The person is presenting his conviction about the claim in place of reasons and evidence.

✍ QUICK QUIZ 7.9
Appeal to Ignorance

Which of the following arguments are appeals to ignorance? For those that are, explain how the criteria apply in the example. For those that are not, portray the argument and explain why you do not consider it to be a fallacy of appeal to ignorance.

1. You haven't shown me that abortion is wrong, so it must be OK.

    This is a fallacy of appeal to ignorance. No evidence has been shown either way. The person draws a conclusion in the absence of the evidence.

2. You need to show me that passive euthanasia is wrong. So far, I haven't seen an argument against it.

    This is not a fallacy. It is a call for the argument partner to supply an argument. The challenger is not asserting a conclusion because of the lack of proof but simply demanding a reason.

    I haven't seen an argument against passive euthanasia.
    _____
    ∴ You need to show me that it is wrong.

3. Nessie [the Loch Ness monster] must exist. No one has been able to show that she doesn't.

    This is a fallacy of appeal to ignorance. The arguer concludes that Nessie exists because no one has been able to show that she doesn't. No evidence has been offered either way.

✍ QUICK QUIZ 7.10
Loaded Presupposition

Which of the following arguments are fallacies of loaded presupposition? For those that are, explain how the criteria for this fallacy apply in the example. For those that are not, portray the argument and explain why you do not consider it to be a fallacy of loaded presupposition.

1. We cannot accept the fiscally unsound and morally bankrupt policies of the opposition. They would only lead us down a path we should not take.

    This commits several fallacies, including loaded presupposition. It presumes that the policies are fiscally unsound and morally bankrupt and implies that we should not accept them. However, no argument has been given as to why they are unsound or bankrupt. Without further context in which these claims have been proven, this is a fallacy of loaded presupposition.

2. The objectionable notion that intelligence is genetically determined is one of the central tenets of sociobiology.

   This commits the fallacy of loaded presupposition by presupposing that the claim that intelligence is genetically determined is objectionable. However, if that claim is defended in the passage, it would not be a fallacy of loaded presupposition but a summary of what has been shown.

3. When did you stop beating your wife?

   This is a fallacy of loaded presupposition. It presupposes that the person has assaulted his wife in the past. If uttered after this has been established, it would not be an instance of loaded presupposition.

✑ QUICK QUIZ 7.11
Begging the Question

Which of the following arguments are fallacies of begging the question? For those that are, explain how the criteria apply in the example. For those that are not, portray the argument and explain why you do not consider it to be a fallacy of begging the question.

Euthanasia is wrong because it involves helping someone to end his or her life.

   This is a begging the question fallacy. It offers as a reason the definition of the key term, *euthanasia.* In effect, the arguer is saying that euthanasia is wrong because it is euthanasia. The arguer could salvage this argument by presenting reasons why helping someone to end his or her life is wrong. Without that, it begs the question.

2. Women are less rational than men because they can't reason as well as men.

   This begs the question. "Can't reason as well" means the same as being "less rational," which is what the arguer is attempting to show.

3. Democracy is a form of government in which the leaders are elected and represent the will of the people. Using that definition, the government of Vulcan is not a democracy. The so-called elections are shams, and the leaders represent only the will of the power brokers.

   This is not a begging the question fallacy. A definition is given. It is then shown that the government in Vulcan does not live up to the definition.

   > **Democracy is a form of government in which the leaders are elected and represent the will of the people**
   > **The elections are shams.**
   > **The leaders represent only the will of the powerbrokers.**
   > _____
   > ∴ **The government of Vulcan does not fulfill the definitions for a democracy.**

✍ QUICK QUIZ 7.12
Common Practice/Popularity

Which of the following arguments are appeals to common practice or popularity? For those that are, explain how the criteria for this fallacy apply in the example. For those that are not, portray the argument and explain why you do not consider it to be a fallacy of appeal to common practice or popularity.

1. You're an essentialist? No one believes in essentialism anymore.

   This is a fallacy of popularity (common sentiment): Since no one believes in it, it must be wrong. No independent reasons are offered.

2. The Canadian legal system is based on the core values of tolerance, equality, respect, and social justice. This proposal violates all of these and should be rejected.

   This is not a fallacy of common belief. Although there does appear to be an appeal to the common values that are the foundation of the Canadian legal system, I believe that the appeal is legitimate in this case. The arguer is showing that a given proposal violates fundamental values that are at the core of the legal system. These have been and could be defended, if required.

   The Canadian legal system is based on the core values of tolerance, equality, respect, and social justice.
   This proposal violates all of these.
   _____
   ∴ **This proposal should be rejected.**

3. I don't see how you can argue that pornography is beneficial. Society disagrees and rightfully bans it.

   This is a fallacy of appeal to common belief and common practice. If the person has given arguments, then those need to be addressed.

✍ QUICK QUIZ 7.13
Faulty Appeal to Authority

Which of the following arguments are faulty appeals to authority? For those that are, explain how the criteria apply in the example. For those that are not, portray the argument and explain why you do not consider it to be a fallacy of faulty appeal to authority.

1. Don Cherry, a noted hockey announcer, appears as a spokesman for a leading auto insurance company, claiming that it has the lowest rates in the industry.

   This is a faulty appeal to authority. Auto insurance rates can be a field of knowledge about which someone could be an authority. Don Cherry may be

an expert on hockey, but he is not an expert on auto insurance rates. His support is based on his own personal experience.

2. My art history professor says that the *Mona Lisa* is the most beautiful painting in the Western world. I guess it must be.

   This is a faulty appeal to authority. Although there can be experts in art history, there is likely to be a fair bit of contention and lack of consensus within the field about what makes something "the most beautiful painting."

3. A: There are only about 30,000 genes in the human genome.

   B: How do you know that?

   A: I read a study that claimed that.

   I read a study that claimed that.

   ─────────────────────────────

   ∴   **There are only about 30,000 genes in the human genome.**

   This may or may not be a fallacy of faulty appeal to authority. It appears to be one, because the authorities have not been identified. Although person A may not immediately remember the study, the authors, or the source, if he or she can provide this information, this argument would not be a faulty appeal on these grounds (however, we would still have to determine whether it met the expert in field and consensus criteria). Unless the studies and experts are or can be identified, claims such as "studies have shown" or "experts agree" risk being a form of faulty appeal to authority. In everyday discussion, we sometimes take on trust our dialogue partner's claim that he or she has read a study that has proven something, without demanding that the study and authors be identified. However, in principle, he or she should be able to provide that information if challenged. Not being able to does constitute a faulty appeal to authority.

✍ QUICK QUIZ 7.14
Hasty Generalization

Which of the following arguments are hasty generalizations? For those that are, explain how the criteria for this fallacy apply in the example. For those that are not, portray the argument and explain why you do not consider it to be a fallacy of hasty generalization.

1. Book prices sure have gone up. I bought my texts for the fall, and they were double the cost of last year's.

   This is a fallacy of hasty generalization. It is based on a sample of one student. Many things other than prices having gone up might explain the difference in prices. The student may be in more advanced courses for which the textbook prices are higher. Such a claim may not be intended as an

argument. It may be an expression of disbelief about the high cost of textbooks.

2. I have asked six of the ten support staff what they would like for lunch. They all agreed on the salmon. Since everyone wants it, we should order salmon for everyone.

   Although this would normally be a significantly large enough sample, if a critical factor has been overlooked, the generalization may be hasty. For example, if one or more of the support staff not surveyed is a vegetarian or does not like fish, then the generalization that everyone will like it is false. The problem here is in ensuring that the sample is representative, not that it is sufficiently large enough. Therefore, we need to know what would be a relevant consideration for drawing the conclusion. Being a vegetarian or not liking salmon would be relevant in this circumstance.

3. People who support euthanasia also support abortion. Liz supports euthanasia, so she must support abortion.

   This is not a fallacy of hasty generalization. There is a generalization in the premises, and it is false, but it is not a fallacy of hasty generalization because the generalization is simply asserted and not supported. See the difference between general claims and generalizations in Module 5, Section 5.4.

   People who support euthanasia also support abortion.
   Liz supports euthanasia.

   ∴ **She must support abortion.**

✍ QUICK QUIZ 7.15
False Cause

Which of the following arguments are fallacies of false cause? For those that are, explain how the criteria for this fallacy apply in the example. For those that are not, portray the argument and explain why you do not consider it to be a fallacy of false cause.

1. A recent government study has found that smoking and education are inversely related. The lower a person's education, the more likely he or she is to smoke and the more difficulty that person has in quitting smoking. Obviously, being less educated causes people to smoke. The solution to getting people to stop smoking, therefore, is to develop a more educated populace.

   This argument commits the false cause fallacy. It draws a causal conclusion (lower education causes people to smoke more) from a correlation (that smoking and lower education are correlated). There could easily be a third factor—both smoking and lower education are related to family or socioeconomic background, or smoking affects educational achievement. Temporal priority is not clearly established in the correlation.

2. When the city repaved the street in front of my house on Monday, severe vibrations shook my house. Tuesday it rained, and the foundation of my house started leaking. The vibrations obviously cracked the foundation in my basement. The city should be held responsible for damaging the foundation of my house.

> **This seems to be a reasonable inference, not a false cause fallacy. There is temporal priority, spatial connection, and a possible mechanism; however, the leak and the road repairs could be coincidental—that is, other factors could have coincidentally produced the effect. We cannot rule out all coincidences.**
>
> **When the city repaved the street in front of my house on Monday, severe vibrations shook my house.**
> **Tuesday it rained and the foundation of my house started to leak.**
> _____
> **∴ The vibrations cracked the foundation of my basement.**
>
> **[If the vibrations cracked my foundation, the city should be held responsible.**
> _____
> **∴ The city should be held responsible for damaging my foundation.**

3. Several South Korean scientists have announced that they have found a prevention for stomach cancer. They fed kim chi (pickled cabbage) to a test group of subjects and compared their rates of stomach cancer with those of people who did not eat the kim chi. Those fed the kim chi had a twenty-five percent lower rate of stomach cancer than those who did not eat the cabbage. The scientists have concluded that kim chi has an inhibiting effect on the development of stomach cancer.

> **This is a false cause fallacy. There appears to be covariance. However, there is no mechanism.**

✍ QUICK QUIZ 7.16
Slippery Slope

Which of the following arguments are slippery slope fallacies? For those that are, explain how the criteria for this fallacy apply in the example. For those that are not, portray the argument and explain why you do not consider it to be a fallacy of slippery slope.

1. We can't allow abortion. Once we start killing innocent babies in the womb, there is nothing to stop us from killing the elderly, the disabled, or anyone deemed undesirable. We become no better than the Nazis with their gas chambers!

> **This is a slippery slope fallacy. It slides from allowing abortion to performing involuntary euthanasia. It also uses some loaded language.**

2. I can't take that first drink. I'm an alcoholic. I know that if I have one drink, I will be in the gutter tomorrow. I can't stop myself.

> **This is not a slippery slope fallacy. The individual is giving reasons why he or she, as an alcoholic, can't take a drink. Although this looks superficially like a slippery slope—there is a move from one event through a sequence of events to an undesirable consequence—the causal mechanism is obvious. Alcoholics do have trouble stopping after one drink.**
>
> > **I'm an alcoholic.**
> > **If I take one drink, I will be in the gutter tomorrow.**
> > **[I don't want to be in the gutter tomorrow.]**
> > _____
> > **∴ I can't take that first drink.**

3. Argument given in response to a proposal to fund a separate school for black students who are at special risk of dropping out of the school system: We can't fund schools exclusively for black students. If we do, then every ethnic and religious group will want its own school, and that will be the end of public education. And we don't want that to happen.

> **This is a slippery slope. Allowing one special separate school for one purpose does not necessarily lead to the consequences outlined—that every ethnic and religious group will want its own school. The school is being proposed for a particular group of students identified as being at risk in the school system. The other groups are not necessarily at risk in the same way.**

✍ QUICK QUIZ 7.17
False Dichotomy

Which of the following arguments are fallacies of false dichotomy? For those that are, explain how the criteria for this fallacy apply in the example. For those that are not, portray the argument and explain why you do not consider it to be a fallacy of false dichotomy.

1. *George Bush in a speech to the American people:* "If you are not supporting us, then you are supporting the terrorists. Democratic opposition in Congress is only helping the terrorists in Iraq."

> **This is a false dichotomy: One either supports President Bush's policies or supports the terrorists. Bush is allowing no other possible position, although these are not the only two.**

2. Either we save for a down payment on a house by cutting out all luxuries or we allow ourselves the luxuries of lattes, new clothes, and vacations and forgo saving for a house. I, personally, can't forgo the little luxuries of life. So it looks like we won't get the down payment for a house.

This is a false dichotomy. It poses two extremes—save by cutting out everything or not save at all. However, there are a range of intermediate positions.

3. Either we raise taxes and break an election promise or we don't raise taxes and keep an election promise. However, we need the additional revenue from taxes. So it looks like we'll have to break an election promise.

> **This is a case of an exclusive disjunction: Either raise taxes or don't raise taxes. There is no third alternative here. It is not a false dichotomy.**
>
> > **Either we raise taxes and break an election promise or we don't raise taxes and keep an election promise.**
> > **We will raise taxes.**
> > _____
> > **∴ We will break an election promise.**

✍ QUICK QUIZ 7.18
Equivocation

Which of the following arguments are fallacies of equivocation? For those that are, explain how the criteria for this fallacy apply in the example. For those that are not, portray the argument and explain why you do not consider it to be a fallacy of equivocation.

1. Men and women are clearly not equal. They differ in various attributes. Men are stronger; women, more verbal. So how can one say that we ought to treat them equally?

> **This is a fallacy of equivocation. The equivocation is on the term *equal*. In one use, it means "substantively equal," or equal in terms of the properties they possess—strength and verbal expressiveness. In the other use, the speaker is talking about moral equality. These are not the same.**

2. Active euthanasia is morally justified. When a doctor administers a lethal injection, he or she is not killing the patient. Rather, the disease is killing the patient. If a person is responsible only when he or she actually kills someone, then the doctor is not responsible for the death. The disease is.

> **This equivocates on *kill*. In one sense, the disease "kills" by being the factor that is causing the person's body to fail and die. Without further intervention (and possibly even with), it will end the life of the patient. In a second sense, one would claim that administering a lethal injection kills the patient (brings about the end of someone's life). In this sense, the doctor appears to be killing the patient. The author of this passage seems to want to reserve *kill* only for the disease as a cause, not for the doctor's intervention. The author seems to be saying that since the disease will bring about the end of the person's life that any other intervention is "not killing," although this runs against other uses of the term. In this sense, there are two notions of *kill* being used in this passage.**

3. We shouldn't teach critical reasoning because critical reasoning teaches people to argue and arguments create conflict and dissent between people.

    There is equivocation on *argue* and *arguments*. *Argue* is used to mean "giving reasons," and *argument* is used to mean "a quarrel."

✍ QUICK QUIZ 7.19
Faulty Analogy

Which of the following arguments are faulty analogies? For those that are, explain how the criteria for this fallacy apply in the example. For those that are not, portray the argument and explain why you do not consider it to be a fallacy of faulty analogy.

1. The state is like a ship. Just as a ship needs a strong captain—one who insists on unyielding obedience—to command it, the state requires a strong leader whom all the citizens must obey.

    This compares the state to a ship:
    *   **Both need leaders. (implicit)**
    *   **The ship needs a strong leader who insists on unyielding obedience**

    Therefore, the state needs a strong leader who insists on unyielding obedience.

    OR

Analogs:	**state, ship**
Properties identified:	**need leader (implicit)**
Properties inferred:	**need strong leader who insists on unyielding obedience**

    This is a faulty analogy. While a ship might need a strong captain, governments, especially democratic ones, are not like ships. Leaders are accountable to those who elect them, and leadership in democracies is shared.

2. Business is a struggle for survival in which only the most competitive should survive. For this reason, the government should not provide support to businesses. If businesses cannot survive on their own, they should not be supported by government handouts.

Analogs:	**business, struggle for survival (evolution)**
Properties identified:	**both competitive; only the most competitive should survive**
Properties inferred:	**no outside support (government for business)**

This is a faulty analogy. In nature, no creature or species survives on its own. Many are involved in a symbiotic relationship. Humans and the many microbes that inhabit them depend on one another for survival. Even if nature involved a competitive struggle of all against all, nature and business are not the same. The argument treats businesses as analogous to either individuals or species. Neither analogy is correct. Businesses are part of a larger whole, and what happens with some businesses affects the survival of individuals not involved in those businesses. For example, not maintaining agriculture within a society could result in the failure of the entire society.

3. Nature is a book open to everyone to read. If we do not understand it, it is simply because we have not read it carefully enough. And like a book, nature requires an author. Its author is God.

Analogs:	**nature, book**
Properties identified:	**both can be read; not understanding means we haven't read it properly**
Properties inferred:	**both require an author; the author of the book of nature is God**

This is a faulty analogy. There is a difference in how a book is read and how nature is "read." Books are written in a specific language. Although nature can be "read" through discovering the laws of nature, these "laws" are not written, nor are they in a specific language.

✍ QUICK QUIZ 7.20
Straw Person

Which of the following arguments are straw person fallacies? For those that are, explain how the criteria for this fallacy apply in the example. For those that are not, portray the argument and explain why you do not consider it to be a fallacy of straw person.

1. *Original source—biology text:* Although we have many transition fossils for the large families, we have not yet found such transition fossils for many specific species. And we have none for the soft-body species. Nor are we likely to find any, since these creatures do not produce fossils.

   Argument: Even evolutionists admit that evolution is impossible. If evolution were true, then we should find many fossils for transition species. Yet a noted biology text claims that we don't have fossil remains showing any transition species, nor are we ever likely to.

   This is a straw person fallacy. The critic ignores the claim that we have discovered transition fossils for the large families, focuses on the claim that we do not have them for some species, and makes the claim that we do not have transition fossils for any species, whereas the biology text says only that there are no fossils for soft-body species. This is an omission of nuance and making a claim absolute.

2. Lara: "Unless we construct a nuclear power plant in this area within the next ten years, we will not be able to meet the significantly growing demands for electrical power in the province."

Arkadi: "What you are saying is that you don't care what happens to the plant life and wildlife in the area or even to human lives that might be dislocated by the building of this plant."

This is a straw person fallacy. Lara has made a conditional claim that we may not be able to meet the growing demands of electrical power without a new nuclear plant. Arkadi has attributed to her a quite different claim—that she doesn't care about the effects of building such a plant. Lara has said nothing like this. If the argument continues, it could turn into a red herring.

3. The core claim in evolution is that species evolve over time. Yet we have no direct evidence of this. The best we have is fossil evidence or DNA evidence. But neither establishes that evolution has occurred. Both are compatible with the hypothesis that species are fixed and do not change.

This is not a straw person fallacy. It states a core claim of evolution, identifies the evidence, and claims (rightly or wrongly) that the evidence does not establish that evolution has occurred. Disagreeing about the facts and inferences is not a straw person.

> **The core claim of evolutionary theory is that species evolve over time.**
> **We have no direct evidence of this.**
> **The best evidence we have for evolution is fossil evidence and DNA evidence.**
> **Neither establishes that evolution has occurred.**
> **Both are compatible with the hypothesis that species are fixed and do not change.**

_____

∴ **[The core claim of evolution is not established by the evidence.]**

✍ QUICK QUIZ 7.21
Red Herring

Which of the following arguments are red herring fallacies? For those that are, explain how the criteria for this fallacy apply in the example. For those that are not, portray the argument and explain why you do not consider it to be a red herring fallacy.

1. Eugenics is a failed science. After all, it was used by the Nazis as a justification to eliminate over six million people—Jews, gypsies, homosexuals, and the mentally challenged.

The reasons given are not relevant to proving that eugenics is a failed science. Rather, the speaker identifies how the Nazis used eugenics, which

sidetracks us from what is relevant and needs to be shown—how and why eugenics became a failed science.

2. In response to the charge that she has mismanaged the union, been ineffectual as chair, played partisan politics, and been ineffectual in negotiations, Chandra Johnson argues that the charges should be dismissed because they are merely an attempt to discredit her because she is a woman and the members obviously don't believe a woman should run a union.

   A series of charges has been levelled against the union head. Rather than responding to those charges, the speaker accuses the critics of discriminating against a woman, which is irrelevant to the substance of the charges and constitutes a red herring.

3. My opponent has argued that we should implement a national child care program that would ensure that all parents have access to universal child care for all children up to the age of six. While there are good reasons for a program like this, and my opponent has advanced them, there is one critical and overwhelming objection—the cost. We, as a society, simply do not have the resources to fund this project and, therefore, we can't introduce such a program.

   This is not a red herring. A relevant consideration for any proposed policy is its feasibility, and that includes cost. This is a challenge based on implications.

   > **We do not have the resources to fund this project, even though it is a good project.**
   > _____
   > **∴ We can't introduce such a program.**

✍ QUICK QUIZ 7.22
Genetic Fallacy

Which of the following arguments are genetic fallacies? For those that are, explain how the criteria for this fallacy apply in the example. For those that are not, portray the argument and explain why you do not consider it to be a genetic fallacy.

1. Sergei: "As a rule of thumb, you can convert miles to kilometres by multiplying miles by 1.6."

   Pravar: "Don't you know that you shouldn't say 'rule of thumb'? It's a sexist term. It refers to a nineteenth-century English law that says that a man can beat his wife as long as he uses a stick no bigger than the diameter of his thumb. By using it, you are condoning wife abuse."

   This is a genetic fallacy. Pravar appeals to the origins of the term *rule of thumb* to challenge Sergei's use of it. However, words change meaning over time. We have to examine the context to understand the intended meaning of the term. (This could also be treated as a red herring since the introducing of the origins of the term diverts attention away from the original discussion about converting miles to kilometres.

2. Liberalism as a political philosophy and guide for social policy is a nineteenth-century idea. How could it possibly provide guidance in the twenty-first century?

> **Liberalism is being dismissed as a guide to twenty-first-century politics because it originated in the nineteenth century. This is a genetic fallacy. Liberalism's origins in the past are not sufficient grounds for rejecting it today.**

3. We have to rethink liberalism. It was founded in the nineteenth century as a guideline for social reform. However, many of the assumptions on which it was based no longer stand.

> **This is not a genetic fallacy. It gives reasons for rethinking liberalism— namely, that the assumptions on which it was founded no longer stand.**

> > **Liberalism was founded in the nineteenth century as a guideline for social reform.**
> > **Many of the assumptions on which liberalism was based no longer stand.**
> > **[If the assumptions on which a program for social reform was based are no longer true, then we need to rethink that program.**
> > _____
> > ∴ **We need to rethink liberalism.**

✍ QUICK QUIZ 7.23
Neutralizing a Fallacy

In each of the following, use the six-step method for neutralizing a fallacy.

1. A number of peace activists are challenging the war on terrorism. People who challenge the government in a time of war are not true Canadians. We shouldn't listen to them.

> **Background claim: A number of peace activists are challenging the war on terrorism.**

> > **2. People who challenge the government in a time of war are not true Canadians.**
> > _____
> > ∴ **1. We shouldn't listen to them.**

> **Name of fallacy: Poisoning the well.**

> **Criteria for the fallacy: An argument commits the poisoning the well fallacy when it discredits the person giving the argument before that person can present his or her argument.**

> **How the argument fits the criteria: Those who oppose the war are being dismissed as "not true Canadians," as not having the interests of Canada at**

heart. In a wartime situation, this could amount to calling the objectors "traitors."

Challenge: The peace activists' arguments against the war on terrorism have been dismissed before they have been heard. According to the argument and respect principles, we have an obligation in argumentation to hear and assess the arguments.

2. The government is hiding the remains of several UFO crashes, including alien bodies, in "Area 51," a top-secret area of an air-force base in the Southwest. While the government has denied this claim, it has never proven that it is false. So I am inclined to believe that it is true.

> 2. While the government has denied this claim, it has never proven that it is false.
> _____
> ∴ 1. The government is hiding the remains of several UFO crashes, including alien bodies, in "Area 51," a top-secret area of an air-force base in the Southwest.

Name of fallacy: Appeal to ignorance.

Criteria for the fallacy: An appeal to ignorance occurs when one arguer's not proving a claim is used as the sole reason for the truth of the opposite.

How the argument fits the criteria: The arguer is claiming that his opponent's not proving that the claim about UFO remains is false must mean that it is true.

Challenge: No evidence is given for either claim. Without evidence, we cannot conclude that either claim is true. This violates the argument and resolution principles.

3. Look, if you allow euthanasia of people even in irreversible comas, the next thing you know, they will be euthanizing anyone in a coma. Then it will be people with terminal illnesses, and, before long, they will be wanting to kill anyone who has become an inconvenience.

> 2. If you allow euthanasia of people even in irreversible comas, the next thing you know they will be euthanizing anyone in a coma.
> 3. If we euthanize anyone in a coma, then they will start euthanizing people with terminal illnesses.
> 4. If we euthanize people with terminal illnesses, then before long, they will be wanting to kill anyone who has become an inconvenience.
> 5. [We should not euthanize people simply because they are inconvenient.]
> _____
> ∴ 1. [We should not allow euthanasia, even in cases of people in irreversible comas.]

Name of fallacy: Slippery slope.

Criteria for the fallacy: A slippery slope fallacy is committed when one event is alleged as leading to a distant consequence, which is undesirable. The sequence assumes a set of causal steps, none of which are established and some of which are questionable.

How the argument fits the criteria: Allowing euthanasia for individuals in terminal comas is alleged to lead to killing anyone who has become inconvenient, which is both undesirable and a distant outcome from the original proposal. The argument alleges a quick slide from using euthanasia in one specific kind of case to a much broader use in society.

Challenge: There are at least three steps in this argument—(1) patients in irreversible comas; (2) anyone in a coma; (3) anyone who is inconvenient. The reasons that may be relevant for making the case for patients in irreversible comas are not likely to apply to all individuals in comas, much less to those who are "inconvenient." There is a quick slide from one to the others without the arguer showing why one will inevitably lead to the others.

✍ QUICK QUIZ 7.24
Putting It All Together

For each of the three questions in 7.23, write a prose paragraph that puts the critique together.

1. The arguer is claiming that we shouldn't listen to peace activists opposing the war because anyone who challenges the government is not a true Canadian. This commits a poisoning the well fallacy in which a person tries to discredit one side of an argument before that side can be presented. In this case, the peace activists are discredited and their arguments ignored by their being labelled as "not true Canadians" simply for raising objections to the war on terrorism. This violates the basic principles of argumentation that require us to give and respond to arguments.

2. The arguer is claiming that the government is hiding the remains of several UFO crashes in a top-secret area of a U.S. air-force base. His or her reason is that the opponent (and the government) has not proven that this claim is false. Rather than offering independent evidence for the claim, the arguer relies on an appeal to ignorance in which the one side's inability or failure to provide reasons for its claim (or to show its opponent's is false) is taken as evidence for the opposite. In this case, neither side has been able to provide reasons or evidence for its claims; therefore, neither side can declare that its claim is true.

3. The arguer claims that if we allow euthanasia for individuals in irreversible comas, this will lead to killing anyone who is "inconvenient." Since that is unacceptable, we should not allow euthanasia for individuals in irreversible comas. This slippery slope fallacy moves from the first step—allowing euthanasia in a restricted set of cases—to widespread killing of individuals in cases quite different without establishing how this will occur. The causal connection between the first step and the final step in the sequence is

neither obvious nor inevitable. To make his or her case, the arguer would have to show that killing those who are "inconvenient" would be an inevitable consequence of allowing euthanasia in the more limited cases.

✍ QUICK QUIZ 7.25
Hasty Generalization, False Cause, Slippery Slope

Identify and explain which fallacy is committed in each of the following. Explain how each might be confused with one of its look-alikes.

1. *Said in a campaign for mayor:* My opponent is opposed to increasing the number of police officers, yet there have been an increased number of crimes, especially crimes involving guns, this year in the city. If we don't put more police on the street, then the streets will degenerate into disorder and chaos with the thugs running everything. We don't want the criminals and thugs running this city. We have to have more police on the street.

   This argument commits the fallacy of slippery slope: If we don't have more police, the assumed increase in gun crime will result in disorder and chaos with the thugs running the city. Although this could simply be political hyperbole, as stated, it is a slippery slope.

2. We have proof that marijuana causes violent behaviour. In a murder trial in Alabama, the prosecution established that the defendant, previously a model young man, had been smoking marijuana. He became inflamed—nay, possessed—by overwhelming lust and slew a rival for his girlfriend's affections. This is not the only case like this. In New York, several youths were smoking marijuana. They went on a rampage, smashing everything in their apartment. In San Francisco, an arsonist torched several buildings—this, after he became a regular marijuana user.

   The speaker is trying to establish that smoking marijuana causes violent behaviour. He gives three cases from three separate cities of individuals who smoked marijuana and became violent. This is both a false cause and hasty generalization. What the speaker has given is a simple correlation (not even a covariance), which is not enough to justify a causal connection. The speaker is also making a generalization from these three cases to all smoking of marijuana.

3. *A newspaper report of a scientific research study:* Psychologists have discovered that most male scientists make their major discoveries in their late twenties and thirties, which is also the period when their sexual interest is at its peak. Therefore, the psychologists concluded, male scientists strive to achieve to attract the attention of women. Scientific inquiry is driven by sexual desire.

   This argument commits the false cause fallacy. The psychologists are trying to make a causal connection between scientists trying to attract women and their making major discoveries. They are claiming that sexual interest causes scientists to make major discoveries. What they have, at best, is a correlation. They don't have covariance. A third factor could independently cause both:

age. One might argue that younger men put more effort into their work and, at the same time, have a higher sexual interest.

✍ QUICK QUIZ 7.26
Ad Hominem, Poisoning the Well, Genetic Fallacy

Identify and explain which fallacy is committed in each of the following. Explain how each might be confused with one of its look-alikes.

1. Aristotle's comments on women can safely be ignored, for they simply reflect the patriarchal society of the fifth century B.C.E.

   This is a genetic fallacy. Aristotle is associated with a patriarchal society. His ideas arose in the context of that society, so what he says about women must be patriarchal. In the context, this is also a poisoning the well, since it invites the listener to dismiss Aristotle's views without considering them.

2. We should reject the arguments in *The Bell Curve* that blacks have lower IQs than whites and are disproportionately involved in social problems, because the authors are known racists.

   This is a poisoning the well. The authors of *The Bell Curve* have presented arguments, which are being dismissed without being considered because the authors are allegedly racists.

3. Pravar: "Martina Lieberman in the biology department claims that gay men are born that way. She claims that the evidence shows that brains of gay men are structurally different from the brains of straight men. So we do have proof that there is a biological basis to being gay."

   Sergei: "Of course she's going to say that. She's a lesbian, isn't she?"

   This is an ad hominem. Martina Lieberman's ideas are being dismissed because she is a lesbian and she is arguing about the biological basis of homosexuality. The suggestion is that her sexual orientation somehow makes her biased, yet no bias has been shown.

✍ QUICK QUIZ 7.27
Fallacy ... or Not?

In each of the following, identify whether or not a fallacy is committed. If a fallacy is committed, explain and neutralize the fallacy. If it is not, explain how the argument might be confused with a fallacy.

1. Yan is insensitive to the suffering of animals because he eats meat. And all meat eaters are insensitive to the suffering of animals.

This is not a fallacy. Because it contains a false general claim—all meats eaters are insensitive to the suffering of animals—it may be mistaken for a hasty generalization.

2. Unless we find a way to stop the indiscriminate use of guns by gang members, violence on the streets is likely to increase. And the increase in violence will likely mean that more bystanders will be injured and killed, and we don't want that. We must stop the violence.

   This looks like a slippery slope. If we don't stop the gun violence, more innocent people will be harmed and killed. However, it is not a slippery slope because the arguer limits the claim (*more*) and suggests that the outcome is not inevitable but simply likely.

3. Professor Harrison is a convicted sex offender. He has been convicted twice of sexual assault. I do not believe he should be allowed to teach in a school where he will come into contact with teens and others who could be at risk of being assaulted.

   Although it could be mistaken for one, this is not an *ad hominem*. Professor Harrison's behaviour is directly relevant to whether or not he should teach in a school; this is not an attack on him.

4. Carl Sagan, an astronomer who researched global warming on Venus and has investigated the effects of global warming on the earth, has claimed that unless we limit automobiles and industry, human life as we know it will be seriously threatened by 2030. Although other experts disagree, we need to consider Sagan's arguments.

   Although this could be mistaken for a faulty appeal to authority, it is not. There is a field of knowledge about global warming. However, there is not consensus on that knowledge. The speaker is not suggesting that we accept Sagan's opinion as expert opinion but that we consider his arguments. A faulty appeal to authority would simply recommend accepting his arguments as expert opinion.

5. George Bush lied to the American people and the world when he said that he had proof that Saddam Hussein had weapons of mass destruction. He lied to the American people and the world when he claimed that he had proof that Saddam Hussein was part of the axis of evil that was fuelling terrorism. He lied to the American people about his war record in the Vietnam War. He lied about his involvement in various financial scandals. [Take all of this as true for the sake of argument.] Now he is asking us to trust him when he says that U.S. intentions in Iraq are honourable. I say all that we have to do is look at the record.

   This is not an *ad hominem*, although it looks like one. George Bush is asking that people trust his intentions. That requires that we assess his integrity. The speaker is challenging that integrity and giving reasons to doubt Bush's intentions.

EXERCISES

The following are the instructions for the completion of Exercises 7.1, 7.2, 7.3, 7.4, and 7.6:

Follow your instructor's directions to either

(a) identify whether or not a fallacy is committed in the passage. If a fallacy is committed, provide a full analysis and neutralization of it using the model for neutralizing a fallacy; if a fallacy is not committed, explain why the passage might be confused with a fallacy.

OR

(b) identify whether or not a fallacy is committed in the passage. If a fallacy is committed, provide a short-form analysis of it (putting it together); if a fallacy is not committed, explain why the passage might be confused with a fallacy.

The fallacies are defined in Module 7, Section 7.3 of the textbook.

✍ EXERCISE 7.1
Fallacies 1 to 4

1. Are you sure that you want to openly oppose the proposal to amalgamate with the Canadian Chiropractic College? After all, both the president and the dean are strongly in favour, and you haven't gotten tenure yet.

2. I've come before you to ask that you rehire Professor Yang. I realize that Mr. Yang does not have a Ph.D., and I am aware that he has yet to publish his first article. But Mr. Yang is over forty now, and he has a wife and two high-school-aged children to support. It will be very difficult for him to find another teaching job at his age. I'm sure you would agree.

3. It's no wonder you think that promiscuity is all right. You've never had a good relationship with a man. So it's not strange that you'd resort to recreational sex.

4. Anyone who challenges M. Bouchard, a leading separatist, is not a true Quebecker.

5. *Retort to #4:* And anyone who doesn't is obviously not a true Canadian.

6. *A lawyer makes the following plea on behalf of his client in the sentencing phase of a trial:* Rather than putting the witnesses through a gruelling trial, my client has admitted his guilt. He is truly remorseful for embezzling the money from his clients and is seeking to repay them, as you have heard. As you have also heard, his embezzling was the result of a drug and alcohol addiction for which he is being treated. We ask that Your Honour take these factors into consideration and impose a lenient sentence so that my client can continue his rehabilitation and continue to repay his victims.

7. *Said by striker to coworker crossing a picket line:* You shouldn't cross picket lines, you know. You never know what could happen to your car.

8. Background: Arthur Schopenhauer, a nineteenth-century philosopher wrote a famous essay denouncing women.

   Lecturer: We needn't take Schopenhauer's arguments and misogyny seriously: Any psychiatrist would explain that Schopenhauer's attitude, as expressed in this essay, is a result of the strained relationship between him and his mother.

9. *Said to a white middle-aged male teaching a course on race and gender:* You can't teach about women, race, and discrimination. You are a white, middle-aged, privileged male. What can you know?

10. The absurd arguments of my opponent don't deserve the dignity of a reply.

11. I don't think we should take David Suzuki's arguments about global warming that seriously. After all, the David Suzuki Foundation, which he and his wife developed, combats global warming; he is just trying to get more money for his foundation.

12. Every year, 35,000 to 45,000 people die of sudden cardiac arrest. Give now to the Canadian Heart and Stroke Foundation.

EXERCISE 7.2
Fallacies 5 to 11

13. It's obvious who the next mayor of the city should be: David Peters. He's the best candidate. Look at all he's done for the city.

14. We should impeach the solicitor general. There have been many allegations of unethical conduct on her part. However, she has done nothing to demonstrate her innocence.

15. Capital punishment for murderers and rapists is quite justified; there are a number of good reasons for putting to death people who commit such crimes.

16. Student: "I think I deserve a better grade than this on the second question."

    Professor: "Could be. Why do you think so?"

    Student: "You think my answer's wrong?"

    Professor: "Well, your answer *is* wrong."

    Student: "Maybe you think so, but I don't. You can't mark it wrong just because my answer doesn't fit your opinion."

17. I will not commit this act because it is unjust. I know it is unjust because my conscience tells me so, and my conscience tells me so because the act is unjust.

18. *Professor to student:* "How often have you plagiarized before this and not gotten caught?"

19. It is obvious that the Liberals are corrupt. How could anyone doubt it?

20. Blacks must be happy with their situation these days. There haven't been any protest marches or loud voices of dissent for some time now.

21. Asked to explain why a payroll cheque bounced, the owner of a professional basketball team replied, "Obviously, we didn't have enough money in the bank."

22. Student to professor (about a paper the student got a low mark on): "About this paper—why don't you like me?"

23. *Said by someone proposing that a new tax levy be implemented:* "We think our proposal is a good one and should be implemented. You need to give us compelling reasons why it isn't.

24. You have to show me that pornography is not harmful. Otherwise, I contend that we have a clear obligation to ban it.

🖎 EXERCISE 7.3
Fallacies 12 to 19

25. Students have to be taught respect for authority. Everyone agrees that the time has come to reintroduce the lash into the public school system. *Appeal to authority.*

26. Wayne Gretzky, the all-star hockey player, uses Advil for his rheumatism. If he recommends it, it must be good. *Faulty Appeal to Authority*

27. From a recent survey of a large number of representatively selected people in Toronto, it was discovered that less than two percent of Canadians engage in hunting for sport. Therefore, most Canadians are not hunters.

28. *Parent to teenager:* "If I let you have the car to go to the dance on Saturday, then pretty soon, you'll be wanting it to go to school, and I won't have any way of getting to work. No. You're not getting the car.

Ad Hominem

29. When it comes to race relations, you are either part of the solution or part of the problem.

30. If you took a lecture course with Professor Smith, you would know that lectures are a lousy way of learning. (Formulate as an argument.) *premises.*
Hasty Generalization.

31. Because human bodies become less active as they grow older and because they eventually die, it is reasonable to expect that political bodies will become less and less active the longer they are in existence, and they, too, will eventually die.

Premises: Human bodies become less active
political body Faulty Analogy

32. All three sex offenders arrested this month by municipal authorities have previous records for the same crime. It seems that once a sex offender, always a sex offender. *Hasty Generalization*

33. It is hard for me to see how my neighbours and I can be blamed for discrimination when it comes to deciding who is to live in our condominium building. We make discriminations all through life. If people are not allowed to discriminate, how can they make decisions between right and wrong. Indeed, how can they even act responsibly if they must be indiscriminate in their choices? *Equivocation*

34. How can you argue that gambling should be banned? Gambling is something we can't avoid—an integral part of human experience. People gamble every time they get into their cars or decide to get married. *Equivocation. Risk: Gambling: betting money Car: You could get into an accident.*

35. Nobody sticks to the one hundred kilometres per hour speed limit. Almost everybody drives one-twenty. The speed limit really ought to be raised twenty kilometres an hour. *Common Belief.*

36. Linus Pauling, a double Nobel laureate in chemistry and peace, recommends the use of megadoses of Vitamin C to prevent colds. If I want to prevent colds this winter, I should follow Pauling's advice. *Faulty Appeal to Authority*

37. The late eighteenth-century/early nineteenth-century social reformer Thomas Malthus, noting that sober and industrious farmers owned at least one cow while those who had none were usually lazy and drunken, proposed that the government give a cow to farmers who had none in order to make them sober and industrious. *False Cause*

38. This country is like a machine. No matter who operates it, it will run in essentially the same way, so it really doesn't make any difference who is prime minister or which party is in power. *Faulty Analogy*

39. Solar energy can't meet all of our energy needs now, nor will it ever be able to. We must abandon the notion that it will and continue investing in nuclear energy. *Hasty Generalization*

40. During a full moon, there are always more admissions to emergency rooms. This shows that the moon has an effect on people's behaviour. *False Cause*

41. I can show you that God exists. You acknowledge that the laws of physics exist. And laws imply a lawmaker. Since man did not make the laws of physics, someone else must have. The only possibility is a supreme lawmaker we call God. *Faulty Dichotomy*

✎ EXERCISE 7.4
Fallacies 20 to 22

42. Daniele: "What do you think of nuclear power plants, Theresa? Do you think we ought to have more of them?"

    Theresa: "Well ..." *Red-Herring*

[handwritten: Red-Herring ↓]

[handwritten: Straw Man ↘] Daniele: "Well, we should develop nuclear power, and I'll tell you why. I'm sick and tired of these antinuclear environmentalists always complaining about something or other. What a bunch of troublemakers. They find something wrong with everything."

43. *Letter to the editor:* The recent Supreme Court decision outlawing a moment of silence for prayer in public schools is scandalous. Evidently, the American Civil Liberties Union and the other radical groups will not be satisfied until every last man, women, and child in the country is an atheist. I'm fed up.

[handwritten: Genetic Fallacy] 44. A good Christian should not dance because dancing was originally used in pagan mystery cults as a way of worshipping pagan gods.

[handwritten: straw-man ↘] 45. The evolutionists claim that man evolved from apes. But this couldn't be true. Apes and men don't look at all alike.

46. Parent A: "I think it would be a good idea for us to encourage the children to watch less television and get more physical exercise."

Parent B: "You think I've let the kids become a bunch of lazy, unhealthy television addicts, don't you?" *[handwritten: Loaded Presupposition]*

[handwritten: Red-Herring] 47. The present method of evaluating public school teachers, which, at best, is an occasional perfunctory check by an administrator, is quite inadequate. If a teacher turns out to be a poor one, there is presently no effective way of getting rid of him or her. Therefore, teachers should be hired for a "term of service," after which they would reenter the job market, seeking jobs through the usual screening process.

[handwritten: Genetic Fallacy or False Dichotomy] 48. You're not going to wear a wedding ring, are you? Don't you know that wedding rings originally symbolized the ankle chains worn by women to prevent them from running away from their husbands? I wouldn't have thought you would be party to such a sexist practice.

49. You want my opinion of the new proposal for increased bus service? It's just another proposal by a mayor with few ideas to try to establish some pretext for reelection. Like all politicians, he will promise us anything to get reelected, and then he won't deliver.
[handwritten: Red-Herring]

🖎 EXERCISE 7.5
Look-Alikes and Fallacy/No Fallacy

Below are passages that may or may not be fallacies and, if fallacies, may contain look-alikes. For each, briefly identify the argument, including implicit arguments (i.e., arguments with implicit conclusions), if there is one. If there is no argument, explain why. If there is an argument and it contains a fallacy, briefly explain the fallacy and how it is committed. If the passage contains an argument and it is not a fallacy, explain why it might be mistaken for one.

50. At a trial, a defence lawyer, in his summation speech, claims the evidence he has produced proves that his client is innocent. He also claims that some of the prosecution's evidence,

although not the critical parts, is ambiguous and could be interpreted in favour of his client. He ignores evidence that places his client at the scene of the crime at the time of the crime.

Appeal to Ignorance

51. I asked my priest what the Church's stand on in vitro fertilization is. He told me that the Pope has said that it is the same as adultery and, hence, immoral. Being a Catholic, I have to treat it as immoral. *Appeal to Authority*

52. All of the Van Evrys—Vance, George, Jeb—have favoured the elite classes. [Take this as a given] Susan is a Van Evry, so she will favour the elite classes. *Hasty Gen*

[53.] It is obvious that the fiscally irresponsible proposal should be rejected. It is fiscally irresponsible because it proposes to spend money we don't have and have no means of raising. It is fiscally irresponsible because it addresses something that is not a need. And it is fiscally irresponsible because it will drain our already low reserves.

54. My ethics professor has argued that of all the ethical theorists we've studied this term, Kant [a philosopher] has the best argument on abortion. I have to defer to his expert opinion and agree that Kant does have the best argument on abortion. *Appeal to Authority*

55. Over the past five years, each summer has gotten warmer and drier in this region. This summer is likely to be warmer and drier yet. *Hasty Gen*

56. The car has been stalling, the gas mileage is down, and the acceleration is poor. The likely cause is a problem with the carburetor. *Slippery slope*

57. Professor Rumball claims that he is not racist and that his theory is scientific. However, his recent papers have been published in a journal that supports white supremacy, and his work is funded by a white-supremacist organization. Moreover, he selectively includes scientific work that can be interpreted to support his claims, ignoring major areas of research that refute his claims. That is not a sign of reputable science. His work is racist and unscientific. *Genetic Fallacy*

58. John, I don't care what your friends are doing. You have a curfew. If you break it again, you are grounded. *False Dichotomy*

Appeal to Ig

59. No one has proved that the fetus does not have rights. And since it is immoral to kill someone who has rights, it is immoral to kill a fetus.

60. I think the reason Gina and Aisha have been so rude and irritable lately is that the customers have not been tipping as well. *Not Fallacy*

61. Either we develop genetically modified foods or the human race will starve to death. I think the choice is obvious. *False Dichotomy*

62. Monogamy within marriage is the only justifiable form of sexual relations. For it is unacceptable to have sex with more than one person or to have sex outside of marriage. *Begging the question*

63. I know that Bev has a hearing loss. She has had a difficult time getting a job because employers seem unwilling to accommodate people with hearing loss. I think we should hire

her and do what is necessary to accommodate her. She more than meets the basic qualifications for the job. *Appeal to Emotion*

☙ EXERCISE 7.6
Additional Passages for Analysis

The passages in this section come from all sections of Module 7 and may include look-alikes and some arguments that are not fallacies.

64. The legalization of euthanasia is just the first step along a path that will inevitably lead to the destruction of our civilization. Once we legalize euthanasia, we will lose all respect for life. And this will bring an end to civilization as we know it. *Slippery Slope.*

65. Ms. Noor argues that a woman has a right to decide what happens inside her own body and that the state is not entitled to interfere with that right. I say that we cannot stand by and simply allow pregnant teenagers to use abortion as a morning-after form of birth control, and Ms. Noor is wrong to demand that right. *Straw Man*

66. Fred: "We need to look more carefully at the evidence for global warming. After all, the weather the past few years has been quite unusual, with major winter storms in Vancouver and warm winters in the east."

    Slippery Slope

    Sally: "Since when did you become an environmentalist? Next, you'll be opposing nuclear power and wanting everyone to stop using cars and start riding bicycles. It's not that warm."

67. *Chair of an ethics committee deciding who is to get an organ that has just become available:* "I know that candidate A is a better tissue match and has a much better chance of recovery, but candidate B has had a much longer wait, and that wait has been hard on his family. I think we should give the kidney to Candidate B." *Appeal to Emotion*

68. Background: Thirty students at the university's law school have been accused of misrepresenting their first-term grades to prospective employers by sending them inflated grade reports (they reported getting mostly or all As when their actual grades were lower).

    Faculty member: "The students are under an incredible pressure, and they should be excused for giving in to the pressure." *Hasty Generalization*

69. Background: A proposal has been made for the Canadian Memorial Chiropractic College to become part of York University and for York to offer doctorates in chiropractic.

    Defender of the proposal: "The critics of this proposal haven't shown that chiropractic is not a science, so we must accept that it does have a scientific foundation. And universities do teach science. *Appeal to Ignorance, Shifting the Burden of Proof.*

70. Background: Same as #69.

144

Critic of the proposal: "Two years ago, a woman died after receiving a chiropractic manipulation. The chiropractor killed her! If chiropractic is so unsafe, I don't see why we should give the field credibility by accepting it into the university." *Hasty Gen*

71. Background: Same as #69.

    Faculty member defending the proposal: Chiropractic is covered by the Ontario Health Insurance Program and by the university health insurance. So the opponents who claim that there is no scientific merit to chiropractic, including some of my colleagues in the faculty of science are clearly mistaken. Since it is scientific, we should accept the proposal. *Red-Herring.*

72. Background: Three incidents of racism have been reported at the university's law school in the last three weeks. One involved the defacing of a photo on the Black Caucus bulletin board. Two others involved anonymous racist notes sent to two students.

    Editorial in student newspaper: The university must move to stop the pervasive racism at the law school, or the reputation not only of the school but of the entire university will suffer. *Slippery slope*

73. Background: Same as #72.

    Editorial in student newspaper: Students cannot keep silent on this. You are either part of the problem or part of the solution. *False Dichotomy*

74. Background: Same as #72.

    Editorial in student newspaper: We have to stop this now. If we don't, people of colour and women will feel unwelcome in law schools, and we will go back to having an all-white, male legal system. *Slippery Slope*

75. I don't see why I should accept Professor Jones's arguments that much of what people call pornography is not harmful. After all, he is male and is simply reflecting his gender bias. *Ad hominem*

76. Dr. Hugh Chintala, head of the pediatric unit at General Hospital, has said that we should not use extraordinary measures to keep children with severe birth defects alive. I think we should follow his advice. *Appeal to Authority*

77. We shouldn't raise hydroelectric rates (electricity rates in Saskatchewan are government regulated). I can barely afford to pay my electric bills now, and higher rates will mean I have to cut back on other things. Also, it will make it more difficult for businesses to operate in Saskatchewan and likely cause them to flee Saskatchewan for other jurisdictions. No case can be made for raising hydroelectric rates.

78. There were three murders on the weekend in the city, all involving guns. This is becoming a much less safe city in which to live. We are in the middle of a violent crime wave. *Hasty Gen*

79. John Allen Muhammad, having been convicted of the Washington sniper shootings, should not be sentenced to death for murdering several people in those shootings. He is a loving father, and to execute him would deprive his children of their father. *Appeal to Emotion*

80. It is commonly accepted that euthanasia is wrong. That's why it should remain illegal. *Appeal to Common Belief*

81. It is obvious that polygamy is wrong. The idea of having more than one spouse is simply unacceptable to any right-thinking, moral person. *Self-evident truth.*

82. Professor Xiao, a biologist, has argued that the evidence for evolution is overwhelming, that virtually all biologists accept that evolution has occurred. But how can we accept a doctrine that holds that a dinosaur hatched an egg and a bird emerged from that egg? Such a position makes no sense. Things just don't happen that way. *Straw Man*

83. *A professor speaking*: "After being away from the university for two years on research leave, I came back this year to discover that the students have improved considerably. All three of my classes have averages considerably above those of my previous classes, and the students seem unusually dedicated. I believe that the students are much better than they were three years ago." *Hasty Generalization*

84. *Excerpt of a letter from a student to an instructor:* I should be given an extension on the essay that was due three weeks ago because I need to get a good mark in this course so I can go to teachers' college next year. My other courses are really demanding of my time and energy, and I haven't had the opportunity to start researching my paper for this course. *Appeal to Emotion*

85. Sex education in public schools has become more prevalent over the past fifteen years. At the same time, the incidence of AIDS has skyrocketed. I conclude that sex education is responsible for the increase in AIDS cases. *False cause*

86. Wilhelm: "I believe that abortion is morally acceptable. After all, a woman should have a right to her own body."

Jane: "I disagree completely. Dr. Johan Skarn says that abortion is always morally wrong, regardless of the situation. He has to be right. After all, he is a respected expert in his field."

Wilhelm: "I've never heard of Dr. Skarn. Who is he?"

Jane: "He's the guy that won the Nobel Prize in physics for his work on cold fusion." *Faulty Appeal to Authority*

87. Either we enforce mandatory drug testing in the workplace or productivity will continue to decline. And we don't want productivity to decline, so we must enforce mandatory drug testing. *False Dichotomy*

88. A former provincial premier responding to various presentations by teachers' groups in favour of more funding for public education: "Of course that's what we would expect them to say. They are only concerned about losing their jobs." *Ad-hominem*

89. Social problems are like a pimple that eventually cures itself if left alone. Government programs are like a big, clumsy thumb that, if they squeeze the pimple, actually do more harm than good. We should let the social problems resolve themselves without government interference. *Equivocation*

90. Of course the environmentalists favour restricting the use of pesticides. The environmentalists actually want small family farms to fail. We need to continue using pesticides. *Ad hominem*

91. James: "I think capital punishment is justified."

    Tusha: "Why?"

    James: "Because those the state kills have no qualms about killing others. So why should we have any qualms about killing them?" *Appeal to Ignorance*

92. I don't know why you bother going to Professor Mulic's lectures. Don't you know that she's a lesbian? *Ad hominem*

93. I didn't see any sign saying no rollerblading, so I assumed it was all right to rollerblade through the halls. *Appeal to ignorance*

94. I'm sorry, Mr. King, but we cannot approve your loan application. We have no evidence that you have met any monthly installment payments. *Not fallacy? or shifting the burden of proof*

95. Friend: "Did you get the job?" *False Dichotomy*

    You: "No. I sent in my application over two months ago and haven't heard from them, so I must not have gotten the job."

96. I really can't take your arguments very seriously, son. A sixteen-year-old just hasn't lived long enough to know what life is about. *Ad-hominem*

97. The government proposes to cut waste and mismanagement in military spending. But this will simply weaken our ability to do our peacekeeping duties by eliminating what we need to keep up our essential military commitments.

98. It is true that several researchers have testified that these hallucinogenic drugs are harmless and nonaddictive, but these same researchers have admitted to taking these drugs themselves. We should certainly disregard their views. *Poisoning the well*

99. The chiropractors have failed entirely in their attempts to establish a scientific basis for their concepts. This question can now be settled once and for all. Chiropractic has no basis in science. *Appeal to Ignorance*

100. No responsible scientist has proved that electromagnetic field radiation causes any harmful effects. Therefore, we can disregard the alarmists. *Appeal to Ignorance*

101. No breath of scandal has ever touched the honourable MP. Therefore, he must be incorruptibly honest. *Appeal to ignorance*

102. *Professor:* "Unless someone wishes to add something further to the discussion of this absurd issue, I suggest we move on to the next topic." *Not Fallacy*

103. I don't understand this demand for equal pay for women. None of the women in my office have voiced any discontent with their salaries. *Hasty Generalization*

104. I'm in favour of legalized gambling. Those opposed to it simply think that anything fun is sinful. *Straw Man*

105. I do not believe that we have an obligation to redistribute wealth to the less fortunate. What people earn is rightfully theirs. No one else has a claim on it. *Not Fallacy*

106. Student: "Professor MacKinzie, in your lecture, you argued that all men are rapists and seek to dominate women through rape. But I don't see how your argument actually supported that. Could you elaborate, please?"

Professor: "I don't see how you could fall for that patriarchal view of the world that men aren't rapists. Of course all men are rapists. Women don't rape women. Who are the abusers of women? Who make and consume pornography?" *Self-Evident Truth*

107. "The tax system in this country is unfair and ridiculous! Just ask anyone!" *Self Evident Truth*

108. C'mon, George, the river's waiting and everyone's going to be there. You want me to tell 'em you're going to worry on Saturday about a test you don't take until Tuesday? What're people going to think?

109. *Letter to the editor:* I strongly object to the proposed sale of alcoholic beverages at the County Golf Course. The idea of allowing people to drink wherever and whenever they please is positively disgraceful and can only lead to more alcoholism and all the problems it produces—drunk driving, perverted parties, and who knows what else. *Slippery Slope*

110. Using as textbooks works with profane and obscene words in them is immoral because there are no good reasons for exposing our children to vulgar, disrespectful, and ugly words. *Straw Man*

False Analogy 111. People who have to have a cup of coffee every morning before they can function have no less a problem than alcoholics who have to have their alcohol each day to sustain them.

112. I'm not getting married again. I was married once and I'm convinced all men are rotten. *Hasty Generalization*

113. I have had five ABC products—an mp3 player, a portable CD player, and three answering machines. All have broken within a month of being purchased. ABC makes inferior merchandise. *Hasty Gen*

114. *Landlord to tenant after the third service call in two weeks to repair a furnace:* "I can't help but think that you are the cause of the problem. We never had any trouble with the furnace until you moved in." *Genetic Fallacy or False Cause*

False Cause 115. Today's movies and TV shows are full of degenerate and violent images. Is it any wonder our society has become more degenerate and violent since the rise of such programming?

116. All kinds of groups are demanding equal rights in employment. Pretty soon you'll have to be a black–Aboriginal lesbian sole-support mother even to be able to apply for a job. *Ad-Hominem*

117. Eighty percent of the young people who are heavy drug users have serious difficulties relating to their parents. Thus, we can conclude that a stricter enforcement of our drug prohibitions could significantly reduce the domestic problems of these young people.

Hasty Generalization

118. Ever since the Abella Commission said that Canada should have affirmative action, we have had nothing but trouble from various minority groups demanding their "rights" and redress for past problems. We wouldn't be in this mess if it weren't for the Abella Commission.

Slippery Slope

119. After George went to university, he started drinking and using drugs. Obviously, university is a bad influence on young people.

Self-Evident Truth

120. Philosophy has never been taught at the high school level, and I see no reason to start it now. If philosophy were suitable for the high school curriculum, it would have been introduced long ago.

121. You shouldn't take philosophy. *Philo* means "lover," and *sophists* were Greeks who taught people how to persuade other people of anything. They didn't believe in the idea of truth. You don't want to become a con artist do you?

Genetic Fallacy of False Dichotomy

122. But, René, you have to go to university. Both of your parents went to university. So did both of your grandparents. No one in our family for the past two generations has not been a university graduate.

123. It is necessary to force other people to accept our religious beliefs about an afterlife, just as force must be used to prevent a delirious person from leaping over the edge of a cliff. It's for their own good.

Appeal to Force

124. Why should we sentimentalize over a few hundred thousand Native people who were ruined when our great civilization was being built? Maybe they did suffer injustices, but, you know, you can't make an omelet without breaking a few eggs.

Red Herring

125. What is taught on this campus should depend entirely on what students are interested in. After all, consuming knowledge is like consuming anything else in our society. The teacher is the seller; the student is the buyer. Buyers determine what they want to buy, so students should determine what they want to learn.

Equivocation — *Consuming: absorbing Knowledge or Using a Product*

126. More and more young people are attending high school and colleges today than ever before. Yet there is more juvenile delinquency and more alienation among the young. Clearly, today's young people are being corrupted by their education.

False Cause

127. Twenty-five years after graduation, alumni of Dalhousie have an average income five times that of people of the same age with no college education. If a person wants to be wealthy, he or she should attend Dalhousie.

Hasty Generalization

128. The institution of marriage is as old as human history and thus must be considered sacred.

Genetic Fallacy

129. The golden rule is basic to every system of ethics ever devised. Everyone accepts it in some form or other. It is, therefore, an undeniably sound moral principle.

Common Practice

130. Smoking marijuana is illegal. If there were nothing wrong with it, then it wouldn't be illegal. So there must be something wrong with it. *Begging the Question*

131. All it takes is one joint to start you on the road to being an addict. If you try it and like it, you'll want more, and the more you smoke, the more dependent you'll become. Then, you'll try the harder stuff and finally end up a complete addict. *Simple Explanation of what will happen*

132. Studies show that alcoholics tend to be severely undernourished. This shows that a poor diet contributes to alcoholism. *False Cause*

133. You either side with the strikers or with the administration in this labour dispute. And you can't side with the administration after how badly they have treated you. So you have to side with the strikers. *False Dichotomy*

134. We should start shopping at that new grocery store that just opened on Main Street. I stopped to pick up some milk and bread, and its prices are better than those at the store we usually go to. *Hasty Generalization*

135. Because every part of the human body has a particular function, the human organism itself must have some essential or particular function. *False Analogy*

136. James Watson, discoverer of the molecular structure of DNA, Nobel laureate, and former director of the Human Genome Project, probably knows more about genes and genetics than any person alive. He believes that people with defective genes should not be allowed to have children, that it will only drag down the character of the human race. I think we should take his advice. *Appeal to Authority*

137. Even the ancient Egyptians believed in some form of life after death. So there must be some truth in the idea. *Genetic Fallacy*

138. Homosexuality must be wrong because most societies, past and present, have forbidden it. *Genetic Fallacy* *Common practic*

139. The government is now forcing us to register our handguns. Next it will force us to register all of our guns. Then it will take them away. We'll be set up for a police state. *Slippery Slope*

140. Reality is made up of more than material objects—there is also spirit. The spiritual aspect of reality is demonstrated by man's interest in such things as art and religion. *Straw Man*

141. I read in the paper that experts believe that the stock market is in for another correction. I'd better cash in my high-tech stocks. *Appeal to Authority*

142. In their book *The Bell Curve,* Richard Herrnstein and Charles Murray cite psychologist Richard Lynn no less than twenty times on the relationship between race and IQ. They don't identify any challenges to Lynn's work, so it is safe to conclude that Lynn must be right—there must be a relationship between IQ and race. *Appeal to Authority*

143. Canadians are opposed to gun control. A survey done in rural Kootenay County showed that seventy-eight percent of the respondents were opposed to gun control.

Hasty Generalization

144. *A picketer on the union picket lines:* "If we allow one vehicle to cross 'on emergency grounds,' we will have to allow everyone who claims an emergency to get through the lines quickly, and then we might as well stop picketing. No one gets through without having to wait their turn." *Slippery Slope*

145. A Nova Scotia rehabilitation hospital brought in pets periodically to cheer up patients and give them a break from the rigour of treatment. One day, a German shepherd nuzzled and licked the face of a boy who had been in a coma for several weeks. One week later, the boy awoke from the coma. The boy's family and the hospital credited the attention of the dog for the awakening. *Hasty Generalization*

146. *Student speaker:* "Student fees have jumped by more than three hundred percent in just two years! This is outrageous! The premier is working for a balanced budget, but it'll be on the backs of us students, the people who have the least to spend! It seems pretty clear that these increased student fees are undermining higher education in this province!" *Red Herring*

147. Marxism is clearly an anti-Semitic doctrine. In a letter Karl Marx wrote to his friend Friedrich Engels and in an essay outlining the basics of his theory, Marx expressed anti-Semitic sentiments. This shows that Marxism arose from Marx's early anti-Semitism and has never lost that taint. *Genetic Fallacy*

148. *Philosophy professor in lecture:* "The essence of women's liberation is that women have the same rights as men to be sexually irresponsible." *Loaded presupposition*

149. If you think the feminist arguments against pornography are wrong, as you have been arguing, then you must be in favour of men abusing women. *False Dichotomy*

150. Proponent: "Unless we find some economical way of dealing with the city's garbage in the next few years, we will end up with a polluted and toxic environment."

    Opponent: "What you're saying is that you couldn't care less what happens to the wildlife and plant life or even the human lives that might be harmed by another mega-dump in the area!" *Straw Person*

151. Evolutionists claim that man evolved from chimpanzees. So when are you inviting your cousin Charlie the chimp for supper? *Genetic Fallacy*

152. Evolution amounts to the claim that one day a bird hatched from a reptile egg. And that is clearly impossible. So evolution is false. *Genetic Fallacy*

153. *Conservative:* "The Liberals have challenged the government's spending and claimed that we have been wasteful of public funds. I need only point out to you that under our administration we have been involved in peacekeeping throughout the world, been ranked as the best nation in the world to live, and provided additional funds for health care." *Red Herring*

154. During the Watergate scandal of the early seventies, Richard Nixon's practice of secretly tape-recording conversations with White House guests (a violation of U.S. law) was excused by Nixon apologists on the grounds that several former U.S. presidents had done the same thing. *Hasty Generalization*

Straw-Man

155. Despite all the studies and the public outcry, it's still true that nobody has ever actually *seen* cigarette smoking cause cancer. All the anti-smoking people can do is talk about statistics.

156. *Philippe to Sharon:* "What's wrong with you taking my name when we get married? I know that marriage is an equal partnership, as you say, but it wouldn't mean that we aren't equal just because you have my name. It would really be embarrassing to me if we got married and you refused to take my name. In fact, I don't think I would want to be part of a relationship where you would show me that kind of disrespect." *False Dichotomy*

157. Leili: "In summary, let me say that after careful and serious reflection on this matter, I must conclude that there is no logical, moral, or legal justification for discriminating against a person on the basis of sex. Therefore, I wholeheartedly support the government's proposed anti-discrimination law."

Jay: "Look, if you want men to be excluded from the job market and end up on welfare, then you go right ahead and support it." *Red Herring*

158. A: "True love never ends in separation or divorce."

B: "What about your brother and his wife? I thought they were truly in love, but they got divorced."

C: "Well, that was obviously not true love." *Self-Evident Truth*

159. Researchers have found that seventy percent of the gay men in the study have a particular gene in common, whereas only ten percent of straight men have the same version of the gene. This clearly shows that genes cause homosexuality. *Hasty Generalization*

160. Background: Stockwell Day, when leader of the opposition and on the campaign trail, commented that Lake Erie flows from east to west, when, in fact, if flows from west to east.

One of Day's opponents: "You shouldn't vote for Stockwell Day. He doesn't even know which way Lake Erie flows. *Straw Man or Ad-hominem*

Loaded Presupposition

161. *Lawyer cross-examining the defendant in a murder trial:* "You say that you should not be convicted. Do you mean that you acted in self-defence when you stabbed your lover?"

Poisoning the well

162. The environment minister has argued that greenhouse gases are not significant and that Canada need not live up to the Kyoto Accord obligations. However, we don't have to respond to this. That is exactly what one would expect a member of this government to say.

163. You haven't presented evidence to show that the greenhouse emissions are harmful, so I think we can safely conclude that they are not harmful. *Appeal to Ignorance*

164. The price of liberty is eternal vigilance. The moment that we stop guarding against even the slightest infringement of our liberties, we are giving our lives over to the totalitarian control of the state. *False Dichotomy*

165. Dr. Mary Martin, who teaches anatomy at the local community college, claims that gay men are born that way. She claims that the brains of gay men are structurally different from the brains of straight men. Since she is an anatomist, we have proof that there is a biological basis to being gay. *Appeal to Faulty Authority*

166. The brains of men and women are structurally different. Men and women have fundamental differences in their linguistic, spatial, and mathematical abilities. It is obvious that the differences in their brains are responsible for the differences in their abilities in these areas. *False Cause* *Straw Man*

167. A: Despite what most people think, capitalism is actually based on ethical principles. John Locke argued that it is the best system for protecting rights, and Adam Smith argued that it produced the greatest good for the greatest number.

    B: Hogwash. Capitalism is simply a justification for people to act on the basis of their own greed and their base personal wants. Greed and the pursuit of individual self-interest aren't ethical.

168. The human body is like a well-oiled machine. Just as every part in a machine has a function, so, too, does every part in the human body. And just as a machine has no superfluous or extra parts, neither does the human body. And, therefore, since a machine has to have a designer, so, too, must the human body. We call this designer "God." *False Analogy*

169. Democracy is the only legitimate political system, for to be legitimate, a political system must have the leaders elected by those who are governed by them. *Straw Man*

170. Professor Wallace has argued that the evidence for the cancer drug is promising. However, we would expect him to say that since his work is funded by a major pharmaceutical company that stands to profit if the drug is successful. *Circumstancial Ad Hominem*

171. One in every five women has an eating disorder of some kind. This is the finding of a survey of more than one hundred thousand female college students. *Hasty Gen*

172. Montreal is a really ugly city. I took the train from Quebec City to Montreal then to Ottawa. While the countryside was spectacular, Montreal was full of abandoned warehouses, with litter all over the place. I didn't leave the train station. Montreal sure was a disappointment. *Hasty Gen*

173. Margaret Somerville is a noted Canadian ethicist. She claims that gay marriage is bad for children and, hence, should not be legalized. Since she has studied the literature carefully and is a widely known and respected scholar in this area, I think we should follow her recommendations. *Appeal to Faulty Authority*

174. Not improving our security to match the Americans' would be an invitation to terrorists. It would be like putting waterproof siding on the side of a house and not fixing a leaky roof. We have to fix the roof and beef up our security. *Equivocation*

175. It is clear that raising hydroelectric rates will cause a hardship for everyone in New Brunswick. Consumers, businesses, and the not-for-profit sector all agree on this. We can't raise electric rates. *Preloaded supposition* *Slippery slope*

176. Maggie's stance is based on a position that was defended and ultimately refuted at the end of the nineteenth century. She is simply appealing to a long-lost faulty theory that has long been disproved. *Genetic Fallacy*

177. Patrice: "I think we should consider donating some of our time this Christmas to helping at the local food bank. We have some time, and people need our help."

Andrew: "That's absurd. I won't deprive our kids of Christmas." *Red Herring*

177. Student: "I need a three-day extension on my essay. I've had a family crisis and need a little more time to finish the assignment."

Professor: "Absolutely not. If I give you an extension, then everyone will be asking for one. I might as well not set deadlines and let students hand in papers whenever they feel like it." *Slippery Slope*

178. Professors Silva and Lewis have engaged in misquotation and *ad hominem* attacks in earlier stages of this debate. I don't see why we should give a hearing to their arguments now. After all, they have shown that they have no concern for the truth. *poisoning the well*

179. It is obvious that cultural explanations of social behaviour are incomplete. You can't explain cultural phenomena without invoking other factors. *Self-Evident Truth*

180. Either we take decisive and drastic action now to stop global warming or we can see the end of life on earth as we know it within a hundred years. Since the government is proposing no action until 2040, I guess we and our descendants are going to have to start considering a radically changed form of life on earth. *False Dichotomy*

181. Marriage has always meant the union of one man and one woman to create a family. Therefore, that is what the true and only meaning of marriage can be. *Genetic Fallacy*

182. "We can't fire Yvonne. She is a single mother and has a family to support. What will happen to her kids?" *Appeal to Emotion*

183. Most Canadian students are spending five to ten hours a day outside of class working on their schoolwork, contrary to what many teachers think. A survey of one hundred and seventy-five students at the University of British Columbia found that one hundred and thirty of the students reported spending five to ten hours a day on schoolwork; thirty admitted to spending less time; and fifteen, more time. The survey was done of students emerging from the undergraduate library on three consecutive weekday evenings in November. *Hasty Gen*

184. The cost of health care is increasing yearly. I ask you whether you would prefer to accept this proposal and spend the additional money or cut ten years off your life. The answer is clear. We must spend more money on health care. *False Dichotomy*

185. The charges against the police over racial profiling are ludicrous. They would never do something like that. *Self-Evident Truth* *Appeal to Ignorance*

186. I am going to buy a video iPod because my sister says it's the best, and we usually like the same things. *Hasty Gen*

187. If you don't stop smoking, you will die. That is a horrible death. You wouldn't want to die that way. *False Dichotomy*

188. Victoria is the best candidate because she is better than everyone else. *Self-Evident Truth*

189. The argument is valid because the premises support the conclusion. *Self-Evident Truth*

190. Raising the minimum wage will cause more unemployment. There will be less money to distribute among a fixed pool of workers. *Slippery Slope*

191. Why listen to him? He's just an environmentalist who prefers trees to people. *Circumstantial Ad-hom*

192. I'm not going to the new James Bond movie. I saw three previous ones, and none of them were any good. *Hasty Gen*

193. My psychology professor has been discussing the relationship between psychology and evolution. He claims that the basic structures of our minds were laid down in the Pleistocene era (1.8 billion to 10,000 years ago) and that they haven't changed significantly since then. According to him, some of our mental structures are more adapted to our lives as cavemen than to modern society. I guess that explains why we have so much trouble with stress in our fast-moving societies. The cavemen didn't have those things to deal with. *Red Herring or Genetic Fallacy*

194. *Woman to a male coworker who has found out that she has been falsifying her expense reports*: If you tell my boss on me, I'll accuse you of sexual harassment. And you wouldn't want to go through that. So, don't report me. *Appeal to force/Threat*

195. Only two suspects had the opportunity to steal the money—Anitha and Haroum. But Haroum doesn't have the computer skills required. So Anitha must be the thief. *False Dichotomy*

196. Although Aristotle's works were written in a society that supported slavery and the subjugation of women, some of his ideas are still worth considering. His ethics provide an enlightened look at human virtue, and his biology has much to teach modern biologists. *Red Herring*

197. My watch says it is 5:15. The radio says it is 5:15. And my computer says it is 5:15. It is obvious that it is 5:15. *Self Evident truth*

198. A truly civilized society would not invoke the death penalty. Since we consider ourselves civilized, we should not have capital punishment.

199. We should support animal testing, because testing potentially harmful products on humans is not justified. *Straw Man.*

200. Animal experimentation is justified because we have laws that allow it. *Not Fallacy*

MODULE 8: ANALYZING AND ASSESSING EXTENDED ARGUMENTS

Passage for Analysis

This passage is reprinted here from the main text so that you can analyze it and follow along.

An Idea Whose Time Has Come

The government has no choice but to legalize the possession and sale of marijuana. First, individuals have a right to engage in whatever activities they choose as long as they don't harm others. This is a basic assumption of our society. We allow people to ingest alcohol and nicotine, to eat unhealthy foods, and to engage in risky behaviour such as hang-gliding and scuba diving. The use of marijuana puts no one but users at risk. Therefore, we should allow people to use marijuana.

Second, no one has conclusively established it is harmful.

Third, legalizing it will make money for the government through taxes and will curtail various evils, such as the proliferation of grow-ops and the use of illegal marijuana profits to fund other criminal activities.

It might be argued that using marijuana can harm others. For example, it might be claimed that people will use marijuana and then drive. However, drunk drivers kill people, yet we don't ban alcohol. Rather, we try to prevent people from driving while impaired.

[handwritten margin notes: "As long as that behaviour harms no one but themselves?" and "Elegalizing it?"]

QUICK QUIZ ANSWERS

✎ QUICK QUIZ 8.1
Read the Passage

Read the passage, and then answer the questions below. The answers given here are suggestions. Yours may differ, especially as we get into more complicated passages and passages that can be constructed in different ways. Where your answers differ, ask yourself why they differ. Are they simply different ways of analyzing the passage? Do they reflect different understandings of the passage?

1. Write a brief summary of the main point after first reading (don't reread yet).

   We should legalize the sale and possession of marijuana.

2. What is your hypothesis about the main point (conclusion) of the passage?

   People have a right to do what they want; there is no proof of harm; and the sale of marijuana will make money for the government through taxation.

3. What questions do you have about the argument of the text?

   - **How do we know marijuana harms no one but the user?**
   - **What about a pregnant woman using it?**
   - **Will that harm the fetus?**
   - **How will we detect if someone is using it and driving?**

✍ QUICK QUIZ 8.2
Annotate the Passage

An Idea Whose Time Has Come

1
[The government has no choice but to legalize the possession and sale of
2
marijuana.] First, [individuals have a right to engage in whatever activities

they choose as long as they don't harm others.] [This {the right of individuals
3
to engage in whatever activities they choose as long as they don't harm

others} is a basic assumption of our society.] [We allow people to ingest
4
alcohol and nicotine, to eat unhealthy foods, and to engage in risky behaviour

such as hang-gliding and scuba diving {as long as that behaviour harms no
5
one but themselves}.] [The use of marijuana puts no one but users at risk.]
6
Therefore, [we should allow people to use marijuana.]
7
Second, [no one has conclusively established it is harmful.]
8
Third, [legalizing it will make money for the government through taxes] and
9
[{legalizing it} will curtail various evils, such as the proliferation of grow-ops

and the use of illegal marijuana profits to fund other criminal activities.]

10

It might be argued that [using marijuana can harm others]. For example, [it

11

might be claimed that people will use marijuana and then drive.] However,

12

[drunk drivers kill people, yet we don't ban alcohol.] Rather, [we try to

13

prevent people from driving while impaired.]

✍ QUICK QUIZ 8.3
Clarify Meaning

1. Examine the text for clarity and precision of meaning. Are there concepts whose meaning is unclear? Does a dictionary help in the clarification of the meaning? If not, can you paraphrase to clarify the meaning or come up with alternative possible meanings?

> There are several clarifications I would make of this passage. The first is a qualification. All of the arguments address the recreational use, not the medical. I would limit the argument to that.
>
> Claim 2 puzzles me: It is an overly general claim that seems to have exceptions. I will need to qualify or limit this in some way. This will emerge in the argument analysis and through counterexamples.
>
> I am also a bit puzzled by what the author means by "conclusively established" in claim 7. If he means "establish beyond all reasonable doubt," then this may be stronger than is necessary and beyond what we would normally accept. We often restrict or limit potentially harmful drugs and food ingredients on lesser criteria. This may become a criticism on the grounds of being an overly strict criterion.

2. Are there any hidden implications in the premises?

> Claim 7 presupposes that one of the major grounds for prohibiting something is its being harmful to either the user or others.

✍ QUICK QUIZ 8.4
Portray Structure

1. Portray the structure of the argument in the marijuana passage.

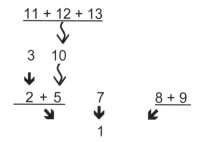

Note that this constitutes an objection to the argument and a response to that objection. We diagram an objection or challenge and a response to the challenge with wavy arrows.

2. How many lines of argument are there?

   There are three lines of argument.

3. What names would you give the lines of argument?

   The first is the autonomy argument; the second is the no proof of harm argument; and the third is the benefits (taxes and curtailing of crime) argument.

✍ QUICK QUIZ 8.5
Assess Cogency

1. Supply missing premises for the arguments in the marijuana passage.

2. Using the topics model or the argument patterns, assess the arguments for validity.

3. Assess the arguments for cogency.

4. Explain and justify your assessments.

These questions are all addressed in the assessments below.

> **The Autonomy Argument:**
>
> 2. **Individuals have a right to engage in whatever activities they choose as long as they don't harm others.**
> 5. **The use of marijuana puts no one but users at risk.**
> A. **[If someone has a right to something and the exercise of that right causes no harm to anyone other than the person whose right it is, then it should be legalized.]**
> _____
> ∴ 1. **Marijuana should be legalized.**
>
> **Supplying A as a missing premise makes the argument valid—affirming the antecedent.**
>
> **Claim 10, a potential challenge to 5, is answered by claims 11, 12, and 13. However, these do not comprise a good response. One particular example— alcohol and driving—is identified, and then the argument is generalized to**

marijuana use and driving. What is needed is a more general defence of claim 5—that what is objectionable is not marijuana per se but using it and then driving, which *could* cause harm to others. We shouldn't ban either of these activities, which, in themselves may be acceptable, but instead ban the combination of the two things. With this, I think that the objection is handled and premise 5 stands strong.

The main problem is with premise 2, not premise 5. The claim states that individuals have a right to engage in any activity they choose as long as it does not harm others. Although causing or potentially causing harm to others is grounds for curtailing an activity, the lack of harming others is not in itself grounds for allowing that activity and enshrining it as legally justified. I am prohibited from selling myself into slavery even though it would cause harm to no one but myself. Premise 2 as stated is false, and thus the argument is not cogent.

The No Proof of Harm Argument:

> 7. No one has conclusively established that marijuana is harmful.

> ∴ 1. The government should legalize the possession and sale of marijuana.

This argument commits the fallacy of appeal to ignorance. As such, this line of reasoning is not acceptable. It might be possible to develop it, however, by arguing more extensively about the conditions under which something such as recreational drugs should be legal.

The Benefits Argument:

> 8. Legalizing marijuana will make money for the government through taxes.
> 9. Legalizing marijuana will curtail various evils, such as other illegal activities.
> B. [If something will make money for the government and curtail other illegal activities, then it should be legalized.]

> ∴ 1. The possession and sale of marijuana should be legalized.

This argument is valid—affirming the antecedent. I will grant premises 8 and 9. The problem is with the missing premise. Many things could produce benefits for the government—increasing the rates of taxation to usurious levels will make money; executing anyone convicted of a serious crime would likely curtail other illegal activities. However, we don't simply do things because they benefit the government. Benefits must be weighed against costs, harms, and rights.

Although the argument is valid, it is not obviously cogent. More is needed to establish the missing premise (and probably to qualify and limit it). Once that is done, the arguer would need to show that the benefits outweigh the harms and costs and do not infringe rights.

Using notation symbols, we can provide an annotation for our arrow diagram:

$$\underline{11 + 12 + 13}$$
$$\downarrow$$

3   10
$$\downarrow$$

$\underline{2[?] + 5 + A}$ 7 $\underline{8 + 9 + B[?]}$
   ↘ V   ↓ X/F   ↙ V
               1

✎ QUICK QUIZ 8.6
Give an Overall Assessment

Give an overall assessment of the arguments in the marijuana passage using the criteria outlined in this section. What are the possible merits of the argument? Are there any considerations worth pursuing?

> The author has given three lines of argument. One is clearly a fallacy. Each of the other two, though valid, has questionable premises that render each argument not cogent as presented. If the challenges to claim 2 could be addressed, this would be a much stronger argument. The benefits argument could be improved by turning it into a balance of considerations argument (see Module 12, Section 12.6) and by arguing that the benefits of legalizing marijuana outweigh the harms. The potential harms would also need to be addressed.

✎ QUICK QUIZ 8.7
Write Your Own Critique

Write your critique of the marijuana passage using the criteria outlined in this section.

> The passage "An Idea Whose Time Has Come" presents three arguments for the conclusion that the government should legalize the sale and possession of marijuana.
>
> The autonomy argument asserts that individuals have a right to engage in activities as long as they don't harm others. Although this can be made valid, the missing premise—that we should not restrict autonomy unless it causes harm to others—is too general. It would allow for selling oneself into slavery, which we do not permit. A more careful defence of this argument would give the author a stronger case.
>
> The no proof of harm argument asserts that since there is no proof of harm, we should legalize the possession and sale of marijuana. This is a fallacy of appeal to ignorance.

The third line of argument, the benefits argument, asserts that since legalizing marijuana would produce benefits to the government through taxation and the curtailing of other evils, it should be legalized. Although this is a valid argument, the missing premise—that if something produces benefits, it should be legalized—is false. Legalizing marijuana may also produce harms—for example, increased incidence of lung cancer. The argument needs to weigh the harms against the benefits.

The author raises and addresses an objection that can be issued against the autonomy argument—that using marijuana can harm others. The author responds by drawing a parallel with drinking and driving. Neither, by itself, causes harm to others; however, put together, they can. We handle the problem of impaired driving by banning that, not the separate elements.

Although this is a good response, it does not overcome the fact that the basic argument has a false premise and is not cogent.

Overall, the author has not provided a single cogent argument to establish his or her conclusion. If the author could strengthen the autonomy argument by showing the conditions under which things should be legalized and when they should not be, and if he or she could improve the benefits argument by weighing the costs against the benefits, there would be a stronger case.

EXERCISES

✎ EXERCISE 8.1

For each of the following passages, do an extended argument analysis using the technique outlined in this module. Then write a critique using your analysis.

PASSAGE 1: Eliminate the Gun Registry

The government's gun registration program has failed. It did not stop the Dawson College shooting nor the two previous rampages in Montreal. All three crimes were committed by individuals using legally acquired weapons. More important, recent statistics show that while the incidence of crime—homicides, robbery—involving guns has decreased over the past ten years in the United States, it has increased in Canada. In the United States, not only is there no gun registry, but citizens are actually being encouraged to carry guns. Twenty-six states have recently passed laws allowing citizens to carry handguns and have made it easier for them to get handgun licences.

Not only has the gun registry program failed; it has had the effect of a steamroller crushing a butterfly. The gun registry program has two main

162

functions: (1) to decrease the use of guns for criminal activity, and (2) to reduce the number of domestic murders because of easy access to guns. The registry has had no effect on either of these.

Most crimes are committed with unregistered and illegal handguns, often either stolen from individuals who have registered their guns or with guns illegally imported from the United States. A gun registry doesn't address that problem. Criminals will still get guns; law-abiding citizens won't. In fact, a gun registry can actually facilitate criminals getting guns because it tells the criminals who has the guns and from where they can be stolen.

The gun registry, by itself, does not reduce the number of domestic murders. The number is, first of all, already low. And if someone is going to kill a spouse or other family member, that person will use whatever is available. If guns aren't available, he or she will use knives or clubs. Registering handguns will not change that.

Nor will it stop the killing of police officers. Few police officers in Canada are killed with guns. And when they have been, the guns have either been legally acquired, which the gun registry does nothing to prevent, or they have been illegal, which the gun registry also does nothing to prevent.

The gun registry is simply not effective. It should be eliminated.

PASSAGE 2: No New Fees

Over each of the past seven years, there has been a referendum on campus in which students have been asked to vote on adding additional auxiliary fees to the official fees the university charges. All but one of these has passed. The result is that we students are now being "taxed" an additional eight percent over what we pay in tuition. Only a small number of students even bother to vote in such elections, and usually they are the ones who will benefit from such unjust fees. Last year only four percent of the student body voted. This year, we have an additional three proposals that will add, according to the students advocating these proposals, a "negligible" amount to our fees. But such negligible proposals are killing us by inches. Each year the province increases the official fees it charges. And each year, a small number of students pile additional unjust taxes on us.

These "supplemental" fees benefit the few at the expense of the many. The proposals last year were for funding a gay and lesbian centre, providing additional funding to the campus radio station, and funding two campus political lobby organizations—a global-warming lobby group and an environmental advocacy group. None of these benefits more than a handful of students. The official membership of all of these combined is less than one percent of the total student body. Yet every student on campus is paying to support these.

These fees are not democratic. Only a small number of students vote for them. And they benefit only a miniscule percentage of the student body.

Many students are already pushing the limit in their efforts to pay for their university education. These additional fees constitute one more amount students have to borrow to continue their education. And we will pay for these for years after we complete our education. We have to stop the unjust imposition of these unfair and undemocratic taxes. Vote no in the upcoming elections.

PASSAGE 3: Hate Speech and Free Speech

Should we ban hate speech on campus? Groups critical of Israel are accused of uttering hate speech; groups defending Israel are accused of uttering hate speech. Groups critical of, or defending, Islam or Palestine or U.S. policies in Iraq are all accused of uttering hate speech. A university professor criticizes a funding body as having a disproportionate number of supporters of Israel and is accused of being racist and uttering hate speech. Pornography is hate speech against women. The response of some universities has been to pass policies and codes that prohibit speech that offends any ethnic or religious group, race, gender, or sexual orientation.

This benefits no one except perhaps the university administration, who can control dissent and maintain a semblance of public order. But this creates a semblance of order at the expense of silencing discourse; it harms our basic liberties and free speech.

Freedom of speech is a fundamental right of any society that claims to be democratic. And it is especially valuable in an institution of learning such as a university. The basic argument was aptly put by John Stuart Mill in *On Liberty* in 1859: Freedom of speech is basic to human autonomy and to the discovery of truth. Autonomy is the ability of an individual to make decisions and act on those decisions without constraint in order to pursue his or her own interests as he or she best defines those interests. An individual develops autonomy by being exposed to, examining critically, and choosing from various possible options. Limiting options by preventing exposure to some ideas inhibits the person's ability to choose, and thereby inhibits the development of the self.

Freedom of speech is fundamental to the discovery of truth and the investigation of ideas. If an idea is false, suppressing it prevents us from learning that it is false and why it is false. If it is true, we're prevented from challenging it and discovering why it is true. Mill argues that failure to challenge and discover the grounds for believing something that is true results in our treating the idea as a dead dogma. And if a belief is partially true and partially false, its suppression stops us from examining it to discover what is true and what is false. Any and all ideas must be available to be examined or we risk not knowing part of the truth. Suppressing ideas, even ones we consider abhorrent, absurd, racist, sexist, or against our religion, implies that we already know the truth and that we cannot be mistaken about it.

For these reasons, free speech is fundamental to a free society and for free inquiry.

Thus, for a university to implement such codes, even in the name of tolerance, is to violate a basic premise on which the university operates—the search for truth.

Moreover, as has been seen time after time, attempts to suppress free speech not only are rarely effective but are often used against those they are designed to protect—the subordinate and persecuted groups in society. In authoritarian societies, suppression of free speech has been turned against the dissenters and those who protest. In Canada, a law introduced to suppress certain kinds of pornography that objectified women was used against lesbian erotica—not against heterosexual or violent pornography, its intended target. See, for example, the Canada Customs case involving Little Sisters bookstore in Vancouver.

This is not surprising. As with any law, it is far more likely to be used to protect the powerful and suppress the powerless. Those in power get to define who is and who is not uttering hate speech. This rarely serves the interests of the persecuted groups and is often used more as a means of protecting a privileged position and maintaining social order than protecting the rights of the powerless. Expelling students and banning speech and assembly do not address the underlying issue of prejudice. If an assembly erupts into violence, then the authorities have grounds for discipline, not because hate speech is used but because the protesters have shifted from speech to action.

But shouldn't we prevent speech that causes discomfort, offence, or emotional pain, that tells lies and misrepresents, that attacks whole groups of people? No, for two very simple reasons. Suppression of offensive and hate speech does not solve the underlying problem of prejudice and inequality. Rather, it directs our attention away from such evils. Nor does it make the offensive beliefs go away. They are simply removed from a given forum. In the age of the Internet, people can publish whatever they want online. Suppressing them in academic discourse, however, means that these views cannot be exposed for what they are—lies, hatred, bias, misrepresentations—which is a far more effective means of neutralizing such materials and for giving the individuals holding such views reasons to change them.

Rather than allowing reasoned discourse to be hijacked or suppressed, we must work harder to ensure that we encourage free speech, so we can expose the lies and learn from the process. And that involves establishing a more tolerant and egalitarian atmosphere in which the rational discussion of, and disagreement over, deeply held, conflicting, and emotional views can occur. And that requires that we not limit freedom of speech.

PASSAGE 4[3]: Rap and Moral Character

Various critics have railed against the alleged harms of rap music. It is misogynistic and promotes violence (especially toward women), crass materialism, and street crime. Virtually all of the arguments about rap focus on its alleged effects—harmful or, occasionally, beneficial. Yet such arguments are difficult to prove. While not suggesting we abandon approaches like this, the focus on effects ignores another important moral argument—rap music is both a sign of and contributes to a form of corruption of moral character.

Morality is not simply about actions, consequences, and effects on others. It is also about oneself and the development of one's own character. Being self-centred, cowardly, or weak-willed may not harm others, but we do

---

[3] This essay was inspired by Susan Dwyer, "Caught in the Web: Sexual Fantasizing, Character, and Cyberpornography." Wesley Cragg and Christine Koggel, eds. *Contemporary Moral Issues,* Fifth Edition. Toronto: McGraw-Hill Ryerson, 2005.

judge such things in terms of morality. Who we are and the motives for our actions are important. Two people may do the same thing but for different reasons. We, justifiably, judge them differently. Two nephews may be attentive to their elderly aunt, taking her places, buying groceries, seeing to her welfare. If we judged them solely in terms of the consequences of their actions, there would be no difference between them. But maybe one nephew has no love for his aunt and helps her solely out of hope that he will benefit in her will. The other maybe helps her because he loves her and is concerned about her well-being. We judge their actions differently because of intent. Even the legal system considers motive and character. A person who pushes a man in front of a moving bus with the intent of killing him is judged differently than one who stumbles and pushes the man accidentally. Character is important in morally assessing ourselves and others.

Rap both indicates and contributes to a corrupt personal character. Rap lyrics (and accompanying videos) are full of images of "hos" and pimps, guns, violence, the killing of cops, dissing and being dissed, dominance, and drug dealing. It is rife with jewellery-wearing thugs promoting crass materialism and hostile sexual stereotyping. Women are subjected to the crudest form of sexual subjugation—as merely the sexual playthings of violent men—to be used, pimped out, and discarded.

The imagery is unrelenting. And it glorifies a world of misogyny, where crass materialism by any means, where violence as a primary means of settling disagreements, and where illegal activity—drug dealing, stealing, killing cops—are considered normal and desirable.

People who choose to listen to and watch such material on a regular basis are saying something about their own moral character, about what they value, about who they are. They are endorsing the behaviours the genre exemplifies. Seeking out such material is like seeking out and choosing to watch portrayals of atrocities, such as rapes, executions, and real-life violence, all of which are available in our culture and on the Internet.

One could argue that people might listen to rap only for the music and not pay attention to the lyrics. In response, consider the following parallel. Imagine that a genre of music emerged that had interesting music but whose lyrics and accompanying videos were entirely devoted to the denigration of a particular race and the superiority of another. I doubt that we would believe that self-described nonracist people listened only for the artistry of the music and ignored the lyrics. But even if this was the case, we would likely still find a moral failing in that. Their failure to see and condemn the message of the lyrics would itself be a moral failing. Finally, even if *some* individuals failed to recognize the message of the lyrics, that cannot be true of everyone who listens to the material. If it was simply the music and not the lyrics that was important, other lyrics would develop. This singular vision would not be as pervasive in the genre. Other genres are not as unrelenting and uniform in their vision of the world.

The state cannot prevent us from corrupting our character, nor should it. However, that does not prevent me, as an individual, from deploring the corruption of character in rap. We make a decision when we choose to listen to music. The choice to persistently listen to a form of music that celebrates thugs, violence, drug dealing, crass materialism, and the denigration of women shows a corruption of character and deserves moral censure.

PASSAGE 5: Sports Build Character?

It's often claimed that sports build character. We encourage children to participate in them because it teaches them important life lessons. Yet evidence from contemporary sports shows the lie in this. They may teach us about life in some ways, but they do not necessarily teach the lessons we want our children to learn.

Professional athletes, the role models of many children and adolescents (and many adults), have far from exemplary characters. In fact, away from the playing field, they exemplify some of the worst elements of our society. They engage in sexual assault, fraud, illegal gambling, sexism, materialism, barroom violence, drunk driving, and illegal drug use. This is what we want our children to emulate? This is being a role model?

Some would say that we need to separate the players' personal lives from their professional or on-field activities. First, that is an artificial distinction. The idea of being a role model does not come with boundaries. A role model exemplifies characteristics we find admirable. The fact that someone performs admirably on the playing field just shows technical proficiency. What makes that person a role model is what he or she does with the whole of life. Babe Ruth was a great baseball player. He could be considered a good role model only if we don't know about his womanizing, drinking, and other off-field activities. If we deem him a role model to be emulated despite knowing of these serious shortcomings, then we are treating those behaviours as desirable.

Second, players themselves often replicate on the field what they do in their personal lives. Contemporary sports emphasize winning at all costs. Using steroids and other illegal means—corked bats, spitballs, illegal hockey sticks—to get an edge, bending and breaking the rules of the game, lying, intimidating others, and using violence are seemingly justified by the pursuit of winning. Personal standards and integrity often take a back seat to achieving the corporate goal, in this case, winning.

In this respect, sports is little different from the wider society. The goal is to win and as long as the rules (the law) don't prohibit something, anything is considered fair game.

And this filters down into amateur sports. It is newsworthy when a high-school long-distance runner stops to help a fallen runner, thereby losing the chance to go on to the regionals—newsworthy because no one else stopped. It is newsworthy when a Norwegian skier, possibly at his own expense, gives a ski pole to a Canadian who broke his during an Olympic race. That is sportsmanship. And it is newsworthy because it is all too rare.

Sports may instill values and provide role models. However, these are not necessarily the values we want our children, or the rest of society, to learn nor the role models we want them to emulate.

PASSAGE 6: In Defense of Astrology

Astrology needs to be taken more seriously as an art and science that can contribute to human well-being. A great deal of evidence points to the truth of astrology.

Astrology has been practised for over six thousand years, and millions of people have based their lives and life choices on it. Until the eighteenth century, astrology was even used as a form of medical diagnosis. Its diagnoses and prescriptions were considered at the time to be far more reliable and efficacious than those of the medical practitioners of the time.

Since the middle of the twentieth century, countless scientific studies that have ultimately supported the basic principles of astrology have been conducted. Michel Gauquelin, a noted French statistician, spent much of his life using statistical methods to investigate astrology; he established the truth of a number of claims, including the Mars effect, which proved a relationship between the planet Mars and outstanding athletes.

Every year at New Year's, astrologers make predictions about what will happen in the coming twelve months. These predictions have a high rate of success. Jeanne Dixon, a noted astrologer, even predicted the assassination of President John F. Kennedy, demonstrating that those who claim that astrological predictions are vague are wrong.

Probably most important, astrologers make analyses of individual personality traits based on the twelve-sign system of astrology. In one study, ninety-six percent of those surveyed reported that such analyses of personality were "incredibly accurate." If nothing else proves the truth of astrology, this does.

Some psychologists have taken to using astrology as a means of diagnosing and treating their clients. Studies of the clients show that many claim that such treatment has been incredibly effective. Again, this supports the basic claims of astrology.

PASSAGE 7: The Loch Ness Monster

Arguments for the existence of the Loch Ness monster have persisted for almost one hundred and fifty years. The Loch Ness monster is alleged to be a prehistoric dinosaur inhabiting Loch Ness in Scotland. The primary evidence for it has been eyewitness testimony, some photographs, and several videos. None of the evidence supports the claims that the loch is inhabited by such a creature. And other evidence suggests that it is unlikely that such a creature exists.

Eyewitness testimony is notoriously unreliable. People have testified to seeing all kinds of things that don't exist and have made claims about things that could not have happened in the way described—witches flying on brooms, which violates the basic laws of physics; UFOs making right-angled turns at an incredibly high speed, which, again, violates the laws of physics; the existence of trolls and fairies. Eyewitness accounts usually sprout from only brief observations—seconds, not minutes or hours—under conditions of surprise. Such conditions contribute to unreliable observation.

Virtually all of the photos and videos presented as evidence are of poor quality. A viewer with no knowledge of what he or she was supposed to be seeing would not be able to identify it as a prehistoric sea monster.

Other evidence, however, calls these claims into further doubt. A systematic and exhaustive sonar study of the loch in 2003 found nothing that would match the identified characteristics of a living creature the purported size of the monster in the loch.

Basic biology also challenges the theory of a dinosaur in the loch. A breeding population of any kind of creature is necessary to sustain a species over time, and neither the environmental conditions nor the size of the loch would support one, much less a breeding population, of dinosaurs. Also, since sunlight does not penetrate much below the surface, the growth of algae and plankton, small fish and larger fish up the food chain would be limited. No matter what the monster eats, there is simply not enough food in the loch to sustain it, much less its family members.

Finally, formed about 10,000 years ago, the loch is still fairly new. Since it is a freshwater loch, those supporting the theory have to explain how the creature survived prior to the formation of the loch and how it has survived (and reproduced) in the loch to the present day.

✍ EXERCISE 8.2
Analyzing Someone Else's Argument

Find a passage containing an extended argument (perhaps from a textbook for another course, a magazine or journal, or the Internet) and analyze it using the tools of this module. Write a critique using your analysis.

✍ EXERCISE 8.3
Analyzing Your Own Writing

Select one of your own essays written for another course. Analyze it using the skills of this module, then rewrite it to address the challenges you raise in your analysis.

MODULE 9: CONCEPTUAL ANALYSIS

QUICK QUIZ ANSWERS

The answers to the Quick Quizzes in this module differ somewhat from those in previous modules. The answers given are suggested answers that illustrate the possibilities. Your answers will depend on the cases you generate and how you analyze them.

For Quick Quizzes 9.1 through 9.6, we will use the following case for analysis:

> **I am talking with a friend and say that since I have been in the country for thirty years, I no longer feel like an immigrant and am going to apply for my citizenship papers. My friend says, "You will always be an immigrant. The only people who aren't are First Nations people."**

✍ QUICK QUIZ 9.1
Paradigm Cases

1. What is the issue?

   What is an immigrant? Are all non-Native people immigrants?

2. Identify the question(s) of concept in this passage.

   Concept needing to be clarified: "immigrant." The term's use in the passage seems to be at odds with the way we would normally use the term *immigrant*. I normally don't describe people who have lived in Canada all of their lives as "immigrants."

3. Generate three paradigm cases of each concept and identify the possible criteria that emerge from those cases.

   Paradigm cases and criteria:

   1. **Last month, my cousin Geon moved to Canada from Australia.**

      Criterion: An immigrant is someone (1) who moves from one country into another.

      This doesn't capture the full notion of what an immigrant is.

   2. **Last month, my cousin Geon moved to Canada from Australia and plans to live here permanently.**

Criteria: An immigrant is someone who (1) moves from one country to another (2) with the intent of taking up permanent residence.

This better captures the idea of what an immigrant is.

3.   **Last year, my cousin Geon moved to Canada from Australia after receiving permanent residence status. He now identifies Canada as his place of permanent residence ("home") and is integrating into Canadian society.**

Criteria: An immigrant is someone who (1) moves from one country to another (2) with the intent of taking up permanent residence, and (3) who has been legally admitted to the destination country and (4) intends to become a member of the society to which he or she has moved.

This case is better than 2 in that it distinguishes between visitors who stay, refugees, and those who have been through the legal proceedings. We need other examples to distinguish between legal and illegal immigrants and refugees.

✍ QUICK QUIZ 9.2
Contrary Cases

For the case in Quick Quiz 9.1, generate three contrary cases and identify their possible criteria. Compare these criteria with those developed in Quick Quiz 9.1 and modify the criteria if necessary.

1.   Marcia just moved to Canada from Barbados to accept an executive position. She plans on returning to Barbados in two years.

   Marcia is not an immigrant because she does not plan on making Canada her permanent home. This is covered by the original criteria developed in Quick Quiz 9.1: An immigrant is someone who (1) moves from one country to another (2) with the intent of taking up permanent residence, and (3) who has been legally admitted to the destination country. Marcia does not meet the second criterion.

2.   Riza has come to Canada as a student from the Philippines.

   Riza is not an immigrant. She is in Canada to study and then will return home. Since she has no intention of staying, I would not call her an immigrant. Riza does not meet the second criterion developed in Quick Quiz 9.1.

3.   My parents came to Canada. I was born here. My parents were immigrants, but I would not call myself an immigrant.

   An immigrant is someone who moves to a country. Their children are not normally considered immigrants. This fails to meet criterion 1 developed in Quick Quiz 9.1.

✍ QUICK QUIZ 9.3
Mixed Cases

For the case in Quick Quiz 9.1, generate three mixed cases and identify their possible criteria. Compare these criteria with those developed in Quick Quizzes 9.1 and 9.2, and modify the criteria if necessary. Explain what makes these cases mixed cases.

1. Jian, 35, has moved to Canada and taken up residence in order to get his Canadian citizenship. After getting his citizenship, he intends to return to Hong Kong to work. He may come back to Canada when he retires, although he identifies Hong Kong as his home.

    This case is difficult. It partially fits the criteria. When Jian first moves to Canada with the intention of applying for Canadian citizenship, we would probably say he is an immigrant even if we know that he doesn't intend to stay permanently. Once he moves back to Hong Kong, we would no longer call him an immigrant, partially because he still identifies Hong Kong as his home. The criterion not met is the intention of permanent residence. Canada is simply a residence of convenience.

2. Anwar moved to Canada from Lebanon and applied for Canadian citizenship. After eight years in Canada, Anwar feels homesick and moves back to Lebanon with the intent of staying there.

    This case is similar to the first. Where it differs is that Anwar came to Canada with the intent of remaining here. We might say that Anwar was an immigrant but has moved back to his original home. As long as Anwar intended to make Canada his home, we might call him an immigrant. Once he gives that up, I would no longer call him an immigrant: He does not meet the criterion of intending permanent residence.

3. Anwar moved to Canada from Lebanon and applied for Canadian citizenship. After eight years in Canada, he feels homesick and moves back to Lebanon. He now spends six months of the year in Lebanon and six months in Canada.

    This situation poses challenges. Anwar was an immigrant. The question is whether we still call him an immigrant once he ceases to live full-time in Canada. The case would be clearer if Anwar had to live elsewhere because of business but saw Canada as his home and intended to return here.

✍ QUICK QUIZ 9.4
Borderline Cases

For the case in Quick Quiz 9.1, generate three borderline cases and identify their possible criteria. Compare these criteria with those developed in Quick Quizzes 9.1, 9.2, and 9.3, and modify the criteria if necessary. Explain what makes these cases borderline cases.

1. Paolo entered Canada as a visitor five years ago. He has found a job in the construction industry and brought his family to Canada. They also entered on visitors' permits.

   We would normally call Paolo an illegal immigrant. Although he has not followed the procedures for being a legal immigrant, he has moved to Canada with the intention of staying. He therefore meets the criteria we set above for being an immigrant.

2. Kwan is a refugee. He moved to Canada last month and was given refugee status.

   The question with this case is whether we want to call Kwan an "immigrant" or a "refugee," or whether the idea of an immigrant includes that of a refugee. We often distinguish between the two on the grounds that a refugee normally has no choice but to leave his or her home country and not return. If we want to distinguish this, we might add voluntary to the first criterion.

3. Regina and Elzear are married. They moved to Canada thirty years ago. Elzear has learned the language and integrated into the wider Canadian society. Regina still speaks only her native language, lives in a community of others from her home country, and associates only with them. She still thinks of her country of origin as home and returns every year to spend a few months there.

   We would tend not to call Elzear an immigrant. He has been in Canada for thirty years and has made it his home. Regina, however, is an awkward case. Although she has moved to a new country, she does not consider it home. She is more of a permanent visitor than an immigrant. This suggests that the notion of an immigrant includes the idea of someone in transition from one permanent home to another. It also suggests that applying the term immigrant to someone involves an intent to make one's home in and become part of the new country. It is not clear that Regina has done that. In this sense, the concept of immigrant seems to involve a notion of self-identification.

   This case suggests the following criteria: An immigrant is someone who (1) moves from one country to another (2) voluntarily (3) with the intent of taking up permanent residence in the new country and making it his or her home; and (4) identifies with the new country.

✍ QUICK QUIZ 9.5
Related Concepts

For the case in Quick Quiz 9.1, generate three related concepts and identify their possible criteria. Compare these criteria with those developed in Quick Quizzes 9.1, 9.2, 9.3, and 9.4, and modify the criteria if necessary. Explain what makes these related concepts.

Related concepts have been identified in the preceding cases and include:

- **immigrant**
- **refugee**
- **illegal immigrant**
- **student**
- **temporary worker**

✍ QUICK QUIZ 9.6
Imaginary Cases

For the case in Quick Quiz 9.1, generate three imaginary cases, at least one of which is a science-fiction case, and identify the possible criteria found in those cases. Compare these criteria with those developed in Quick Quizzes 9.1, 9.2, 9.3, 9.4, and 9.5, and modify the criteria if necessary. Explain what makes these cases imaginary cases.

All of the preceding cases are imaginary in the sense that they are not based on real situations of real people.

1. **A group of explorers arrive on an uninhabited island and settle it. They bring their customs, values, and institutions with them, and establish these as the basis for their new society.**

We would not consider the settlers immigrants. We distinguish between settling an uninhabited land and immigrating to an already inhabited land. The idea of immigration involves the notion of moving into an area that already has a population. In the same way, nomadic tribes are not immigrants.

2. The same explorers arrive at an isolated island, but it is already inhabited. The explorers settle on the island and impose their values and customs on the local inhabitants.

The explorers are still not immigrants; they are colonizers. Although they have moved and intend to stay, their goal is not to become part of the new home but to impose their own institutions, values, and culture onto the people already living there.

3. Captain Kirk and the crew of the *Starship Enterprise* crash on the planet Hmung in a star system far, far away. The *Enterprise* is nonfunctional. The crew will spend the rest of their lives on the planet. The inhabitants of the planet welcome them and invite them to settle, provided that they respect the laws and customs of Hmung. Although initially resistant, within ten years, the crew members have accepted Hmung as their new home.

Although this meets some of the criteria—moving to a new land, assimilating—we would not call the crew of the Enterprise immigrants. The situation fails to meet several criteria—the crew did not come to Hmung voluntarily, nor did they come with the intent of settling permanently.

✍ QUICK QUIZ 9.7
Synthesize the Criteria

Examine the criteria developed in each of the cases for the analysis of the concept in Quick Quizzes 9.1 through 9.6 and synthesize them into one set of criteria.

> **An immigrant is someone who (1) moves from one country to another (2) voluntarily (3) with the intent of taking up permanent residence in the new country and making it his or her home; (4) identifies with the new country; and (5) is in the process of becoming part of the new country.**

✍ QUICK QUIZ 9.8
Critique Your Criteria

Identify possible challenges that might be made to the criteria you identified in Quick Quiz 9.7. Develop those challenges, and then respond to them by modifying your criteria.

> **The criteria do not address the issue of how long a person is considered an immigrant or when that person shifts from being an immigrant to being a Canadian.**

> **Challenge:** **Mika and Michael's parents moved to Canada before they were born. Mika and Michael have been raised as Canadians. Although their parents tended to live near and associate exclusively with those from their home country, Mika and Michael speak English fluently and have assimilated to Canadian society. Are they immigrants?**

> *Although their parents have remained immigrants, Mika and Michael clearly are not. They are Canadians (we may hyphenate them as X-Canadian, where X is the country of origin). This makes the notion of becoming part of the wider society a key criterion for the immigrant designation.*

> **Challenge:** **Nora and Ned's parents came to Canada before Nora and Ned were born. Nora and Ned have been raised as Canadians but have a strong identification with their country of origin. They speak both English and the language of their parents. Although they have assimilated to Canadian society, they also have a strong respect for and adherence to the values and culture of their parents' country of origin.**

> *Again, we would not consider Nora and Ned immigrants. They are Canadians. It appears that along with the other conditions, the notion of whether someone has assimilated to Canadian culture (and identifies him- or herself as Canadian) is essential to distinguishing immigrants from Canadians. It is not their length of stay in Canada so much as their identification with Canada and their efforts to assimilate that seem to determine whether or not they are considered immigrants.*

Challenge: Jean-Philippe's ancestors arrived in Canada three hundred years ago. He speaks French and English, is assimilated within Canadian society and identifies himself as a Franco-Canadian. Is he an immigrant?

Jean-Philippe is not an immigrant in any normal sense of the term. He is not in a state of transition. He sees himself as Canadian and is part of Canadian society.

✍ QUICK QUIZ 9.9
Results in Context and Results in Language

1. How well do your criteria in Quick Quiz 9.8 answer the question of concept from the original context in which it arose? Explain.

2. What are the practical results of your conceptual analysis on the way the concept is used in the language? Explain.

> The set of criteria identified in Quick Quiz 9.7 articulates what we normally mean by *immigrant*. Native Canadians are not immigrants, although they may have been "settlers" when they first arrived in North America. Nor were the original English and French arrivals immigrants—they were "colonizers." We normally distinguish between immigrants and "natives"—those who have been in a country a sufficient length of time and have assimilated to Canadian society. Calling all Canadians except Aboriginal peoples *immigrants* goes against the usual use of the term. The speaker would be invoking only one of the criteria for being an immigrant—having originated from some other place—but ignoring the remaining criteria, such as assimilation to and identification with the dominant culture. We don't normally refer to descendants of the original French and English settlers in Canada as *immigrants.* To do so would distort the language and make it impossible to draw distinctions between longtime residents who have assimilated to Canadian culture and recent arrivals who are still in the process of assimilating.
>
> Insofar as the speaker is simply pointing to the fact that Aboriginal peoples were in North America long before others arrived, his or her use of *immigrant* is an extended application of the concept.

✍ QUICK QUIZ 9.10
Write Up Your Analysis

Briefly write a presentation of your conceptual analysis aimed at explaining it to other students who have not done this analysis. Follow the guidelines for presenting a conceptual analysis.

Are We All Immigrants?

The author of the passage claims that only Indigenous peoples are Canadian and that all others are immigrants. I find this puzzling since we normally don't describe people who have spent their whole lives in this country as immigrants. Through a conceptual analysis of the concept of "immigrant," I will show that the term *immigrant* is being stretched beyond its normal meaning.

A paradigm case of an immigrant is my cousin Geon, who moved to Canada to take up permanent residency here just last month. He is someone we would clearly call an immigrant. The criteria we use for calling him an immigrant include (1) someone who moves from one country to another (2) with the intent of taking up permanent residence and (3) becoming a member of the country to which he is moving. This seems to apply to Geon. He is unquestionably an immigrant.

But what about Kwan, who arrived with his family at the same time as Geon? He and his family are refugees. I would not normally count them as immigrants. An immigrant is someone who voluntarily leaves a home country and moves to another with the intent of making a new home in the second country, whereas a refugee is someone who is fleeing poor conditions in his or her homeland and seeking a better place to live. Since we normally draw a distinction between refugees and immigrants, I will maintain the distinction by including in my criteria the following condition: (4) the person moves to the new country voluntarily rather than as a result of conditions that force the person out of his or her home country.

Consider then the case of Regina, who moved here with her husband. She still speaks her native language, has made little effort to learn English or French, and lives in proximity to and associates only with others from her home country. Is she an immigrant? I would suggest that she is. The notion of an immigrant includes someone who is in process of becoming a member of the country or culture. In this case, Regina has not made that transition. Since she is still in the process of assimilating to the new culture, I would consider her an immigrant. This adds the following criteria to our set: (5) an immigrant is someone who has not yet assimilated to the culture and language of the new host country and (6) does not yet identify him- or herself as a Canadian. To test this, let us consider what we might say about Regina's husband, Elzear. He has learned English and integrated into the wider Canadian society. He sees Canada as his home. I would suggest that Elzear is no longer an immigrant, but a native.

We can get closer to our situation by considering two parallel cases, those of Mika and Ned. Both of them were born and raised in Canada. However, Mika has assimilated to Canadian culture, speaks English, and has many Canadian friends. Ned, on the other hand, identifies with his parents' country of origin, retains his parents' language, although he speaks English as well, and longs to return to his parents' country of origin, although he is a Canadian citizen. I would not be willing to call Mika an immigrant. However, I might be willing to call Ned one, even though he was born in Canada. An important criterion is whether or not the individual identifies with the country to which they have moved and seeks to assimilate to (become a member of) that country and its culture. Under no condition would I call someone whose ancestors came to this country three hundred years ago and who considers him- or herself Canadian an immigrant.

This analysis of *immigrant* suggests that an immigrant is someone who (1) moves from one country to another (2) voluntarily (3) for the purpose of taking up permanent residence and (4) becoming a member of the country to which he or she is moving, (5) identifies with the new country, and (6) has not yet assimilated to the culture and language of the new host country.

With these criteria, it is easy to see that the author's applying the label "immigrant" to everyone who is not Indigenous is a misuse of the concept as it is normally used. We usually don't apply the concept "immigrant" to someone who was born and raised in this country and definitely not to someone whose parents and ancestors were born and raised in this country. To use the concept in this way would require a revision of the term's use and would mean that we cannot distinguish among those who have just arrived in this country, such as Alan, those who identify with another country and its culture, such as Regina, and those who have assimilated and consider themselves Canadian, such as Elzear or Mika.

Some Comments on the Essay

This essay does not precisely follow the steps outlined nor use every case developed in the initial analysis. In transforming an original analysis into an essay format, we often have to rewrite and revise the material we have created to make it easier and clearer for the audience to follow.

This essay is a model, not a template. A template is a pattern that one imposes on other things. Using this essay as a template for the topics you are discussing will likely result in a poor analysis. A model, on the other hand, serves as an example of one way something can be done. It needs to be used critically.

The writing of any essay is a critical-thinking and problem-solving activity. The writer must determine his or her goals, the best means for accomplishing them, and the most effective way of conveying ideas to the reader. There is always a purpose (or purposes) for writing an essay—and it's not getting something on paper that can be turned in to an instructor. If the writer doesn't address the requirements of the essay and successfully convey his or her ideas, then the writer has not accomplished what he or she set out to do. Submitting a paper is a necessary, but not a sufficient, condition for fulfilling the assignment requirements and getting a grade.

In this particular case, I have both a specific purpose (to give a conceptual analysis of "immigrant" so that I can clarify what an immigrant is and understand how the term applies to the passage in question) and a general purpose (to display that I know the skills and techniques of conceptual analysis). How I compose and present my paper should satisfy these goals.

One nice feature of the above analysis is that part of the defence of the criteria comes through the challenging of the original criteria. By testing the criteria and suggesting improvements, I am more likely to convince the reader that these are good criteria. Had I adopted a strategy of simply presenting my criteria after the first case and then using additional cases that simply confirmed the original criteria, I am likely to leave the impression in my reader's mind that I haven't really challenged the criteria or thoroughly thought it through. Under some conditions, this might be a good strategy. However, if the remaining cases are simply further examples, rather than tests and challenges, of the criteria, then the reader is likely to have doubts both about the criteria and how they were arrived at.

A challenge need not result in a revision of the criteria. Serious challenges, however, do raise new and interesting issues about the criteria. Challenges that don't are probably more examples or illustrations than tests. Illustrations and examples show what has already been established; they do not advance the argument.

All analyses are done in a particular context. If the criteria you develop and the cases you choose in developing those criteria do not help in addressing the passage under discussion, then you are going off topic.

EXERCISES

✍ EXERCISE 9.1
Conceptual Analysis Exercises

For each of the following,

a. identify the issue;
b. identify the question of concept;
c. identify three paradigm, contrary, mixed, borderline, and imaginary cases for each concept needing clarification;
d. analyze the concept for criteria of use and synthesize the criteria;
e. apply the criteria to the original issue and show how it addresses it; and
f. show how the proposed criteria would affect the use in the language.

The first six below are taken from the beginning of Module 9.

1. Is artificial insemination by donor (i.e., the fertilizing of a woman's egg using sperm of someone other than her husband) adultery? Because she has become pregnant by someone other than her husband, in some legal jurisdictions, it is. And according to the Roman Catholic Church, it would constitute adultery. Should we call this adultery? What do we mean by *adultery?*

2. Catharine MacKinnon claims that women in a patriarchal society are unable to consent to have sex with men. Is she using the same notion of *consent* that we use?

3. Is Data on *Star Trek* a moral agent? Can androids be moral agents? What makes someone a moral agent?

4. Albert Carr claims that bluffing is perfectly acceptable in business. Isn't bluffing a form of lying? What might Carr mean by saying bluffing is acceptable?

5. I have read several articles that claim that pornography degrades women. What exactly does *degrade* mean? Does it apply to pornography? What makes something degrading?

6. What does it mean when someone says homosexuality, or any form of sexual activity, is "unnatural"? Does that necessarily mean that it is immoral?

7. No one should blame an addict for his or her addictive behaviour. Everyone has bad habits—many overeat, avoid exercise, swear—and these actions are just as irrational and as persistent as those labelled "addictions" (drinking, gambling, smoking). In fact, the relatively recent identification of gambling addicts and "workaholics" shows just how arbitrary the distinction is. These behaviour rigidities are not "sins." They're just part of the human condition and require understanding, not sitting in judgment.

8. Grading students is a form of punishment—indeed, sometimes quite a severe form of punishment as far as their careers or scholarship plans are concerned, and associating punishment with education is a surefire way to turn people off it. Therefore, grading should be abolished.

9. That plant you are cutting is in intense pain; see the jump in the graph of the electroencephalogram. Plants think and feel.

10. If you don't understand something, you have no right to judge that thing. Being a man, you can't understand what it's like to be a woman and to experience things as a woman does. Only a woman can experience pregnancy (and abortion). Therefore, only women should have a say on whether or not abortions should be allowed.

11. A: Canada was not a democracy before women were allowed to vote.

    B: Sure it was. We elected our leaders by ballot and had a legislature that represented everyone.

    Analyze the different concepts of democracy being used by A and B.

12. All standards are arbitrary. Just look at temperature scales. We can measure in degrees Celsius or degrees Fahrenheit. Whichever one we choose to use is entirely arbitrary.

13. All of the social sciences are inherently subjective. They involve human subjects, and humans act and behave subjectively.

14. Because fetuses are human, they have a right to life. Therefore, since murder is wrong, abortion is immoral.

15. Pornography objectifies women.

✎ EXERCISE 9.2
Writing an Essay

Your instructor will assign you one of the exercises from Exercise 9.1 above. Using your analyses from the exercise, write an essay presenting your results.

✍ EXERCISE 9.3
Longer Passages

Each of the following are slightly longer passages. For each,

a. identify the question(s) of concept in the passage;
b. explain how each question of concept is central to addressing the issue or analyzing the argument in the passage;
c. do a conceptual analysis to clarify the concept;
d. summarize the criteria you arrive at; and
e. write a brief essay presenting the results of your analysis (if so directed by your instructor).

1. Pornography (sexually explicit material) is a form of hate speech. It preaches lies about women and their sexuality and encourages men to treat women as sexual objects and playthings. Since pornography is a form of hate speech, it should be prohibited, along with other forms of hate speech.

2. Professor X at a Canadian university was charged with sexual harassment. The charge was that he had ogled a female student while she was swimming laps in the university swimming pool. The student claimed that, wearing a face mask and swim fins, he had embarrassed her by swimming alongside her, giving her undue attention, and ogling her. A key feature of the student's testimony was that the professor's actions made her feel uncomfortable. She also testified that she did not speak to the professor about his actions. Professor X claimed that he was nearsighted and that he wore the swim goggles and fins so as to swim better. (There are several issues of concept here.)

3. Intimacy between a man and a woman is not possible in a society in which men and women are not economic and social equals. And there is virtually no society in the world in which men and women are social and economic equals. So intimacy between a man and a woman is not possible.

4. All sexual intercourse in a male-dominated society is rape because a woman in a patriarchal society cannot give consent. And without consent, sex is rape.

5. A professor at a Canadian law school was teaching the stance of Canadian law on the issue of pornography. He randomly assigned half the students in the class to the prosecution side and half to the defence side to prepare a legal brief (formal argument) on a hypothetical anti-pornography law. A number of the female students objected on the grounds that defending pornography contradicted their beliefs and accused the professor of sexual harassment.

6. Affirmative action programs are designed to equalize imbalanced hiring policies and give groups that have traditionally been discriminated against an opportunity to overcome that discrimination. Such programs often contend that where two individuals are equal or approximately equal, then the person from the traditionally discriminated-against group (e.g., women) should be given the job. Critics of such programs accuse them of being sexist.

7. I read in a newspaper the following account:

A church minister in Ottawa, Ontario, has been brought before the courts by the Children's Aid Society on a charge of child abuse. CAS alleges child abuse on the following grounds: "The minister has spanked his four-year-old son on the bare buttocks with a homemade wooden paddle, somewhat resembling a Ping Pong paddle. The spankings were severe enough to make the child's bottom red, but all physical signs of the spankings had disappeared within a twenty-four-hour period. Further, the child appears to have suffered no lasting effects from the spankings." Both the Children's Aid Society lawyer and the minister's lawyer have agreed to these facts. The minister has denied that his actions constituted abuse. He claims that he did this out of love for his child and that not to have done this would have imperiled his child's development. The minister has quoted Biblical passages to support not only his right but his duty to provide such corporal punishment to prevent "willfulness" in his child.

8. A controversy has arisen over whether al Qaeda and Taliban fighters captured in Afghanistan are prisoners of war (POWs) and should therefore be given the rights warranted under the Geneva Convention. If they are prisoners of war, certain minimal standards of treatment must apply. If they are not prisoners of war, they can be treated according to the laws of the society in which they are prisoners—in effect, the criminal laws of that country—which may be harsher or more lenient than the Geneva Convention accords for the treatment of POWs.

The background issue is "How are these people to be treated and what kind of treatment are they entitled to?" Most nations have signed the Geneva Convention, which lays out the minimal standards for the humane treatment of POWS. If these people are indeed POWs, their captors must abide by the laws of the Geneva Convention; if they are not, then no guarantee of humane treatment can be enforced by the international community. For example, in a civil war between two factions within the same nation, there are no minimal conditions for the treatment of prisoners that can be enforced by the Geneva Convention. There may be issues of human rights. However, insofar as the conflict is an internal one, the United Nations has no right to interfere. The issue in the case of the Afghani captives is whether or not they are prisoners of war.

9. A human rights case in British Columbia has raised the issue of what makes someone a woman. A Vancouver rape crisis centre has refused to allow a male-to-female transsexual (someone born with male anatomy who has been surgically reassigned as a female) to act as a rape crisis counsellor on the grounds that "she/he was not a woman." The person involved has lived and interacted with others in society as a woman for twenty years and has been post-operative (without testicles and penis and with a human-constructed vagina) for ten years. She (I will use that pronoun since the person is legally recognized as a woman and self-identifies as a woman) has charged that her rights were violated and that she was discriminated against on the grounds of gender/sex. The British Columbia Human Rights Commission grants that being a woman is a necessary condition for being a rape crisis counsellor in a rape crisis centre.

10. Anita M. Superson defines sexual harassment as follows:

Any behavior (verbal or physical) caused by person A, in the dominant class, directed at another, B, in the subjugated class, that expresses and perpetuates the attitude that B or members of B's sex is/are inferior because of their sex, thereby causing harm to either B and/or members of B's sex. [Superson, Anita M. "A Feminist Definition of Sexual Harassment." Journal of Social Philosophy, vol. 24, no. 1, 1993.]

Using the techniques of conceptual analysis, determine whether this is a good definition of sexual harassment.

MODULE 10: ISSUE ANALYSIS

QUICK QUIZ ANSWERS

✍ QUICK QUIZ 10.1
Identifying Issues

For each of the following topics,

    a. identify whether it is an issue and explain why it is or is not;

    b. if it is an issue, explain whether it meets the criteria for a proper framing of the issue; and

    c. determine what kind of issue it is (factual, conceptual, normative).

1. The morality of abortion.

   This not a complete thought; it is just a topic, not an issue. We cannot determine whether it is a factual, conceptual, or normative question.

2. Abortions have been done illegally by people who are not licensed medical practitioners.

   This is not an issue. It is a factual statement and not controversial.

3. Is abortion ever ethical?

   This is an issue. There is controversy over whether abortion is ethically justifiable. I would consider this not precise enough, though. We need some specification of "ethical for whom"—the mother or the abortion provider? This is a normative (ethical) issue.

4. Should abortion be allowed?

   This is a normative issue. I would consider it imprecise, however, because it could be interpreted as several different questions: Should abortion be legal? Is it ever ethically allowed? It could cover a range of possible conditions: Should abortion be allowed (ethically or legally) to save the life of the mother? Should it ever be allowed (ethically or legally) for eugenic reasons (e.g., sex selection of the fetus or to terminate a fetus that carries a serious genetic disease)? Alternatively, should abortion ever be allowed (ethically or legally) to prevent pain and suffering (on the part of either the fetus or the mother)? Each of the alternatives in brackets represents a separate issue.

   ***Precision* means being as exact and definite as necessary under the circumstances and clearly distinguishing different relevant possibilities. Where an issue is formulated and does not make such distinctions, then all of the relevant possibilities have to be addressed. "Should abortions be allowed?" does not distinguish between a number of different relevant**

possibilities (e.g., legal and ethical framings of the issue), nor does it specify adequately enough parameters—all abortions, late-term abortions, abortions under certain circumstances (rape, incest) or for certain purposes (eugenics, family planning, sex selection). General framing of an issue often is not precise enough.

5. Should abortion for the purpose of preventing the spread of defective genes be allowed?

This is a normative issue. It is reasonably specific. We could make it more precise by adding *legally* before *allowed*.

6. Is a woman ever justified in killing her unborn baby?

This is an issue. It is probably a normative issue, although it could be a factual one if the speaker were asking about the norms within a specific community. The question frames the issue in a loaded way by presuming the fetus is a baby (contentious) and by using the language of one side of the debate ("killing," "baby").

7. Is a woman ever justified in having an abortion?

This is a normative issue. The question frames it as an issue of justification and possibly of a woman's choice. It may be legal, moral, or a question of conscience. This framing is narrower than that in #4 above in that the focus is on the woman's choice and may lead us to ignore other relevant players. Note that this phrasing allows us to assert that a woman is justified in having an abortion even if it is illegal and, in exceptional circumstances, even if it is immoral (if not having an abortion causes a greater moral evil than having one).

8. Is the state ever justified in interfering with a woman's right to choose what to do with her body?

This is a normative issue that focuses on the state's responsibility and how it relates to women. It may also frame the issue in a loaded way by presuming that a woman's right to choose is inherent and overrides most, if not all, other considerations. This choice of language favours one side of the controversy.

✍ QUICK QUIZ 10.2
Identifying Positions and Considerations

For each of the following topics,

    a. identify any possible positions; and
    b. identify all possible considerations you can think of for each position, whether you agree with them or not.

1. Should violent or sexist video games be restricted or banned?

1. **Violent and sexist video games should be censored.**
   Harmful:
   - create antisocial behaviour
   - can lead to violence
   - can increase tolerance for violence; desensitize to violence
   - can lead to objectifying women
   - can lead to callous attitude toward violence and women
   - harm the individual by harming sense of self

2. **Violent video games should be censored, but not sexist ones.**
   Harmful: *See reasons above.*

3. **Sexist video games should be censored, but not violent ones.**
   Harmful: *See reasons above.*
   Disrespectful to women

4. **Neither violent nor sexist video games should be censored.**
   Harm not established:
   - impossible to determine any causal factors when violence is so prevalent in society
   - portrayals of violence are not the same as real violence
   Impossible to police:
   - Internet

By qualifying the scope of each claim, many more positions could be developed—for those under age 16, 17, 18, 21, for example. We could also qualify the kind of violent or sexist video game that should or should not be censored. One danger of focusing on the kind that should be censored is the resulting tendency to presume the assumption of censorship and therefore not to present an argument for why censorship should occur.

2. Should the government fund inexpensive daycare for all working parents?

   1. **The government should fund inexpensive daycare for all working parents.**
      Daycare is an investment in society and future generations

   2. **The government should fund inexpensive daycare only for some working parents.**
      Only some working parents need daycare and can't afford it

   3. **The government should not fund daycare but rather provide other means for helping working parents raise their children.**
      Funding daycare is not the best way of supporting parents—tax reduction is
      Funding daycare takes choices away from parents
      Funding daycare for working parents discriminates against stay-at-home parents

   4. **The government should not fund daycare nor help parents with child care.**
      Not the government's responsibility

Limiting the scope of those parents who should receive daycare would give a larger number of positions.

EXERCISES

EXERCISE 10.1
Developing an Issues Map

Listed below are a number of topics. Select one, define a central issue, and develop an issues map for that topic. (For the context provided in #1, you'll have to first identify a topic before defining an issue.)

1. *News article:* An iPod owner is suing Apple, claiming the volume on his iPod caused his loss of hearing.

2. Mandatory gun registration

3. Downloading copyrighted music and videos from the Internet without paying

4. Legalization of marijuana

5. Using steroids in professional sports

6. Needle exchange programs

EXERCISE 10.2
Developing Arguments on Issues

Using the issues map you made in Exercise 10.1, develop a position you can defend on a central issue.

1. Develop the arguments to support that position.

2. Include challenges and responses.

EXERCISE 10.3
Analyzing an Issue in the Media

Find a controversial topic or popular discussion in the media. Gather articles about the various sides of that topic. Define a central issue, analyze that issue, and present your analysis, either as an issues map or in prose. Make sure that your analysis identifies the issue, the positions, the main arguments, the challenges, and the responses. Clarify any key concepts that may not be clear to a reader.

✍ EXERCISE 10.4
Analyzing an Issue of Your Own

Identify a controversial issue that you have personally encountered—this can be derived from a situation in your personal life, your coursework, or your job. Make sure that the issue is of general concern. Do an analysis of that issue using the tools presented in Module 10. Take a stand on the issue, write your analysis, and defend your position.

MODULE 11: ARGUMENTATION

The answers to the Quick Quizzes in this module differ somewhat from those in previous modules. There may be a variety of good answers. The answers given are suggestions that illustrate the possibilities.

The Quick Quizzes in this module are designed to help develop your verbal argument skills, so they should be done reasonably quickly, without writing out various alternatives. After you have done them verbally, write them down. Then you can think about other possibilities.

QUICK QUIZ ANSWERS

✍ QUICK QUIZ 11.1
Probing Reasons

For each of the brief arguments below, suggest three additional probes (questions) for reasons that B could use to find out more about A's argument. Do not challenge the argument.

1. A: I think we should have more bike lanes in the city because it will encourage more people to ride bikes, and it will reduce traffic.

    B: 1. Why do you think that more bike lanes will encourage more people to ride bikes?
    2. Why is getting more people to ride bikes a good thing?
    3. Why do you think that will reduce traffic?

2. A: Downloading copyrighted music and videos from the Internet without paying for it should not be a crime. After all, it doesn't hurt anyone.

    B: 1. Why do you think downloading copyrighted material doesn't harm anyone?
    2. What do you mean by "hurting someone"?
    3. Is one person hurting another the only basis you would consider for something being a crime?

3. A: I don't think we should allow genetically modified foods to be sold and put into the food chain. After all, we don't know their long-term effects.

    B: 1. Why do you say that we don't know the long-term effects?
    2. What evidence is there that there are long-term effects?
    3. What kind of effects are you concerned about?

Be careful to distinguish among a probe, a challenge, and a simple request for information. A probe is a request for evidence and reasons to develop the understanding and support for the argument. A challenge questions the reasons given. A simple request for information asks for additional information but neither challenges nor develops the argument—for example, do you download music? While this gives us information about the individual, it does not advance the argument.

✐ QUICK QUIZ 11.2
Clarifying Meaning

For each of the brief exchanges below, identify a concept or claim that might need to be clarified and provide B with three questions that would be a probe for meaning of that concept.

1. A: I think pornography exploits women.

    Concept: exploits

    B: 1.   What do you mean by "exploits"?
    2.   How does pornography exploit women?
    3.   Does pornography exploit men?

    Concept: pornography

    B: 1.   Can you give me an example of what you mean by pornography?
    2.   How would you define pornography?
    3.   Does pornography exploit only women?

2. A: Some video games are sexist and encourage violence against women.

    Concept: sexist

    B: 1.   Can you give me an example (other than a video game) of what you mean by "sexist"?
    2.   Which video games do you consider sexist?
    3.   Why do you consider X [name of video game] sexist? (Note that the reason will give us one of the criteria the person has for calling something sexist, and we can use that to start a conceptual analysis.)

    Concept: violence

    B: 1.   What do you mean by violence against women? Can you give an example?
    2.   How do video games cause violence against women?
    3.   Does violence include mental as well as physical abuse?

3. A: Violent video games cause harm.

Concept: harm

B: 1. To whom do they cause harm?
    2. What kind of harm?
    3. What do you mean by "harm"?
    4. What kind of harm do they cause?

Questions 1 and 2 are probes that seek to clarify scope.

✍ QUICK QUIZ 11.3
Generating Counterexamples

For each of the brief exchanges below, without writing out the argument, generate a counterexample verbally.

1. A: I think we should have more bike lanes in the city because it will encourage more people to ride bikes and it will reduce traffic.

> B: Subsidizing the purchase of bikes would also encourage more people to ride them and help reduce traffic. Would you be in favour of government subsidies for buying bikes?

2. A: Downloading copyrighted music and videos from the Internet without paying for it should not be a crime. After all, it doesn't hurt anyone.

> B: In the same way then, photocopying textbooks doesn't hurt anyone. Do you favour photocopying textbooks without buying them?

3. A: I don't think we should allow genetically modified foods to be sold and put into the food chain. After all, we don't know their long-term effects.

> B: We don't know the long-term effects of some cancer drugs. Should we ban those as well?

✍ QUICK QUIZ 11.4
Challenging Meaning

For each of the brief exchanges below, without writing out the argument, generate a challenge for the meaning and give an appropriate response. Use a different kind of challenge for each of the examples.

1. A: We should be allowed to use torture against terrorists to get them to inform us about future terrorist attacks.

> *Meaning challenge:*
> B: So you think it would be OK to beat people and pull out their fingernails in order to get information that would prevent future terrorist attacks?

Response to the challenge:
A: That's not what I mean by *torture.*

Kind of challenge: Counterexample using an example.

2. A: Downloading songs from the Net is not theft.

    Meaning challenge:
    B: What do you mean by theft?

    Response to the challenge:
    A: Stealing someone's property.

    Kind of challenge: Request for clarification/meaning.

3. A: Sexual harassment involves the misuse of power by a man against a woman.

    Meaning challenge:
    B: So if a female manager threatened to fire a male subordinate if he didn't sleep with her, that wouldn't be sexual harassment?

    Response to the challenge:
    A: Yes, that would. I mean any misuse of authority for sexual purposes is sexual harassment.

    Kind of challenge: Counterexample indicating the use of the term is too narrow.

✍ QUICK QUIZ 11.5
Challenging Truth/Acceptability

For each of the brief exchanges below, without writing out the argument, generate a challenge for the truth of a key claim and give an appropriate response.

1. A: Marijuana should be legalized for medical purposes, because it is more effective in treating some conditions than other forms of treatment are.

    B: If cocaine were more effective for relieving pain than other alternatives, would you be willing to legalize it?
    A: Sure.

2. A: I think we should look into the hiring practices of professional schools. Men tend to get far more places than women do.

    B: Looking at the students in my business and law classes, women seem to outnumber men considerably. Why do you say that men outnumber women?
    A: I mean in schools for engineering and science, not business and law.

3. A: We should ban The Adventures of Huckleberry Finn from high school libraries because it promotes racism by using the offensive n-word throughout.

   B: My dictionary uses the n-word. Should we ban it?
   A: That's not what I mean.

✍ QUICK QUIZ 11.6
Stem and Application

In each of the following claims, identify the stem and the application. Provide an alternate application to generate a counterexample.

1. *The Adventures of Huckleberry Finn* is racist because it uses the n-word over two hundred times. And anything that uses the n-word is racist.

   Stem: is racist
   Application: anything that uses the n-word
   New application: my dictionary
   Counterexample: Is a dictionary that includes the n-word racist?

2. It is legitimate to use torture on terrorists because they threaten national security. And it is legitimate to use torture on anyone who threatens national security.

   Stem: using torture on anyone who threatens national security
   Application: terrorists
   New application: journalists
   Counterexample: Some journalists threaten national security by challenging the government. Is it legitimate to use torture on them?

3. UFOs exist. Many people have seen them. (This claim does not contain the general claim that must be inferred.)

   Stem: what many people have seen exists
   Application: UFOs
   New application: witches flying through the air
   Counterexample: Many people have reported seeing witches flying through the air. Do flying witches exist?

✍ QUICK QUIZ 11.7
Challenging and Responding to Counterexamples

For each of the brief exchanges below, without writing out the argument, generate a counterexample and give an appropriate response. Then identify the kind of counterexample (claim, inference) and the kind of response you use.

1. A: Marijuana should be legalized for medical purposes because it is more effective than some other treatments.

B: If crystal meth were a more effective treatment for some illnesses, would you want to legalize it, too?

A: Sure, if it was more effective and the side effects were no greater than other possibilities.

Kind of counterexample: claim counterexample
Kind of response: accept new application and embrace consequences

2. **A:** Astrology must be true because my friend claimed that it worked for her.

B: If your friend claimed that biorhythms worked for her, you would say that the theory of biorhythms must be true?

A: No, that's different. She doesn't believe in biorhythms.

Kind of counterexample: claim counterexample
Kind of response: rejects new application as irrelevant

3. **A:** You can't trust philosophers. My intro philosophy prof misled us on her grading scheme.

B: So if one politician lies to you, that means that they all do?

A: That's not what I mean. I mean you can't trust some philosophers.

Kind of counterexample: inference counterexample; hasty generalization
Kind of response: accepts and changes (modifies scope of) conclusion

✒ QUICK QUIZ 11.8
Challenging and Responding to Implications

For each of the brief exchanges below, without writing out the argument, generate a challenge for the implication and give an appropriate response.

1. **A:** We should introduce more bike lanes because they will reduce car traffic downtown.

B: Wouldn't more bikes coming downtown cause congestion?
A: No. Bikes take up a lot less space than cars.

2. **A:** We should increase tuition in order to increase the quality of education.

B: Wouldn't that mean that fewer lower-income students would not be able to get a university education?
A: We would have to provide more grants for lower-income students.

3. **A:** If we require students to take logic, then they will improve their reasoning, and that is a good thing. Therefore, we should require students to take logic.

B: Wouldn't that reduce the number of courses the students have to take in their majors?
A: Not necessarily. But it would eliminate a possible elective.

✍ QUICK QUIZ 11.9
Challenging and Responding to Fallacies and Dirty Tricks

Identify the dirty trick/fallacy if one is committed and suggest a strategy for handling it.

1. Your argument partner says the following in response to your argument in defence of gay marriage:

    A: You're arguing for gay marriage? Are you homosexual or something?
    B: That's not the issue. If you have a problem with my argument, tell me what it is.

    A tries to label B rather than addressing the argument. B ignores the label and moves the discussion back to his argument.

2. B has quoted Rush Limbaugh's argument that executing Saddam Hussein was a mistake.

    A: You are using Rush Limbaugh as an authority. Don't you know he is just an apologist for a right-wing conservative viewpoint?
    B. He may be. However, he has given an argument here, and I think we should address the argument. After all, even right-wing apologists sometimes have good arguments.

    This may or may not be a dirty trick. If Rush Limbaugh is being quoted as an authority, then it may be a legitimate challenge of him as an authority. If he has given an argument, then the answer acknowledges the label but redirects the focus away from who he is and instead to his arguments.

3. B has been arguing for not teaching creationist theory in biology classes.

    A: That is what's wrong with society today. No one wants to take religion seriously.
    B: That's not what I am encouraging. The issue is whether religion should be taught in science classes. And creationist theory is religion, not science. Challenging the teaching of religion as science is not the same as not taking religion seriously. Do you want religion taught in science classes?

    A's response deflects from B's original argument by moving to a more general complaint. B can redirect the argument back to the issue. Alternatively, B can reformulate A's response as follows: "So should we also teach the astronomy of the Bible in astronomy classes?"

4. B has given an argument for increasing existing taxes and using the increase to pay down the national debt.

    A. Garbage!
    B: Why do you think the position is garbage?

    In asking A for a reason for his dismissal, B will have gone from defending her position to making A defend his.

EXERCISES

🖎 EXERCISE 11.1
Dialogue Analysis: Huckleberry Finn

Reread the Huckleberry Finn dialogue in Exercise 1.3 in this Student Manual and, using the Cell Phone dialogue in Module 11, Section 11.4 as a model, do an analysis of the argumentation moves in that dialogue.

🖎 EXERCISE 11.2
Dialogue Analysis: Drug Testing

Reread the Drug Testing dialogue in Exercise 1.2 in this student manual and, using the Cell Phone dialogue in Module 11, Section 11.4 as a model, do an analysis of the argumentation moves in that dialogue.

In-Class Listening and Verbal Arguing Exercises

General Instructions

In the in-class listening and arguing exercises that follow, students will assume one of the following roles:

Speaker: This is the primary speaker—the person presenting the argument.

Responder: This is the person who is actively listening, paraphrasing, or challenging the speaker's arguments.

Referee: The referee carefully observes the dialogue. The referee's role is to keep time and provide constructive feedback on the interaction.

These roles will rotate. Person A in the first iteration of the exercise will be the speaker; Person B, the responder; and Person C, the referee. In the next round, B will be the speaker; C, the responder; and A, the referee. Although the referee appears to have a smaller role, his or her role is as vital as the others.

✎ EXERCISE 11.3
Listening 1

Divide yourselves into groups of three. Label yourselves A, B, and C. In the first round, A will be the speaker; B, the active listener; and C, the referee. A list of topics is given below.

A: Select one of the topics from the list and speak about it for two or three minutes. You may give an argument or simply state an opinion or belief on that topic.

B: Listen actively and provide feedback on what you understand A to have said. You may attend not only to the content of the message but also to emotions and body language to help identify what is important and what is not.

A: If you judge that B's paraphrase is accurate, move on to the next round. If you judge that it is not accurate, restate and clarify, and B will paraphrase again.

C: Function as a referee. After A and B have agreed on what A said, you debrief them by providing your own observations and analysis. If A and B disagree on what was said (or agree when they should not), you can intervene to point out any further observations.

After the first round, rotate roles. A becomes the referee; B, the speaker; and C, the listener. Proceed as before. Continue rotating until each person has had an opportunity to play all three roles at least once.

List of Topics

1. Using cell phones and iPods in classes
2. Downloading copyrighted materials from the Net
3. Pornography
4. Your current courses
5. A current controversial news topic
7. Capital punishment
8. Teachers' strikes
9. Use of cell phones while driving
10. Use of cell phones and iPods while walking
11. Minimum wage increase
12. Fast food restaurants' responsibility for obesity
13. Pick some topic of interest to the speaker

Debriefing

1. Did you have any difficulties in playing any of the roles? What were they? Why do you think they occurred? What could you do to handle those difficulties if you encounter them in the future?

2. Did your group find it difficult to provide active listening and feedback? What challenges were there? Briefly describe and characterize them.

3. As a referee, did you notice anything about the patterns of feedback in your group?

4. What did you learn about listening and feedback from the exercise?

5. What barriers to effective listening did you discover in this exercise? How could you overcome them?

6. Do you have any other observations or comments on the exercise and what you learned from it?

Topics for Exercises 11.4 to 11.10

The following topics can be used for the remaining exercises. Each can be negated or otherwise modified.

1. We should have a two-tier medical system.
2. The government should provide free daycare centres for working mothers.
3. Use of cell phones while driving should be prohibited.
4. The legal drinking age should be raised/lowered.
5. The government should censor obscene and adult material on the Internet.
6. Pornography is degrading.
7. Cloning of humans should be banned.
8. Abortion should be available on demand.
9. Women make better managers than men.
10. Capital punishment should be reinstated.
11. Workers should share in management decisions.
12. Prostitution should be legalized (decriminalized).
13. Birth-control information should be made available to every youth at puberty.
14. Housewives should be paid for housework.
15. Workers should share in the profits of a company.
16. Feminism is a mistake.
17. The social emphasis on masculine traits over feminine ones is a mistake.
18. There should be no sex outside of marriage.
19. Sex outside of marriage should be encouraged.
20. Teachers should have the right to strike.
21. Homosexual couples should not be allowed to marry.
22. We should abolish the right to strike.
23. We should deregulate tuition and allow universities to charge whatever they want.
24. People convicted of a first offence for drunk driving should automatically lose their license for five years.
25. Everything is fair in business as long as you are making a profit.
26. We should not get rid of the mandatory age of retirement.

🖎 EXERCISE 11.4
Paraphrase

    A: Select a topic of interest and speak for thirty seconds on that topic. This should not be an argument.

    B: Listen to A. When A is through, paraphrase what A has said, paying attention to both content and emotion.

    A: Listen to B's paraphrase and confirm or correct as necessary.

    C: Listen to both and paraphrase what you have heard.

Rotate roles so that each person gets to be A, B, and C at least once. Debrief in terms of both content and process. See debriefing notes for 11.3. In addition, answer the following questions:

1. Was the paraphrase accurate?

2. Did the speaker tend to add or leave out material?

3. Was this material important?

4. Did the speaker tend to accept incomplete or inaccurate paraphrases?

5. What difficulties did each person encounter in each role in this exercise?

6. Do you have any further observations or comments on the process, task, or the content?

Report your debriefing to the class.

🖎 EXERCISE 11.5
Discussion

This exercise is an extended version of Exercise 11.4.

    A: Select a topic of interest and speak on that topic.

    B: Listen to A and paraphrase A's comments.

    A: Confirm or correct as necessary and continue speaking about the topic.

    B: Paraphrase new information A has added and encourage A to develop the topic further.

A&B: Continue for two minutes, going back and forth. B should not add his or her own comments or respond to what A says other than to actively listen and paraphrase.

C: Listen to both and, at the end of the discussion, say what you have heard and comment on B's paraphrasing.

Rotate roles so that each person gets to be A, B, and C at least once. Debrief both process and content and report to the class.

✍ EXERCISE 11.6
Probing

A: Select a topic of interest and briefly (30 seconds) state an opinion on that topic.

B: Probe A's position on that topic by
asking for clarification of meaning;
asking for connection between the stated issue or argument and other issues;
asking for further reasons; and
asking for reasons for those reasons.

C: Act as referee, listening and reporting what you hear.

Rotate roles so that each person gets to be A, B, and C at least once. Debrief and report to the class.

✍ EXERCISE 11.7
Arguing 1

A: Select a topic of interest and present a claim on that topic.

B: Ask "Why?"

A: Give a reason for the claim.

B: Formulate the missing premise from the claim and reason, and state it explicitly (in normal discussion we would not do this). Identify the more general reason and give a counterexample to it.

A: Respond to the counterexample.

C: Listen to both and help, if necessary, in the formulation of the missing premise and counterexample.

Briefly discuss the missing premise formulated, consider other possible ones, and consider possible counterexamples. Rotate roles so that each person gets to be A, B, and C at least once. Debrief and report to the class.

⚅ EXERCISE 11.8
Arguing 2

A: Select a topic of interest and present a claim on that topic (it can be the same as in previous exercises).

B: Ask "Why?"

A: Give a reason for the claim.

B: Formulate the missing premise from the claim and reason and state it explicitly (in normal discussion we would not do this). Identify the more general reason and give a counterexample to it.

A: Respond to the counterexample.

B: Adjust the argument and either (a) generate a new counterexample, (b) reformulate the argument and generate a new counterexample, or (c) clarify the argument and generate a new counterexample.

C: Observe, time, and provide feedback.

Briefly discuss the argumentation. Rotate roles so that each person gets to be A, B, and C. Debrief and report to the class.

⚅ EXERCISE 11.9
Arguing 3

A: Select a topic of interest and make a claim on that topic.

B: Ask "Why?"

A: Give a reason for the claim.

B: Formulate the argument with the missing premise and reason. State the missing premise. Challenge the truth of the more specific reason.

A: Respond to the challenge.

B: Respond to the response with a further challenge either to a specific or general reason.

C: Observe, time, and provide feedback.

Briefly discuss the argumentation. Rotate roles so that each person gets to be A, B, and C. Debrief and report to the class.

✒ EXERCISE 11.10
Arguing 4

A: Select a topic of interest and present a claim on that topic (it can be the same as in previous exercises).

B: Ask "Why?"

A: Give a reason for the claim.

B: Formulate the missing premise and reason and state it explicitly (in normal discussion we would not do this). Identify the more general reason and provide a counterexample to it.

A: Respond to the counterexample.

B: Respond to the response with a further relevant critique.

A&B: Continue the argument and response pattern for one to five minutes, as specified by your instructor.

C: Observe, time, and provide feedback.

Briefly discuss the argumentation. Rotate roles so that each person gets to be A, B, and C at least once. Debrief and report to the class.

✒ EXERCISE 11.11
Arguing 5

Conduct an open argumentation for five minutes using all of the tools of argumentation.

A: Take a position on a topic of your choosing. The topic need not be from the list of topics above.

B: Probe for meaning and reasons, offer feedback and challenges, paraphrase, and, in general, use any argumentation technique to advance the understanding of the position. Help A develop his or her position and challenge that.

A: Respond to challenges and use any other legitimate argumentation techniques to advance the argument.

C: Observe, time, and summarize the argumentation. Serve as coach by providing assistance in terms of giving reasons, challenges, and responses if either A or B gets stuck in the argument. Before you can move into the coach role, however, A or B must request assistance.

MODULE 12: Written Argumentation

QUICK QUIZ ANSWERS

✍ QUICK QUIZ 12.1
Analyzing an Assignment

Use the questions in Module 12, Section 12.3 to analyze the following assignments. Where answers are not clear, identify the questions you would have to ask the instructor.

1. One-page argument assignment for a first-year critical reasoning course:

   Read the attached passage, "The Terri Schiavo Case" and write a one-page (one paragraph) argument on a central moral or policy issue arising from this case as it is presented here. I want to see how you develop your own reasoning on this. Do not simply repeat the arguments in the passage. Your essay will be assessed on how well you frame an interesting and central issue, how well you develop and defend your argument, and how original your argument is. The use of outside materials is discouraged; however, if you use such material, it must be cited appropriately.

   Do an argument analysis and critique of your own paper and submit that as an appendix.

   Since your papers will be marked and returned electronically and will be used for electronic peer review, you must use the following formatting conventions. The paper should be formatted in Microsoft Word or Rich Text Format (not WordPerfect), using an easy-to-read font (e.g., Arial), in 12-point type, black, and flush left.

   Due at midnight, Pacific Standard Time, March 26, 2007, via e-mail.

Point:	**Develop one's own reasoning about the issue**
	Don't repeat existing arguments
Audience:	**Class, instructor**
Context:	**Prefer no outside materials; if used, must be acknowledged**
Constraints:	**Moral or policy issue arising from the case**
	Argument analysis and critique of own argument
	Formatting conventions—see above
Due:	**Midnight, PST, March 26, 2007**
Criteria:	**Framing of interesting and central issue**
	Development and defence of argument
	Originality
	Citing of outside material (if used)

2. Assignment for a second-year English literature course (the class has spent the past three weeks analyzing Mary Shelley's Frankenstein):

   Write an essay on the role of education in Mary Shelley's Frankenstein. The essay should be ten pages and focus only on the primary source (the novel itself).

The paper should use MLA format, cite all material appropriately and include a bibliography.

The essay is due in class on October 1, at the beginning of class. Late papers will be marked down in accordance with the course policies.

Topic:	**Role of education in the novel**
Point:	**Demonstrate understanding of the novel and what was learned**
Audience:	**Class, instructor**
Context:	**MLA format**
Constraints:	**Due date—Oct 1, beginning of class**
	Bibliography
	Ten pages, primary material only
Criteria:	**Good writing (best guess)**
	Demonstration of how to analyze a text and support claims using the text
	Interpretation of text rather than just summary

3. Assignment for a third-year sociology course analyzing ethnicity and race:

Examine the websites given for the Canadian, Irish, and Indian censuses. Find and identify their respective definitions of ethnicity and the questions used in the most recent census to measure ethnicity. Compare and contrast these definitions and relate them to the lectures on ethnicity. What conclusions can you draw about the categories used to identify ethnicity in the respective censuses? Relate this to David's discussion of ethnicity.

Length:	4 pages
Due:	In class March 2, at the beginning of class

Point:	**Demonstrate how to analyze measures of ethnicity as used in various censuses and relate this to David's discussion of ethnicity**
Audience:	**Class, instructor**
Context:	**Concepts of ethnicity in course; David's concept of ethnicity**
Constraints:	**Due date—March 2, beginning of class**
	Length not specified
Criteria:	**Compare and contrast definitions of different censuses**
	Relate this to lectures on ethnicity
	Relate this to David's concepts
	Draw (and support) own conclusions

✍ QUICK QUIZ 12.2
Using Brainteasers

Because of the nature of this exercise, each student will likely generate quite different ideas. The answers given here are intended only to illustrate the possibilities. Not every brainteaser category has been developed in each question.

Use brainteasers to develop ideas on the following topics:

1. Should downloading copyrighted music and videos from the Internet without paying for them be legal?

Beyond the obvious:
- Having downloaded such material, with or without paying, using it on more than one device, or passing it on to friends
- Copying one's own music collection and passing it on to friends
- Apply to podcasts, including podcasts of university lectures
- Some give permission to redistribute; what if they didn't, and each person wanting to hear a university lecture or news broadcast had to pay for it?
- What if such news broadcasts became the only/main way of distributing broadcasts (news, entertainment)?
- What is owned?
- What if copyright holders could develop technology for charging for each time someone listened to or viewed something, as is now done with broadcast music?
- What exactly is copyright and what are people purchasing when they "buy" a song or video on the Internet?
- Spoken-word recordings—what exactly is owned?

Complex:
- The beyond-the-obvious raise issues that could be used to make this more complex—the difference between such things as copyrighted current music and older music (e.g., '30s blues and jazz) that has been reprocessed and re-copyrighted; newscasts; university lectures, etc.

Alternate viewpoints:
- Possible viewpoints—artists spreading their ideas and art and being recognized; various audiences
- Various aims—keeping certain performance styles alive when they are not popular
- Niche recording of ethnic and localized music and dance that do not have a wider audience

Challenge stereotypes, etc.:
- Creators own their creations—not true in all societies; not true in same way in academic world—academics have copyright, but not usually paid for use of academic articles
- Copyright benefits creators—often not true. Copyright is held by corporations, not artists, for much of the materials recorded in the 30s and 40s, for example

Classifications:
- Commercial music (and videos), noncommercial music (and videos), spoken word, broadcasts, informational podcasts, university materials

Comparisons and contrasts:
- Commercial music and videos versus noncommercial ones
- Commercial materials and educational materials
- Recent materials versus older materials (30s and 40s blues, for example)

Metaphors:

- Music as commodity
- Music as property

Bug lists:
- Having to buy music I haven't heard to find out if I like it
- Buying music I haven't heard and finding out I don't like it
- Not being able to buy/find/hear music that is not popular—e.g., 1930s blues, European rock and roll, out-of-print jazz
- Large corporations controlling the music industry and imposing a sameness on the music

Questions:
- What would happen if university courses and lectures, informational materials or newscasts, all copyrighted materials were subject to the same restrictions as copyrighted music?
- Who owns music from the '30s?

Humour and fantasy:
- Imagine a society with no copyright protection or no ownership but where creators are revered.

2. Should marijuana be legalized?

Beyond the obvious:
- Marijuana as religious sacrament (Rastafarians)
- Marijuana as means of social bonding
- Marijuana as political protest
- Autonomy—right of individuals to make decisions about what they will do as long as it doesn't harm others
- Using marijuana for stress relief in a highly stressed world

Complex:
- At least three contexts: medical, religious, recreational

Senses:
- Smell of marijuana
- Heightened senses with its use

Alternate viewpoints:
- As drug
- As enhancement
- As medicine
- As coping mechanism in oppressive society
- Police and enforcement
- Pharmacologists and effects
- Regular users
- Occasional users

Challenge stereotypes:
- Few users are addicts
- Nature of harm
- Extent of harm
- Marijuana only smoked
- *Cheech and Chong*
- Negative attitudes about getting high

Classifications:

- Occasional users, regular users, nonusers, secondhand smoke, costs to society from use of marijuana

Metaphors:
- Getting high

Questions:
- What are the physiological effects of using marijuana?

Humour and fantasy:
- Imagine a society in which no one felt the need to use marijuana or other kinds of drugs. What would such a society look like?
- Imagine a society in which everyone used it.

3. What critical skills, as opposed to discipline-specific skills, should a student learn in university?

Beyond the obvious:
- Social skills
- Group skills
- Clarity and elegance in writing
- Interaction skills
- Develop idea of social skills and the ethics behind them
- Creativity as a critical skill
- Critical skills are usually seen as a means to specific ends—doing well in academia, preparing students for work world
- Develop as ends in themselves. How can critical skills be ends in themselves?
- Related issue—how to make the learning of such skills something students want to do? How to motivate students to want to learn critical skills?

Complex:
- Critical skills are not just those commonly identified but include social skills, interactional skills, and group skills

Senses:
- Visual of student doing argument analysis, writing an essay, talking with others
- Sound bites: "but have you considered ...," "on the other hand ..."
- Dance students performing—what critical skills are involved here (beyond obvious)?
- Other kinds of performance—critical skills involved in those?
- Vision of Nobel laureate in lab teaching grad student—what critical skills are involved?
- In what sense are they critical skills?

Alternate viewpoints:
- Why do we need to learn critical skills?
- What if the curriculum was organized around the skills rather than the content (problem-based learning), so that the students had to provide the content?

Challenge stereotypes:
- Learning is about information transfer; challenge—learning is about learning to learn and developing critical skills
- What is important are critical skills; challenge—developing creativity is more important
- We need to develop critical skills, which can lead to a narrow focus on specific skills and skill development such as argument analysis; challenge—what is important is learning to ask the right questions and developing our own arguments, which is a more open-ended approach
- Critical skills are about being critical, analyzing and critiquing. Different sense of critical—"important." This includes synthesis, creativity, etc.
- Assumption that critical skills need to be taught separately from content
- Assumption that critical skills can be taught with content without separate emphasis and development

Classifications:
- Content, discipline-specific skills, academic skills, life skills, creativity

Comparisons and contrasts:
- Creativity versus critical skills; analytical versus creative/synthetic
- Compare and contrast the various concepts in the previous category: learning as information transfer versus questioning; critical skills versus creativity; critical skills as being critical versus important; skills versus content

Metaphors:
- Learning as a journey, an unending quest
- Critical skills as tools (possibly trite)

Examples:
- My critical-thinking course
- Professor Leightheizer (English) teaching how to interpret a poem or text
- Dr. Krug (sociologist) teaching how to interpret a graph
- My friend Aleksander, a dancer, critiquing another student's performance and incorporating that into his own performance
- Alycia, a cyclist, critiquing another cyclist's riding style and helping him improve his performance

Bug lists:
- Assumption that students don't already have critical skills

Questions:
- What exactly are "critical skills"?
- Why is it important to teach them?
- Can they be taught?
- Can the teaching/learning of them be "fun," challenging?
- Could critical thinking be taught entirely by active learning principles where students have to generate and assess the relevant criteria?

✍ QUICK QUIZ 12.3
Evaluating a Thesis

Examine the following proposed theses for a three-page argument essay on whether the government should crack down on street racing. Identify how each does or does not fit the criteria of a good thesis. Suggest what could be done to improve the ones that do not fit the criteria. Are the theses as stated likely to be interesting to an audience of students who have been discussing the issue for two weeks? Explain.

1. Street racing is dangerous.

   Substantive: yes
   Controversial, interesting, or original: not as stated
   Complex: no
   Clear: yes
   Precise: no (how is it dangerous?)
   Limited in scope: no

   Given the audience, this is likely to be a simple rehashing of the discussions from the class. To be interesting, it needs to be made more original.

2. The government should ban street racing.

   Substantive: yes
   Controversial, interesting, or original: not as stated
   Complex: no
   Clear: reasonably
   Precise: no
   Limited in scope: no

   This is a simple and obvious thesis. It calls for a list of reasons for banning street racing but is not likely to produce much in the way of an interesting argument. It is likely to summarize existing arguments the class has covered so is not likely to be interesting to the audience.

3. Anyone caught engaging in street racing should have his or her car confiscated and face a minimum of two years in jail.

   Substantive: yes
   Controversial, interesting, or original: more interesting than the preceding two
   Complex: yes
   Clear: yes
   Precise: yes
   Limited in scope: yes

   This thesis presupposes that the government should crack down on street racing. Given that, it would be an interesting thesis for the audience, although the audience may have already discussed this. Still, it would be challenging, and it would be useful to work out the reasons.

4. Although street racing can sometimes be dangerous, it would be futile to attempt a ban on all street racing.

> **Substantive: yes**
> **Controversial, interesting, or original: yes (it goes beyond the obvious "yes" or "no")**
> **Complex: yes (it acknowledges one of the major reasons for banning street racing but takes a counterposition)**
> **Clear: yes**
> **Precise: yes**
> **Limited in scope: yes**
>
> **This would likely be an interesting topic for the audience since it requires developing a position that, if discussed, needs substantial support.**

5. A more effective approach to dealing with street racing than further banning an already illegal activity would be educating and imposing curfews on younger drivers.

> **Substantive: yes**
> **Controversial, interesting, or original: yes**
> **Complex: yes (it proposes an alternative to banning)**
> **Clear: yes**
> **Precise: yes**
> **Limited in scope: yes**
>
> **This would likely be an interesting topic for the audience since it requires developing a position that, if discussed, needs substantial support, especially regarding the curfew.**

✍ QUICK QUIZ 12.4
Refining a Thesis

For each of the following possible theses, identify what needs to be established. Where possible, make it a better thesis using the materials in the previous section. Where it already is a good thesis, show how it meets the criteria for a good thesis.

The assignment is to write a two-page argument paper that is to be used as the basis for further discussion of the issue. The students have been studying the specific topic for three weeks.

1. For a first-year sociology course: Criminal behaviour is more a product of the individual's specific interactions with his or her peer group than of general social norms.

> **This is fairly specific. What needs to be established is what constitutes criminal behaviour and how this is a product of specific interactions with an individual's peer group rather than general social norms.**

2. For a second-year urban planning course: We should ban cars in the city.

> **This thesis is overly general. It could be made more precise by specifying which cars, when, and under what conditions. For example, private passenger cars should be banned from the city on weekdays. What would then need to be established to support such a thesis is why anything should be banned, why private passenger cars and not others, and why weekdays and not weekends.**

3. For a first-year course on genetics and society: Although the knowledge gained from genetics promises major gains in agriculture, medicine, and forensics, it also poses serious threats to individual privacy and well-being.

> **This is a fairly good thesis. What has to be established are the benefits of genetics in agriculture, medicine, and forensics; the harm posed in terms of individual privacy and well being; and an argument that the former outweigh the latter.**

4. For a second-year computer ethics course: Maintaining the privacy of individuals is an important concern for those delivering computer services, and every company should have and follow a privacy policy.

> **This thesis could be more precisely formulated: "Every company delivering computer services should have and follow a privacy policy that ensures the privacy of individuals." The writer would then have to establish why a company delivering computer services has to ensure the privacy of individuals and how a policy would accomplish this.**

✍ QUICK QUIZ 12.5
The One-Paragraph Argument

Given the following one-paragraph arguments, identify the thesis and then determine which claims are relevant and which are not relevant to establishing it. Rewrite the passage to organize the claims while eliminating the irrelevant claims.

1. Although marijuana can be used for some medical conditions, it should not be legalized either for medical or recreational use. Marijuana has been used to relieve the nausea that accompanies chemotherapy, for example. It should not be used for medical use because there are other, more effective treatments. Many people claim that marijuana helps them relax and that it is not harmful. But marijuana has proven harmful effects. Moreover, it is an addictive drug. Legalizing it for medical use would be allowing the use of a dangerous drug when more effective drugs are available. For similar reasons, it should not be legalized for recreational purposes: It has harmful effects and is addictive.

> **Thesis: Marijuana should not be legalized for medical or recreational use.**
>
> **1. Marijuana can be used for some medical conditions. (irrelevant— background)**

2. Marijuana has been used to relieve the nausea that accompanies chemotherapy, for example. (irrelevant—background)
3. It should not be used for medical use. (relevant—partial restatement of thesis)
4. There are other, more effective treatments. (relevant—reason, unsupported)
5. Many people claim that marijuana helps them relax. (irrelevant—opposing position, background)
6. Many people claim that it is not harmful. (irrelevant—opposing position, background)
7. Marijuana has proven harmful effects. (relevant—reason, unsupported)
8. Moreover, it is an addictive drug. (relevant—reason, unsupported)
9. Legalizing it for medical use would be allowing the use of a dangerous drug when more effective drugs are available. (relevant—restates reasons)
10. It should not be legalized for recreational purposes. (relevant—restates conclusion)
11. It has harmful effects. (relevant—restates reason)
12. It is addictive. (relevant—restates reason)

Marijuana should not be legalized either for medical or recreational purposes. More effective medical treatments are available. And marijuana, no matter what it is used for, is harmful and addictive.

2. University courses should consist of fewer lectures and make available the information delivered in lectures through materials such as iPod videocasts. Most students have iPods, and video iPods are not expensive. Downloading iPod videos is easy. Many students can't attend class regularly because they have jobs and other commitments. One survey says that over half of all students work at least fifteen hours a week. Some have family commitments as well. Many lecturers are boring. One professor I had simply read from the assigned text. Lectures being available in video format would help ESL students who often need to hear a lecture several times to get its full meaning. Many students are ESL students.

Thesis: University courses should consist of fewer lectures and make available the information delivered in lectures through materials such as iPod videocasts.

1. Most students have iPods. (background—irrelevant—or could be treated as part of a feasibility subargument—relevant)
2. Video iPods are not expensive. (background—irrelevant—or could be treated as part of a feasibility subargument—relevant)
3. Downloading iPod videos is easy. (background—irrelevant—or could be treated as part of a feasibility subargument—relevant)
4. Many students can't attend class regularly. (relevant—reason)
5. They have jobs and other commitments [that prevent them from attending class regularly]. (relevant—reason for 4)
6. One survey says that over half of all students work at least fifteen hours a week. (relevant—reason for 4)
7. Some have family commitments as well. (relevant—reason for 4)

8. Many lecturers are boring. (relevant—possible reason for not attending class; poor reason?)
9. One professor I had simply read from the assigned text. (possible reason for not attending class; it is not clear how a podcast would solve this problem—treat as irrelevant)
10. Lectures being available in video format would help ESL students who often need to hear a lecture several times to get its full meaning. (relevant—reason)
11. Many students are ESL students. (background—irrelevant—or could be treated as part of a not-well-developed argument about how widely useful podcasts would be—relevant)

Universities should use fewer lectures and make available the information delivered in lectures through materials such as iPod videocasts. Many students can't attend classes on a regular basis because of job commitments and family obligations. In addition, podcasting lectures would help ESL students, who often can benefit from hearing a lecture several times in order to understand it.

(This argument partially misses the point. It provides reasons for videocasting lectures, but not for replacing some lectures with videocasts.)

✍ QUICK QUIZ 12.6
The Balance of Considerations Argument

For each of the following issues, identify the alternate positions and competing considerations. Identify possible overriding considerations that would weigh the argument toward one side or the other.

1. Should parents be allowed to spank their children?

   - **Yes, to maintain authority and discipline.**
   - **No, because of harm to the child and the possibility of instilling authoritarian values.**
   - **Sometimes, when reason and other considerations fail.**

   Overriding considerations:
   - **whether obedience to authority or encouragement of autonomy is more important**
   - **whether parents sometimes know more and better than the child**
   - **whether spanking can enforce that**

2. Should the government ban cell phone use while driving?

   - **Yes, because it distracts from driving and may cause harm to others.**
   - **No, because it infringes on individual liberty. Individuals should be allowed to make decisions about their own welfare.**

   Overriding considerations:

- **individual autonomy versus harm to others**
- **whether cell phone use while driving is hazardous (i.e., causes more accidents)**

✐ QUICK QUIZ 12.7
Turning a Simple Argument into Prose

Rewrite each of the following arguments into a fluid prose paragraph that clearly displays the structure of the argument.

1. Background: Tara has submitted an expense form for reimbursement for attending a conference and entertaining a dozen clients and coworker Eli at an expensive dinner.

    1.   Eli claims he was not at the dinner.
    2.   Eli claims that he did not see Tara at any of the sessions at the conference, including the plenary session.
    3.   Eli did see her at the reception and the evening banquet.
    4.   Eli claims that at the time of the dinner, for which Tara is claiming expenses, he was with another company client.
    5.   He has offered to supply the name of the client to his manager.
    6.   Eli is trustworthy.

∴ 7.   Tara has falsified her expense account.
    8.   If someone has falsified expenses, he or she has stolen from the company.

∴ 9.   Tara has stolen from the company.
    10. If someone steals from the company, he or she should be fired.

∴ 11. Tara should be fired.

Tara should be fired. By falsifying her expense account, she has stolen from the company. Theft from the company is unacceptable. Tara says that Eli, who attended the conference with her, was at a dinner she hosted for a dozen clients, which she claimed as an expense. Not only does Eli (who is trustworthy and has offered the name of another client with whom he was dining at the time of the contended dinner) assert that he was not at the dinner but he also claims he did not see Tara at any of the conference sessions, including the plenary, although he did see her at the reception and the evening banquet.

2.   1. If a reorganization results in an increase in morale, greater productivity, and more profits, with no serious detrimental effects, then it is a success.
       2. The reorganization of the ACME bolt company resulted in an increase in morale.
       3. The reorganization of the ACME bolt company resulted in greater productivity.
       4. The reorganization of the ACME bolt company resulted in more profits.
       5. The reorganization of the ACME bolt company had no serious detrimental effects.

    ∴ 6. The reorganization of the ACME bolt company was a success.

The reorganization of the ACME bolt company was a success. It resulted in increased morale, greater productivity, higher profits, and had no serious detrimental effects.

3.   1. Arguers who persistently misuse the principles of logic, quote evidence they know to be false, and use refuted arguments are either grossly deficient in reasoning skills or are not interested in argumentation.
       2. The supporters of intelligent design* persistently misuse the principles of logic, quote evidence they know to be false, and refute arguments.

    ∴ 3. The supporters of intelligent design are either grossly deficient in reasoning skills or are not interested in argumentation.
       4. The supporters of intelligent design are not grossly deficient in reasoning skills.

    ∴ 5. The supporters of intelligent design are not interested in argumentation.

* Supporters of intelligent design are individuals who believe that evolution cannot explain the observed complexity of nature; that the complexity of nature must be explained by appeal to the theory that nature was intelligently designed; and that this can be determined through scientific means.

The supporters of intelligent design are not interested in argumentation. They persistently misuse the principles of logic, quote evidence they know to be false, and refute arguments.

✍ QUICK QUIZ 12.8
Making Prose Clearer

Revise each of the following sentences to make the statements clearer and more forceful.

1. The issue of importance noted by this writer is the extent of control that groups of parents should have over what is being taught in the schools. (from a student essay on the *Huck Finn* dialogue, used with permission)

   The important issue is the control parents should have over what is taught in schools.

2. According to this writer, it is imperative that in light of the issue that we are considering, it should be given further thought.

   We should further consider the issue.

3. There has been a modification to the expectation about the release date of the proposed new edition of the software.

   The release date of the new edition of the software has been changed.

4. In this essay, the reasons why tuition increases by the provincial government should not be implemented will be examined.

   This essay examines why the government should not increase tuition.

5. The crossing of the blue line is an action engaged in by a player acting in the capacity of a forward.

   The forward crosses the blue line.

EXERCISES

✍ EXERCISE 12.1
Three Papers

This is a three-part assignment. Parts 2 and 3 build upon Part 1. This exercise can be used in conjunction with Exercise 12.2.

Part 1: Short Argument Paper 1[4]

Write a one- to two-page paper in which you argue for some position on a specific ethical topic. In selecting a topic, keep in mind that you will have to argue for an opposing view in the second assignment and that the topic will be the basis for all three parts of this assignment.

Here's what you must do:

1. Write a *brief* introduction to the topic. Explain what the ethical issue is, why it is important, and what you are going to do in the paper (thesis and outline of development). This should be no more than five sentences.

2. Present an argument defending your thesis. The conclusion of the argument should be something like "*x* is morally wrong" or "*x* is morally permissible but not obligatory," etc. Your argument *must be valid* if deductive or strongly support the conclusion if inductive.

---

[4] Based on an idea by and used with permission of Dr. Brian Huss, Department of Philosophy, York University.

3. Support *at least* one of your premises, preferably the weakest or most controversial with a subsidiary argument that shows that the weak premise is true or should be accepted. If you have two weak premises in your main argument, you will need two subsidiary arguments. How long this section should be depends a lot on your issue and your argument. Use your best judgment in determining what you need to do to convince your reader of the premise(s).

4. Present at least one challenge to your main argument or supporting argument(s). Put yourself in the shoes of someone who disagrees with you. What would he or she say about your argument? The challenge should not be a counterargument but a challenge to the premises, presuppositions, or implications. Try to make it as convincing as possible. (If you can't come up with a decent criticism, then you have likely chosen a bad topic.) Respond to that challenge.

Do not simply reproduce arguments found in the course text. Your argument should be presented in fluid prose.

Possible Topics

You are not limited to these topics. If you would like to write on a topic other than one relating to morality and values, you should have the topic approved by your instructor first.

1. Abortion (Be specific—*all* cases of abortion, abortion only in the first trimester, abortion when the woman's life is at risk, etc.?)

2. Euthanasia (Active euthanasia or passive? Voluntary or involuntary?)

3. Capital punishment or punishment in general (Is the death penalty a just punishment? If so, when? What justifies punishment? Should we punish people to rehabilitate them, to deter others, or because they deserve to be punished?)

4. Our obligations to different people (Do we owe something to our fellow citizens that we don't owe to foreigners? What about family members versus unrelated people? Friends versus strangers?)

5. The war in Iraq, the war in Afghanistan, war in general (Is a particular war morally permissible? Is war ever just and, if so, under what conditions?)

6. Antiterrorism measures (Is it OK to deny rights to those suspected of taking part in terrorist activities? Perhaps consider the Maher Arar case.)

7. Pornography (Is the production and consumption of pornography morally permissible, or is it unjustified exploitation?)

8. Religion and ethics (Is it necessary to be a religious person to be an ethical person? Are all ethical principles in some way tied to religious principles?)

9. Animals (Are some nonhuman animals persons? Do they have rights? Is it permissible to eat them or make clothes out of them?)

10. Downloading copyrighted material off the Internet.

11. Additional topics as approved by your instructor.

Part 2: Short Argument Paper 2

The second part of the assignment is exactly the same as the first, except that you must now argue the opposite position on whichever topic you chose for the first paper. For example, if in the first paper you argued that the war in Iraq is morally justified, you must now argue that it is morally unjustified. Imagine that there are two different people writing the papers. One thinks *x* and the other thinks not-*x*. Think about how or why reasonable people might disagree about the topic. If, in your first paper, you argued for a view you agree with, then the second paper might be a bit more difficult. Try your best to make a convincing case for the view with which you disagree.

Make sure that the thesis of your second paper really opposes the thesis of your first paper. For example, if in your first paper you argued that abortion is morally permissible in cases of rape or incest, then in your second paper, you must argue that abortion is not morally permissible in cases of rape or incest (or that abortion is not morally permissible in any case). Note that the second paper would not really oppose the first if you argued in the second that abortion is not morally permissible in some other circumstances that do not involve rape or incest.

Part 3: Argument Essay

For this part of the assignment, write a four- to five-page paper on the same topic as you chose for the short argument papers. Choose one side and write a paper in which you develop the best argument you can showing that the view you are defending is correct and that the opposing view is incorrect.

Here's what you must do:

1. Write a brief introduction to the topic. Explain what the ethical issue is and what you are going to do in the paper. Define terms when necessary.

2. Present *at least one* argument for your view (using your instructor's comments from your first two papers).

3. Justify the most controversial premise(s) of your main argument (again, making use of your instructor's comments from your earlier papers).

4. Present an objection to your argument. (Again, your earlier papers might be of use here.)

5. Respond to the objection. Try to convince your reader that the objection fails.

6. Present *at least one* argument for an opposing view.

7. Present a justification for the most controversial premise(s) of your opponent's argument.

8. Raise an objection to your opponent's argument. Try to show conclusively that your opponent's argument is unsound.

9. Show why the arguments for your position outweigh the considerations for the opposing position.

10. Provide a conclusion for the paper.

✍ EXERCISE 12.2
Assignment Analysis 1

Analyze the essay assignments in Exercise 12.1 using the material on analyzing an assignment. Write out your analysis.

✍ EXERCISE 12.3
Assignment Analysis 2

Select an assignment for another course. Analyze that assignment using the questions in Module 12, Section 12.3 in the textbook. Submit a copy of your analysis and your assignment.

✍ EXERCISE 12.4
Brainteasers

Use brainteasers to come up with ideas for the assignments you have done in Exercise 12.1, Parts 1, 2, and 3. Write up and submit.

✍ EXERCISE 12.5
Argument Analysis Appendix

For each of the essays in Exercise 12.1, Parts 1, 2, and 3, construct an argument analysis and critique of your own argument. Put it in standard form and assess it. Identify missing premises and assess for cogency/soundness. This should be no longer than one page for each of the three essays in 12.1.

✒ EXERCISE 12.6
Essay Analysis and Rewrite

Select an essay you have written for a course other than this one. Construct an argument analysis and assessment of the paper. Critique the argument (see module 8). Using your analysis, rewrite the paper to make the argument and paper stronger. Submit the original paper with both your analysis and the rewrite.

✒ EXERCISE 12.7
Clarifying Language in a Paper

Select a paper you have written for another course. Use the techniques for developing reader-based prose (explained in Module 12, Section 12.7) to critique and then rewrite the essay. Write a brief reflective analysis of what you have learned from critiquing and rewriting the original essay. Submit the original essay, the rewritten essay, and the brief reflective analysis.

✒ EXERCISE 12.8
Balance of Considerations Essay

Select one of the topics listed below and develop a balance of considerations argument on that topic. Develop the main lines of arguments, objections, and responses. Using the skills of this module, turn that argument into prose. Submit both the argument structure and the prose version. Make sure that your issue is appropriately limited in scope and that the paper gives fair consideration to the different sides of the issue.

Do not duplicate existing analyses and arguments found in this text.

This assignment requires you to integrate skills from the entire text, especially issue analysis, developing and defending arguments, and conceptual analysis.

Your instructor may request that you write the prose version as an argument essay.

List of Topics

The morality/policy desirability of

- censorship of Internet sites *or* offensive music *or* politically incorrect ideas *or* pornography
- stem cell research
- pornography
- abortion
- euthanasia
- hate speech
- gun control
- other topics offered by your instructor